Village Housing

'Anyone wondering how rural England became "a retirement retreat or playground for the wealthy" should read this stimulating book, which offers a deeper analysis of England's rural housing crisis, combining theory and case studies to investigate the role of property, taxation, financialisation, planning and housebuilders in creating our exclusive countryside.'

– Mark Shucksmith, Newcastle University

'*Village Housing* powerfully sets out the history of the housing crisis in rural England, which in too many places has become a playground for the wealthy. By offering practical ideas through case studies, this insightful book looks at how we can widen access to affordable housing in the countryside and at the multiple benefits that would bring.'

– Kate Henderson, Chief Executive, National Housing Federation

'A fascinating read that superbly frames current opportunities and challenges affecting village housing projects. The book draws out the role that village housing developments have played in supporting and reacting to the changing economic and demographic needs of the countryside, including the connectivity with urban and industrial shifts. It appraises the critical role of public policy, specifically planning policy, and how this has been used as an enabling and disenabling factor, reflecting public attitudes and perceptions of what form villages should take.'

– Martin Collett, Chief Executive, English Rural Housing Association

Village Housing

Constraints and opportunities in rural England

Nick Gallent, Iqbal Hamiduddin, Phoebe Stirling
and Meiling Wu

First published in 2022 by
UCL Press
University College London
Gower Street
London WC1E 6BT

Available to download free: www.uclpress.co.uk

Text © Authors, 2022
Images © copyright holders named in captions, 2022

The authors have asserted their rights under the Copyright, Designs and Patents Act 1988 to be identified as the authors of this work.

A CIP catalogue record for this book is available from The British Library.

Any third-party material in this book is not covered by the book's Creative Commons licence. Details of the copyright ownership and permitted use of third-party material is given in the image (or extract) credit lines. If you would like to reuse any third-party material not covered by the book's Creative Commons licence, you will need to obtain permission directly from the copyright owner.

This book is published under a Creative Commons Attribution-Non-Commercial 4.0 International licence (CC BY-NC 4.0), https://creativecommons.org/licenses/by-nc/4.0/. This licence allows you to share and adapt the work for non-commercial use providing attribution is made to the author and publisher (but not in any way that suggests that they endorse you or your use of the work) and any changes are indicated. Attribution should include the following information:

Gallent, N., Hamiduddin, I., Stirling, P. and Wu, M. 2022. *Village Housing: Constraints and opportunities in rural England.* London: UCL Press. https://doi.org/10.14324/111.9781800083035

Further details about Creative Commons licences are available at https://creativecommons.org/licenses/

ISBN: 978-1-80008-305-9 (Hbk)
ISBN: 978-1-80008-304-2 (Pbk)
ISBN: 978-1-80008-303-5 (PDF)
ISBN: 978-1-80008-306-6 (epub)
DOI: https://doi.org/10.14324/111.9781800083035

Contents

List of figures	vi
List of tables	viii
List of cases	ix
Preface	x
Acknowledgements	xiii
1 The village housing challenge	1
2 Housing markets, planning and land	19
3 Private and public responses: the past	41
4 Planning, community action and neighbourhood planning: the present	89
5 Planning, land, tax and finance	138
6 Self-build and custom housebuilding, off-grid and council-led development: the future	169
7 A future for villages	202
References	213
Index	223

List of figures

0.1	Urban and rural housing affordability.	xi
1.1	Village of Great Chart, Kent. © Nick Gallent.	8
1.2	Cottages, Pluckley, Kent. © Nick Gallent.	10
1.3	Village of Pluckley, Kent. © Nick Gallent.	17
3.1	Interwar council housing, Sherston, Wiltshire. © Iqbal Hamiduddin.	61
3.2	Interwar council housing, Sopworth, Wiltshire. © Iqbal Hamiduddin.	61
3.3	Post-war council housing, Semington, Wiltshire. © Iqbal Hamiduddin.	68
3.4	St Ives town, Cornwall. © Herry Lawford. CC BY 2.0.	82
4.1	Cannomede Cottages, South Tawton, Dartmoor. © Hastoe Housing Association.	95
4.2	Little Stocks Close, Kinlet, Shropshire. © Shropshire Rural HA.	98
4.3	Church Hall Cottage, Chapel Stile, Lake District. © Skelwith and Langdale CLT.	105
4.4	Affordable homes at Conksbury Lane, Youlgrave. © Peak District Rural HA/Youlgrave CLT.	109
4.5	Sustainable homes at Worth Matravers, Dorset. © ARCO2.	113
4.6	Peek Close, Lavenham. © Bryan Panton.	125
4.7	Affordable homes at Bradwell Springs, Derbyshire. © Bradwell CLT.	130
4.8	CGI of Bradwell Springs development, Derbyshire. © Camstead Homes.	131
5.1	Colonsay Harbour, Scalasaig. © dun_deagh. CC BY-SA 2.0.	149
6.1	Graven Hill self-build village, Bicester, South Oxfordshire. © Iqbal Hamiduddin.	175
6.2	Forgebank Cohousing, Halton, Lancashire. © Luke Mills.	181
6.3	Community hub at Tir-y-Gafel, Pembrokeshire. © Tao Paul Wimbush.	186

6.4	Low impact housing at Hockerton, Nottinghamshire. © Rob Annable. CC BY-NC-SA 2.0.	191
6.5	CGI of new council-led development at Park Lanneves, Bodmin, Cornwall. © Treveth Holdings LLP.	196
7.1	Cottages in Wroxton, Oxfordshire. © Elena Gallent Madeddu.	205

List of tables

3.1 Houses completed by local authorities, 1947 to 1959   67
6.1 Selected models of community-led and
self-organised housing   173

List of cases

3.1	The practicalities of building interwar council housing: Staverton and Sherston, Wiltshire	62
3.2	Land assembly for council building: Bradford and Melksham Rural District Council, Wiltshire	68
3.3	The evolution of the third sector: National Agricultural Centre Housing Association	77
3.4	Using general occupancy restrictions in St Ives, Cornwall	83
4.1	Site exception in a national park: South Tawton, Dartmoor National Park	95
4.2	Site exception on private land involving off-site manufacture: Kinlet, Shropshire	98
4.3	Saving a single home from private sale: Chapel Stile, South Lakeland	106
4.4	CLT delivering through a registered provider: Youlgrave, Derbyshire	109
4.5	Delivering sustainable homes on a challenging site: Worth Matravers, Dorset	113
4.6	Incentivising the delivery of 'downsizer' housing through a CRtBO – Ferring, Arun District	120
4.7	'Pro development' neighbourhood planning catalyses mixed approach to development: Lavenham, Babergh District	126
4.8	CLTs as a Neighbourhood Plan delivery vehicle: Bradwell, Derbyshire	131
5.1	The shifting context for community land purchase and planning in Scotland: Colonsay, Argyll and Bute	149
6.1	Graven Hill self-build village, South Oxfordshire	176
6.2	The cohousing model: Forgebank Cohousing, Halton, Lancashire	181
6.3	Low-impact development in Wales: Tir-y-Gafel, Pembrokeshire	187
6.4	Low-impact housing at Hockerton, Nottinghamshire	191
6.5	Council-led housing delivery at Park Lanneves, Bodmin, Cornwall	196

Preface

Housing is more expensive, and less affordable relative to local earnings, in villages than in towns and cities (see Figure 0.1). The crisis of rural housing affordability for working households has been deepening over the last 20 years, although it is rooted in post-war counter-urbanisation. Planning protections for rural areas were strengthened in the second half of the twentieth century and, at the same time, the demand for rural homes amongst urban households gathered pace. That demand has many roots that are peculiar to rural places: nostalgia for the countryside, urban escape, the perceived advantages of rural lifestyles, investment opportunity and the search for identity and status. It also has structural drivers that are common across all areas: widening access to mortgage loans, preferential tax treatment for private housing consumption, increased credit supply as banks connected to financial markets and latterly, historically low interest rates. The peculiar attractions of rural amenity areas, and the scarcity of housing supply in those places combined with the big drivers of housing demand to create a perfect storm for many villages. It pitted adventitious buyers, with their wealth rooted in property and salaried occupations, against rural wage-earners – a competitive mismatch that has since produced gross housing inequalities in many villages.

This book looks more closely at the housing challenge in England's amenity villages. It tracks solutions to date and considers what further actions might be taken to increase the fairness of housing outcomes and thereby support rural economies and alternate rural futures. In a series of chapters examining past, current and future intervention, we look first at the interwar reliance on landowners to provide tied housing and post-war diversification of responses to rising housing access difficulties, including from the public and third sectors. Second, at recent responses that are community-led or rely on new flexibilities in planning intervention. And third, at actions that disrupt established production

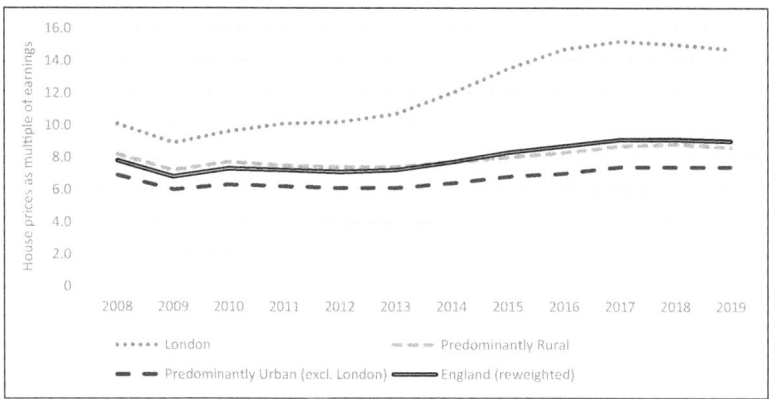

Figure 0.1 Urban and rural housing affordability. This graph shows house prices as a multiple of earnings: ratio of lower quartile house prices to lower quartile residence-based earnings, by local authority rural–urban classification, England, 2008–19, *Source*: Digest of Rural Statistics, Supplementary Data Sets, Worksheet 44, DEFRA, 2021 (See also updated DEFRA, 2022, 126).

processes: self-build, low-impact development and a re-emergence of council provision. These responses to the village housing challenge are set against a broader backdrop of structural constraint – rooted in a planning–land–tax–finance nexus – and opportunities, through reform, to reduce that constraint. The difficulties presented by the planning system and by the private control of land for development are explored in the opening chapters, and consideration is also given to the tax treatment of housing – as a driver of consumption pressure – and the finance of non-market housing in rural areas. Broadly, the planning–land–tax–finance nexus constrains potential responses to the market pressures and housing scarcities that have been witnessed in villages during recent years, but their dissection points to opportunities that might open up the rural housing market to a wider spectrum of entrants, reducing inequality and contributing to alternate rural futures – a more dynamic countryside with greater social and economic vitality.

In the face of *constraint*, we argue that *opportunities* will arise from new planning pathways, from land reforms that promote community stewardship (and community-led housing solutions) and from adjustments to housing/property taxes that calm consumption pressures and help achieve a broader distribution of housing wealth in villages and elsewhere. National data on housing affordability point to a particular challenge facing villages in rural amenity areas. Many have become islands of gentrification, giving exclusive access to rural amenity – often in areas of outstanding natural beauty and in national parks. There is a case for interventions that contribute to the social inclusivity and diversity of villages, restoring their economic function and allowing them to play their part in post-carbon rural futures. This book aims to contribute greater understanding of the village housing problem – framed by the wider cost crisis afflicting advanced economies – and offer glimpses of alternative relationships with planning and land.

Nick Gallent, Iqbal Hamiduddin,
Phoebe Stirling and Meiling Wu, March 2022

Acknowledgements

UCL Grand Challenges provided the funding for the cataloguing of village housing case studies that feature in this book. We are particularly grateful to Ian Scott and James Paskins for their unwavering support and constant encouragement over the last few years, starting with 2016's Rethinking Housing initiative and progressing into case study work on rural housing in Cornwall and the Brecon Beacons National Park between 2019 and 2021. These cases have contributed significant insights to this current work. More broadly, the thinking that has gone into this book has multiple sources, both in terms of past research projects and conversations with colleagues. We are particularly grateful to our collaborators: Mark Scott, Menelaos Gkartzios, Nicola Livingstone, Meri Juntti, Sue Kidd, Dave Shaw, Mark Tewdwr-Jones, Alan Mace, Steve Robinson, Daniela Ciaffi, Dan Durrant and Daniel Fitzpatrick, all of whom have worked on, or are still working on, related projects. There is of course a longer list of colleagues and friends, too numerous to relay in full, who have helped shape our thinking on all aspects of housing analysis. You know who you are – and we are indebted for your insight and friendship.

UCL Press has been publishing an impressive array of work in the recent years, with the open access model enabling it to reach wider audiences. We were keen to benefit from, and hopefully contribute to, its success and thank Chris Penfold for his support in taking forward the original proposal for this book and then guiding it to publication. The brilliant cover design for this book was produced by Gemma Burditt, who can be contacted at burdbits@googlemail.com.

And now the personal thanks: from Nick to Marta, Manuela and Elena (nowadays in height order) for putting up with everything; from Iqbal to Sabahat for permission to sneak off to the boat for writing sessions; from Phoebe to all the wonderful friends and colleagues who have helped and supported her during a year in which she not only worked on this book but also became a mother to Hazel; and from Meiling to her family, for tolerating her bizarre working patterns and occasional crankiness. Finally, the usual disclaimer: this work, including its doubtless imperfections, omissions and any errors is the sole responsibility of the authors.

1
The village housing challenge

Analyses of housing challenges in rural areas have been preoccupied with the entirety of non-metropolitan areas or rural regions. They regularly conclude that the focus of intervention, where needed, must be market towns, leaving lowest tier settlements to the forces of gentrification. In this opening chapter, we contend that there is a particular village challenge – the challenge of ensuring that lower and lowest tier settlements do not lose social balance and become outposts of gentrification in an increasingly exclusive countryside. More generally, we introduce the essentials of the housing challenge in these locations: locally, housing access is determined by economic drivers, including local earnings, constraints on new housing supply and by levels of market intrusion; and structurally, access is limited by the assetisation of housing, which is underpinned by private property rights and the tax treatment of housing relative to other assets. The chapter outlines the structure of the book and its geographical focus.

Introduction

The focus of housing research is set by the apparent scaling of housing problems: where problems congregate, so too does the research community. The collective gaze of that community has been on cities during recent decades. The urban processes that have caused inequalities – across housing, education, healthcare and other domains – are critically important and the concentration of major stresses in large urban centres is undeniable. But another reality is that urbanisation – the movement of people and the concentration of attendant problems – has not been accompanied by the elimination of socio-economic challenges in rural areas, which remain home to a fifth of England's population. Those areas have, in many instances, seen their working populations drift away over the last 100 years, or have been subject to counter-urbanisation and rising wealth and power inequalities. A rural housing problem remains and continues to draw interest from geographers, planners, sociologists and others. Rural housing is frequently seen as a sub-discipline of more generalised housing studies, with its own domains: housing supply and quality, demand and consumption, homelessness, housing class inequalities and so forth. It is also a geographical sub-division: whenever the 'rural' or 'non-metropolitan' prefix (or indeed the urban prefix) is attached to 'housing', the intent is to focus attention on geographical peculiarities and the impact of 'rurality' on the standard concerns of researchers, policymakers or planners. Rural and urban denote different foundations, processes and outcomes.

This book is focused on the sub-discipline of rural housing and the impact of rurality on housing processes and outcomes. But its prefix – that of the 'village' – is even more specific than the rural label for reasons that will become apparent in this introduction. Rural areas, regions or counties are diverse. There is no singular rural place but rather a pattern of rurality that is underpinned by a variety of structuring forces and geographies. Many of these have been noted in past studies and generally separate remoter areas, with sparser settlement, from near-urban metropolitan towns and villages that live in the more direct shadow of urban influence. But in all rural areas there are bigger and smaller places: bigger places, where population concentrates, are advantaged by economies of scale – public and market interventions are drawn to those places; smaller places, on the other hand, may either be deprived of resource or, if they are amenity-rich, attract individual investors. Smaller rural places may either die or gentrify, depending on their place attributes.

This is the basic contextual premise of this book: there is a particular confluence of rurality and scale, found in small villages, that produces a *specific housing challenge* and also generates a set of circumstances that can make it difficult to respond to those challenges. Before looking at that confluence, and the constraints that it produces, one basic question needs answering: what is the rural housing problem?

The rural housing problem

There are many different rural housing problems. Housing access is a significant determinant of social and economic well-being, impacting on family formation, labour mobility and future wealth prospects through asset accumulation. The point was made above that housing problems confronting people and communities in the countryside, at least in the developed world, can appear less urgent than those afflicting urban areas and especially big cities with their more concentrated and visible challenges. The association of housing shortages and low housing quality with crime and safety, unemployment and with various social exclusions has often been viewed as mainly an urban phenomenon. High rates of home ownership in rural areas can provide a false signal of general advantage and mask a range of housing-related challenges. For that reason, rural housing was assigned low priority in the agendas of European and North American researchers until at least the late 1970s. But this has changed over the last 40 years with greater interest now evident in the housing outcomes arising from rural restructuring, which have often been underpinned by new mobilities and by counter-urbanisation (Dunn et al, 1981; Satsangi et al, 2010). Throughout much of this period, Anglophone literatures and perspectives (especially US, UK and Australian) have dominated – but interest in housing outcomes, as a measure of broader rural restructuring, has become an important research focus across many contexts, adding to the richness and diversity of this field.

Evidence of poor housing conditions and supply shortages – compounded by seasonal unemployment, low wages and geographical inaccessibility – has been documented in many rural locations since the 1980s, revealing that the countryside has not been insulated from the many ills, including poverty and social exclusion, afflicting cities (Dunn et al, 1981; Sindt and Guy, 1985; Weber et al, 2005). Notions of the 'rural idyll' – a happy population residing in thatched cottages or the vernacular equivalent – have been discredited and replaced by detailed accounts of structural inequality; a countryside of haves and have nots (Buller and Gilg, 2012). The roots of that inequality run deep. Many British rural communities had endured a century of population loss by the onset of the First World War (Satsangi et al, 2010). As farm incomes declined, so too did housing standards, stranding many households in abject squalor. In the United States, the economic crisis of 1929 to 1932 hit rural areas particularly hard and resulted in the sudden depopulation of regions dependent on farming, and consequent disintegration of communities, leaving abandonment and dereliction in its wake (Danbom, 2017: 185–7). After the Second World War, wider patterns of rural restructuring became an important policy challenge across Europe: depopulation attendant on changing economic circumstances was accelerated in the post-war period by new investment in mechanised farming, which aimed to achieve food security and protect European agriculture from global competition (Hoggart *et al*, 1995). But in all these places, a combination of greater accessibility (as motorways, freeways and autobahn offered wider access to the countryside), personal mobility (provided by private cars), recovering and rising urban wages and, in some instances, nostalgia for rural living (set against the pressures and challenges of urban lifestyles), triggered another critical process that was to shape rural areas for the next 70 years: counter-urbanisation (Fielding, 1982). Counter-urbanisation has numerous components but is generally spilt into a full-time or seasonal return to the countryside or lower-tier non-metropolitan towns. Its full-time form sees retired households, lifestyle downshifters, or salaried commuters moving permanently to rural locations. In its seasonal form, second homes are purchased by urban households who divide their time between rural amenity areas and work-life in the city. From the late 1960s onwards, researchers began to note the decline of traditional 'farming communities', arguing that the social structures of many rural areas were now subject to revolutionary change: communities comprising people sharing the common experience of a land-based occupation were being supplanted by mixed communities dominated by middle-class incomers attracted by rural lifestyles, by lower housing costs and by the greater accessibility of a countryside opened up by post-war investments in road and rail (Newby, 1980).

Counter-urbanisation has generated mixed results for different rural areas. There has, in some instances, been a mismatch in the market power of new and existing households, which has resulted in new exclusions that have been most visible in local housing markets (Shucksmith, 1981). Salaried incomers have been able to dominate those markets, importing equity from urban homes, and pushing house prices in some amenity areas onto a higher track – well out of the reach of the lowest income quartiles (Weekley, 1988; Liu and Roberts, 2013). But at the same time, the infrastructure investments that opened up the countryside have also made urban areas and urban jobs more accessible to existing rural residents. Reduced isolation can bring training, educational, employment and income benefits, presenting new opportunities to rural populations and enabling committed stayers to remain in the countryside. Likewise, the purchase and seasonal use of second homes (which are often extracted from the general housing stock) has brought a spectrum of impacts in both near-urban and remoter rural locations. There is now an expansive literature on this topic (see Hall and Müller, 2018, for a recent review). Where planning systems restrict new development in the countryside, the use of homes by seasonal residents can have a catastrophic impact on housing supply and affordability. This is the case across many parts of the United Kingdom where researchers have viewed second home buying as part of a broader commodification and consumption of the countryside, sometimes with adverse repercussions for existing residents (Brooks, 2021; Gallent *et al*, 2005; Paris, 2019). And yet, this consumption may provide a lifeline to declining rural areas that were already losing population and had few alternative sources of investment and spending. During the period of post-war recovery, the practice of maintaining a rural second home was rediscovered in many parts of Europe, especially across Scandinavia and the Mediterranean south. Once the stock of convertible housing had been exhausted, the production of new purpose-built second homes was encouraged. Second homes in many parts of Europe, and across North America, feature in the tourism and local economic strategies of numerous rural areas.

Counter-urbanisation has the potential to generate resource pressures (that are often felt in local housing markets) while masking rural poverty with imported wealth. It has also brought a social reconfiguration of rural areas that is often expressed in local politics. In very broad terms, counter-urbanisation has generated a divide between groups who continue to see the countryside as a productive space (a place to not only live, but also work, get educated, be young and be old) and those who view it as a space of consumption (an amenity space, for leisure pursuits and for retirement) and investment (a space for prized 'trophy' property in exclusive locations). While this is undoubtedly a simplification (see Harrison, 2019), the latter view has dominated in some amenity areas and is reflected in how people vote in local elections and their expectations of the planning system – which should be concerned with protecting amenity rather than supporting new development opportunities (Gallent *et al*, 2019a). Greater conservatism in rural planning has arguably impeded the supply of new housing while the variety of demand pressures has grown (Sturzaker, 2011). Affluent incomers compete ever more aggressively for land and property while ordinary working households struggle to secure affordable homes, constrained by low rural wages, and frustrated by the way in which some planning systems appear to prioritise environmental goals over social ones.

This narrative is most apparent in countries where nostalgia for the countryside underpins *simultaneous and strong* counter-urbanisation and rural protection pressures. Great Britain and the Netherlands, with their perceived and real land pressures, fall broadly into this type. On the other hand, restrictions on rural development have been less rigid where there is a culture of tolerance toward families meeting their own needs through community initiative and self-build. This tolerance has been manifested in sporadic rural development in southern Europe (especially in Italy – Fera and Ginatempo, 1985), in Eastern Europe (especially Hungary with its long tradition of self-build housing – Wallace *et al*, 2013) and in the Republic of Ireland (Gkartzios and Shucksmith, 2015). Elsewhere, development pressure has been less acute either because of the inaccessibility of rural areas (as in the case of the Nordic periphery – Spiekermann and Aalbu, 2004) or because the stock of vacant rural housing is so great that it has not yet been exhausted, as in France (Buller and Hoggart, 1994).

This brief introduction to the 'rural housing problem' has drawn attention to four themes: the first is counter-urbanisation and external interest in rural housing markets; the second is the strength of rural economies, rural incomes, and the capacity of local households to compete, on equal terms, with market entrants (see also Hodge and Monk, 2004); the third is the social exclusions that counter-urbanisation may generate; and the fourth is the complicating impact of planning systems – whether they accommodate the rhythms of rural restructuring or compound the challenges that new population movements and mobilities generate.

Also, despite rural areas being so different (internationally and intranationally), we can draw attention to a broad binary that is evident from the introduction: while some rural areas have been losing population without replacement, others have been exchanging population through displacement. These could be called *depleting* and *exchanging* areas. *Depleting* areas face significant economic challenges coupled, in some instances, with amenity attributes judged to be of a lower quality than elsewhere: perhaps lowland rural hinterlands in regions suffering economic decline or rural landscapes under mono-cropping that seem to offer fewer amenity attractions. *Exchanging* areas may be subject to economic restructuring – perhaps a shift from productive industries to place-based consumption through tourism – but have higher amenity value. Anchoring (of people and communities) is the central housing problem in depleting areas; perhaps anchoring for an economic reason – the preservation of farming and food security. But the problem in exchanging areas is displacement of a working population by market entrants, with potentially many investors venturing into the housing market (including retiring households or seasonal residents) and a more conservative approach to land use planning for reasons of amenity and equity (housing wealth) protection.

Housing is an *indirect* problem in depleting areas: economic decline drives poverty and the state of housing becomes a symptom of that. On the other hand, housing is a *direct* problem in exchanging areas, with market entrants and mismatched competition becoming the primary agent of change and subsequent driver of socio-economic inequalities. Further, in depleting areas, incomes are insufficient, in absolute terms, to secure decent housing situations *and* the drift away is driven by a lack of economic opportunity. In exchanging areas, incomes are relatively insufficient, causing housing-class based displacement. In both area types, intervention (that is, a response to the housing problem, however contrived) is vital because people, and communities, need to be in these rural areas: to live their lives and support, and be supported by, essential economic activity. More broadly, measures to address rural housing problems are essential, firstly, for reasons of socio-spatial justice – to combat market exclusions; secondly, to support rural economies and new industries, including vital post-carbon transitions; thirdly, to protect rural tourism (and the wider service sector) by ensuring labour supply for this industry; and fourthly, to support the culture and cultural identity of rural areas, including land-based industries. Simply allowing rural areas to transition into 'retirement landscapes' would impact negatively on economic activity and hence on valued landscapes.

Rurality

Rural areas have identifiable housing challenges, which we will contextualise further below – and root in particular types of place. But what is meant by 'rural' and by the idea of rurality? This is an old question – almost an obsession in Western geography – but worth picking up, albeit briefly, here. According to Woods (2010: 30), the contemporary countryside is a complex space, produced by the diverse and dynamic processes of 'imagination, representation, materialization and contestation'. It takes different forms in different contexts and countries. Ideas of the countryside are forever reinvented and reproduced, and underpinned by critical reflection on the observed state of what the countryside is today and what we might want it to be in the future (Woods, 2010: 30). In Latin-rooted languages, the word 'rural' denotes a geographical space beyond cities, but has also become an adjective – rural *people* or *landscapes* – that 'emphasises either connection to the land and agriculture, or to national identity' (Woods, 2005: 4). People in most countries will have a 'know it when you see it' understanding of what constitutes a rural place. The rural is defined by its contrast to urban and semi-urban (or suburban places): emphasis is placed on look and function. Cities are dense (or denser) and rural areas are not; suburbs are less dense than cities, but rural areas are less dense still: there is more 'space' between things. In other words, rural areas are demarked by sparsity: a spacing of things and activities, and it is in those interstitial spaces that rural areas frequently find their function.

In terms of that function, rural areas tend to fit a particular mould: being farmed, forested or places of leisurely pursuit – walking, riding and generally enjoying 'the countryside'. This gives them a particular aesthetic: farming or forested landscapes, gently undulating or topographically striking, and landscapes rich in amenity – where leisurely things can be done, on land, water or in the air. While this may be an Anglocentric perspective, the same sorts of 'know it when you see it' pastiche and subjective 'ruralities' could be presented for other countries.

The earliest attempts to quantify and index rurality sought to move beyond such 'subjective ideas' of rural places (Cloke, 1977) and tried to *measure* the sparsity of settlement or dominance of farming in order to construct taxonomies of rural types. Such 'positivist' delimitations, culminating in indices of rurality, eventually gave way to 'post rurality' perspectives that placed greater emphasis on the meanings and values associated with individuals' experiences of different places rather than their functional character. By the mid-2000s, 'rural' space had become an abstract notion, not necessarily associated with any specific geographical area (Woods, 2005: 4) or any observable function.

Figure 1.1   Village of Great Chart, Kent. © Nick Gallent.

This shift to greater abstraction is evident in the rich literature on this topic. Cloke (1977) started with his index of rurality, which he presented as 'an aid to the possible standardisation of planning solutions in areas with similar problems' (p. 31). Key indicators were used to reveal whether *areas* 'inclined' towards being rural or urban – an approach recently replicated in the geodemographic approach of Webber and Burrows (2017), albeit focused on the inclinations of *people*, read in commercial datasets. The premise of Cloke's index was that what makes a rural area *rural* can be read in key datasets for employment, population, migration, housing conditions, land-use and spatial remoteness. A decade later, Cloke updated his index using new UK Census data (Cloke and Edwards, 1986) but elicited a more critical review from fellow rural geographers. Hoggart (1988) contended that this focus on data mapping, and constructing taxonomies from observable *patterns*, was essentially blind to the *causal processes* that transcend any urban–rural divide, arguing that it is, *inter alia*, the relative importance of competitive, monopoly and state sectors that drives observable spatial outcomes rather than surface issues such as low population density. A few years later, Halfacree (1993) added to this critique. He agreed that statistical descriptions provide only shallow insight into the nature of rurality, and also with another of Hoggart's assertions: that broad socio-cultural divisions do not map neatly onto rural and urban spaces. The 'rural community' trope: that rural areas incubate a greater sense of belonging, attachment and community, had already been discredited by Pahl (1966) who showed that rural places are socially dynamic rather than stable, largely because of counter-urbanising and exchange forces, which bring about a mixing of social behaviours and attachments. But while Halfacree also agreed with Hoggart's emphasis on causal processes, *social representations* of the rural were also held up as a critical dimension of rurality, to be read in lay discourses addressing the nature of the countryside. Hence, the work of these three authors is representative of the broadening vista of rural studies.

Cloke did not remain associated with narrow positivist functionalism for long however. He embraced and developed the transition noted above (Cloke, 2006), but also argued that the detachment of values and meanings ('social representations') from observable function (what rural places 'do' and how they secure their futures) amounts to a 'post rurality' in which a broader disciplinary 'cultural turn' in geography failed to connect adequately with the function and therefore the 'politics of place'. In other words, abstraction had gone too far, prompting Cloke to call for a new fusion of the cultural turn with political and economic materialism: pattern, process and representations are all important. To borrow Louis Sullivan's famous phrase, 'form follows function', and it is the economic processes embedded in rural places that frequently give rise to crucial cultural and socio-political practices that make those places – and make them identifiably 'rural'.

A further layer to this is that the counter-urbanisation noted earlier in this chapter has, in important respects, made many rural areas subordinate to the political and cultural power of cities. That subordination has prompted new discursive representations of the countryside that emphasise the *relational* perspective (Woods, 2010: 44), either the strength or relative weakness of relational ties. Work in the 1990s by Marsden and colleagues has proven particularly useful to many researchers, drawing attention to the ways rurality (and underlying socio-political structures) and rural places change as they become more distant from urban influence and more dominated by *in situ* actors (and power relationships) rather than by relationships with urban centres. The decades of counter-urbanisation that preceded their analysis provides a critical context, as does the 'colonisation' of rural areas by middle-class migrants (Nelson, 2001: 399).

That colonisation transformed the relationship between people, economic production and land (Nelson, 2001: 398) and impacted significantly on the practised politics of rural areas (Marsden *et al*, 1993). Pre-empting Cloke's 'politics of place' challenge, these authors argued that

Figure 1.2 Cottages, Pluckley, Kent. © Nick Gallent.

the politics practised in rural areas is differentiated and determined by contrasting power sources, meaning that spaces can be more, or less, traditional, and subject to continuity or change depending, largely, on the degree to which they have been affected by economic, social and cultural shift. Four political rural spaces were identified: an anti-development 'preserved' countryside, in which incoming middle classes dominate decision-making; a 'contested' countryside beyond commuter catchments, in which landowners and farmers continue to play a leading political role; a 'paternalistic' countryside dominated by landed estates and the monopoly power afforded by landed status; and a 'clientelist' countryside in which relative isolation and 'peripherality' (generating critical welfare challenges) meets strong agricultural corporatism. Remoter rural areas are shaped by processes that are distinctly different from those that dominate in the shadow of cities.

The significance of this for thinking on the nature of rurality (or what it means to 'be rural') is that while functional measures help us visualise the countryside, and constructivist approaches flag lived experiences of rural places, the idea of the differentiated countryside – rooted in critical economic relationships and practised politics – connects to many of the challenges addressed in this book. While there is no direct mapping of our own area types (which serve as broad descriptions of housing problems rather than a rural taxonomy) onto these four distinct ruralities, the idea of practised politics in rural space, arising from critical processes and population exchanges, has clear resonance – particularly for the 'preserved countryside' in which many amenity areas are situated. Our concern, however, is not with the general nature of rurality but rather with a specific challenge within rural places that, because of decades of socio-political restructuring, is embedded in both functional realities (economic, including land market processes; and social, including class-conflict outcomes) and representations, mainly middle-class ones, of rurality and the constraints these impose on housing supply in villages.

Scale

Linked to the above are questions of scale, which are of central concern in this book. Its title – *Village Housing* – is intended to denote a shift in scale and a concern not with the generality of rural regions or with towns, as critical points of investment and intervention, but rather with lowest tier settlements. In the English language, the idea of a village denotes a scale, pattern of sociability and element of separation (or containment) that incubates peculiar socio-political and cultural outcomes. Many are viewed positively, hence the transportation of the 'village' idea into UK urban policy at the end of the 1990s, marked by the goal to create *urban villages*, understood to be ostensibly good things. But then, on the other hand, villages may be viewed as places of social closure, of tradition but not advance (backward and not forward looking or thinking) and of limited social resource, always needing some form of external support. None of these characterisations of villages is critically important in this book, in part because the meaning of 'village' is dynamic, especially between countries. We are concerned with *scale*, not because it might generate particular socio-cultural outcomes, but rather because 'lowest tier' settlements often lose out, in terms of interest and investment, relative to higher tier ones. Our conception of this problem is again rooted in the English experience, often viewed in relation to alternate international circumstances. Rural settlement planning is arguably a historic footnote in the longer story of statutory planning in England, but it is one that continues to shape thinking on rural planning practice. During the 1960s, County Structure Plans (the framework of strategic planning above local development plans) banded settlements according to size and service function (Cloke, 1979; Sillince, 1986). This was, in essence, a formal recognition of extant functional hierarchy (observed by Christaller, 1933), or the natural order that made the smallest hamlets reliant on bigger villages, which were in turn reliant on market towns, which were in turn reliant on principal county towns – centres of government and administration. That hierarchy was rooted in settled agriculture. Villages housed farm workers who needed some services nearby – the church and the blacksmith, meeting spiritual and practical needs – but then needed, at harvest time, to trade produce at the nearest market (situated in a market town). Seasonal dependence on the market town eventually expanded to become daily or weekly dependence: sending children to the 'big school' or heading 'into town' to purchase more than bread and milk. When rural depopulation began to reverse in the 1960s, with counter-urbanisation putting new pressure on rural land and resources, the County Structure Plans responded by fixing that hierarchy, redlining against development in lowest tier settlements and seeking to direct new jobs and housing to designated 'key service centres' including the traditional market towns (Sturzaker, 2019).

But that fixing generated a problem: it was designed to preserve the amenity of a countryside now being consumed for leisure at the expense of farming and other working communities. Counter-urbanisation centred new sources of demand on those smallest villages, with restrictive settlement planning funnelling that demand with the promise that surrounding amenity would never again be threatened by new housing or the expansion of economic activity. The result, for our *depleting* and *exchanging* areas (see earlier) has been either a stifling of new opportunities or the gentrification of villages – specifically these lowest tier settlements. The County Structure Plans have gone but this restrictive approach to development has survived (being 'saved' in local plans following enactment of the Planning and Compulsory Purchase Act 2004). It is a problem, in exchanging areas, because of the ongoing assetisation of homes (see Chapter 2) and the distribution of homes through 'open' market processes: planning drives scarcity; scarcity (of an attractive asset) is a draw to investors; and communities are, over time, reconfigured by market logic (Hoggart and Henderson, 2005). Planning plays a key role in structuring land (and housing) markets in rural areas, sometimes concentrating demand in the smallest villages: and thereby creating a village housing problem that has a clear 'scale' dimension.

Structural constraints

There are clues in the above as to the structures and structural constraints at play in villages. Planning systems play an important role in structuring land markets, affecting land prices and determining housing outcomes (Hilber and Vermeulen, 2016). Those systems interact with population movements and mortgage credit supply to produce inequalities in access to housing resources. More broadly, planning, fiscal policy, credit supply, property rights, stored wealth and legal systems come together to create advantage and disadvantage in open housing markets. But outcomes – the question of who gets housed – are also affected by broader housing delivery systems and particularly the roles of private, public and third sector providers in delivering homes for ownership, private rent or social rent.

The allocation of resource is crucial: regulatory systems allocate land in particular ways; banking systems allocate credit, legal systems allocate rights (including rights over property) and housing systems allocate on a bureaucratic or ability-to-pay basis. The best way to understand the relationships between these factors determining housing outcomes is to observe them in local operation. Relationships are important in two phases: in housing production and in housing consumption (or 'allocation' through the market).

Constraints localised

The nature and impact of factors will change depending on context: stricter or relaxed land use planning; abundant or limited credit; strong or weak legal systems; privatised or public delivery systems. However, we can still say something general about constraints.

First – and in the *production phase* – land must be made available for development. Key settlement policy, or general planning constraint, in England limits the supply of developable land in lowest-tier villages. Therefore (permissioned) land constraint is a critical barrier – with that constraint arising from practised politics, being a choice that is made in light of different economic, social and environmental objectives (Satsangi *et al*, 2010: 102). Second, planning itself is a constraint unless it is flexible enough to respond to the needs of groups who find themselves critically disadvantaged by market allocation (assuming that public policy differentiates between groups and recognises the rights and claims of those with 'local connection' or who are deemed to be 'key workers'). Indeed, planning (or its regulatory dimension) is frequently lambasted by its critics as an obstacle to economic development and housing supply, with 'unreasonable restrictions' responsible for housing shortages and economic inertia (Satsangi *et al*, 2010: 40). Third, we can assume that *private* production finance is not limited where demand (and prices) are high, but finance for affordable community housing may become a barrier if land prices cannot be tamed in some way (it will be too expensive to deliver, and costs cannot be recouped through high sale prices or rents to people on lower incomes). Council housing's 'golden age' – from 1919 until the decades immediately after the Second World War – was rooted in the availability of development land at close to agricultural value (see Chapter 3). That land was available, and priced as it was, because of an absence of speculative demand for private housing. Building council homes on it was the *best use* next to farming – as it was generally only councils bidding for that land. Today, the situation is much changed, with land price rooted in a combination of planning constraint and strong speculative demand in many amenity areas. Land cost massively amplifies the finance challenge for non-market providers.

The nexus of *planning–land–finance* occupies a production phase, structuring housing outcomes. The consumption phase interacts with production – housing production responds to consumption triggers (for instance a queue of buyers looking for homes in a particular place or a queue of people *in need* but with limited financial means). So the *consumption phase* is concerned with those things that structure demand and need.

First, property rights determine legal title and security: freedoms to consume and enjoy residential property. Where those rights are clear and unencumbered, demand can be freely expressed. Second, the expression of that demand will depend – in a market economy – on the availability of individual resource. If housing is allocated through the market (in other words, potential buyers competing with one another) then the chances of success on the part of any individual will depend on wealth, income and credit – and access to credit will depend on wealth (a deposit) and security of income. Past research has shown how different 'domestic property classes' compete against each other in open housing markets, with some enjoying clear advantage (Saunders, 1984; Shucksmith, 1990a). In rural areas, salaried market entrants – moving into rural areas – often outbid those reliant on lower rural wages (Pahl, 1975). Third, not all access is determined by wealth and income. Where there are public and third sector housing options, these may be allocated bureaucratically. But in those situations, young single people – for example – may be relegated behind families with children in allocation systems. Public policy will structure housing access and, critically, may be keener to deliver housing in key settlements than in villages, given consideration of economies of scale. Fourth, patterns of consumption (and access inequalities) will be affected by the assetisation of housing and the incentives to consume non-essential property for investment rather than its housing services (see Chapter 3). And that assetisation is advanced or impeded by the tax treatment of housing: levies charged on second homes, for example, in rural areas and whether these are big enough to discourage investment (given the long term capital appreciation of housing relative to other assets, most notably bank savings). If housing were an unattractive asset then the entire production–consumption dynamic would be changed and we might not be talking about a 'village housing problem', at least not in *exchanging* areas.

So the consumption nexus, interfacing with and driving production, is about rights, wealth and income, credit supply and tax liabilities. Alternatively, it may in some instances be about rules governing bureaucratic allocation – and the patterning of social housing supply. It is consumption drivers that scaffold prices, and affect housing affordability, in many of the case studies presented later in this book, although our principal concern, in the context of those drivers, is how non-market actors can overcome production barriers through a range of land, planning and finance innovations.

Conventional planning and market responses

Governments everywhere have worked to formulate responses to rural housing pressures, but the country we are concerned with in this book, England, has seen its housing, planning and tax policy shaped by a long succession of governments with neo-liberal leanings. They have sought minimum disruption to the ordering of outcomes through the market. In areas of economic stagnation and limited interest in rural property, the public policy response has generally been to anchor population, and provide services, in higher tier settlements – leaving a degree of unmet need and deprivation in 'villages'. The response has been the same in areas of high amenity value and investment demand, but rather than leaving a trail of poverty in its wake, 'key settlement policy' in areas subject to amenity-led migration, has delivered a socio-spatial reconfiguration of rural areas: richer market entrants in the 'villages' and domestic property classes consigned to private renting or requiring welfare support in the 'towns'.

This book is not concerned with investment and bespoke private housing in villages, but rather with public, community or third sector interventions that deliver opportunities for lower income households to live their lives in villages. Public intervention, in particular, has not always delivered those opportunities because of the production-side barriers listed in the last section and also because of a belief that planned interventions should deliver 'best value' from public investment, that is, concentrate delivery, meet the lion's share of needs in one place, and achieve an economy of scale. There is clear logic behind this approach and for some people this pattern of housing provision delivers benefit. But more broadly, conventional planning of this type falls into a 'sustainability trap' (Taylor, 2008), impeding the life cycle of villages, which age, do not renew themselves, become socially imbalanced and do not support labour supply and the health of rural economies (or drive their prosperity). The case for creating housing opportunity in villages rests on a mix of social and economic arguments. On the social side, a mix of age and social groups in villages will support a range of services including schools. That same mix will supply labour to nearby economic activities, including shops and farms. It will support service delivery, including for older retired households who have moved into the villages. Related to all of this, but on the economic side, the 'neo-productivist' countryside (see Gkartzios and Lowe, 2019) remains a place of economic activity that needs nearby labour supply. Where that labour is lacking,

Figure 1.3 Village of Pluckley, Kent. © Nick Gallent.

it will have to be imported (from the key settlements or further afield), driving car dependency and costs. This is the essence of the sustainability trap noted by Taylor. Hence, while conventional planning makes sense in terms of reducing housing delivery costs, it brings a range of negative externalities.

In short, public intervention has absented itself from villages for limited 'economic' reasons but, through key settlement policy, has tightly constrained private development in those same locations. This has conferred great scarcity value on village housing in areas of amenity demand, driving up land and property values (and rents) well beyond the reach of many local households and certainly those on lowest quartile incomes. Where development is possible, within village envelopes, it will invariably be 'high end', or involve the upgrading and extension of existing village housing for wealthy market entrants. Gallent and Robinson's (2012) study of neighbourhood planning in Kentish villages in the late 2000s (see Figures 1.2 and 1.3) flagged numerous examples of high-end conservation: startlingly beautiful archetypal homes adjacent to village greens, sometimes with seven-figure price tags. High level political decisions influence where and how economic and social change happens. Issues such as rural poverty, class conflict or the exploitation of natural resources can be partly explained by state action or inaction (Satsangi et al, 2010: 27). If neither the state nor the market is providing homes for lower income groups in villages then other mechanisms may be necessary to innovate solutions that overcome critical barriers.

Contexts, frameworks and local projects

This book is concerned firstly with the contexts in which village housing challenges arise and might find resolution; secondly with the national and local frameworks that impede or facilitate resolution; and thirdly with the local projects able to illustrate means of overcoming structural barriers relating to planning, land and finance. The book is structured as follows. Chapter 2 takes a direct cue from this introduction, examining more closely the consumption and production forces that shape housing outcomes, not only in rural areas but more widely. It situates rural areas in contemporary housing debate before expanding on the discussion of production barriers introduced in Chapter 1. Chapters 3 and 4 then look at the recent past and current state of intervention in village housing markets. The first of these reflects on 100 years of intervention in England. It notes three important means of aiding housing access: the use of tied housing, public housing interventions (that eventually gave way to third sector delivery), and occupancy restrictions placed on private housing permitted for agricultural workers and later for 'local need' only. Chapter 4 then examines more recent and contemporary approaches, spearheaded by the third sector and communities themselves. It also shines a light on more flexible planning approaches that move away from the conventions flagged in Chapter 1, particularly the granting of exceptional planning permission on farmland, and other land not allocated for housing use in local plans, so as to secure a land subsidy for low-cost housing development. The benefits and drawbacks of this approach are examined, as well as local innovations that have sought to increase the regularity and efficacy of its use. But all past and recent approaches sit within a land and planning framework that is hostile to certain types of development. Therefore Chapter 5 introduces the reforms – planning, land policy, tax and finance – that might support and foster alternate housing outcomes, delivering a different distribution of housing opportunity and wealth. The possibilities that such reforms might present are examined in Chapter 6 and these include low impact off-grid homes, community self-build and a new generation of council housing. Whether that future is attainable, and what its wider economic costs might be, is a question that we end on in Chapter 7.

2
Housing markets, planning and land

This chapter focuses on changing patterns of housing consumption. It examines the financialisation of housing markets and housing assets therein. It relates the assetisation of housing to bank lending preferences and to the defence of asset value through the planning system. The chapter locates rural housing consumption and supply within a broader context. It also provides a more complete theorisation of rural housing consumption by domestic property classes. Housing provides a means of wealth transfer and class reproduction. These systemic roles underpin the consumption of rural housing, which has an asset value that is increased by scarcity and protected by land use policy, mobilised to serve the associational interests of property owners, to the detriment of wider rural populations.

Introduction

It is widely acknowledged that many countries are in the grip of an 'advanced economy housing affordability crisis' (Ryan-Collins, 2021: 480) marked by falling rates of homeownership (or at least a concentration of ownership in fewer hands), rising private rents and general housing inequality, across generations and between key socio-economic groups. That crisis is viewed, by many, as a product of late neo-liberalism, the ascendancy of private interest over shared social responsibility, and the presentation of housing as a financial asset (for investors and owners) rather than as a right (Rolnik, 2013). Housing occupies centre-stage in discussions of global capitalism (Rossi, 2017; Christophers, 2020) and in more focused analyses of growth, prosperity and inequality (Piketty, 2014; Sayer, 2016). But the housing crisis is almost invariably painted as an urban crisis (Wetzstein, 2017), most visible and most pervasive in big cities, well connected to global flows of people and capital. And yet, movements across and within markets are underpinned by both the pursuit of profit and enhanced amenity.

Rural areas, with high amenity and limits on housing supply, can present investors with a prized opportunity. The overlay of multiple planning constraints – for reasons of urban containment or the protection of valued landscapes or areas of scientific significance, or merely to limit development and maintain the openness of countryside – plays its part in generating housing supply scarcity and pushing prices onto a higher track. The generality of rural housing challenges was introduced in the last chapter.

The supply – and hence affordability – challenge in rural areas is well documented and is compounded by reduced availability of social housing and by the limited availability of housing for rent (Bramley and Watkins, 2009: 206), owing to a combination of privatisation policies and a preference, in amenity areas, of renting homes to holidaymakers (Paris, 2019). In England, the Affordable Rural Housing Commission showed that the construction of new homes in rural areas fell by six per cent between 1998 and 2005 while urban housebuilding rose by 29 per cent during the same period. The corresponding figures for affordable housing, between 2001 and 2005, were a rise of three per cent in rural areas and 22 per cent in urban areas. Yet demand has continued to rise amongst commuters, retiring households and second home buyers (Sturzaker, 2010: 1002). It is the mixed function of housing – as investment and utility – that drives demand and shapes patterns of consumption, geographically. The purpose of this chapter is to situate our village housing focus within a broader context, showing how critical land and planning barriers are amplified by the assetisation of housing (the prioritisation of its asset function above its value as a provider of utility), marked by rising land/asset value and the dogged defence of that value by current owners, often through manipulation of the land-use planning system.

But before tracking that narrative, it is important to provide a general overview of the key drivers behind modern housing crises. The causes of 'housing crises' are acknowledged to range from supply-side blockages through to demand-side drivers. On the supply side, there are a number of reasons why too few new homes may be built relative to arising need. The variable application of planning restriction (including stricter application in high-demand amenity areas) may halt development in some locations but wave it through elsewhere. Uncertainty amongst development actors therefore arises, affecting the progress of development schemes where those actors are hesitant to commit the resources for full applications, fearing rejection at the planning stage. It is also the case that the prospect of acquiring planning permission on land allocated, or likely to be allocated, for development, will cause land values to spike. Companies may therefore hang on to land rather than developing it, slowing housing supply but benefiting from rising land values. Supply-side drivers are not restricted to the private sector: a reduction in social housing is bound into a debate on the merits and economy of government investment in this kind of state welfare – whether it makes sense to subsidise 'bricks and mortar' or individuals, supporting the latter's entry into the private housing sector.

The demand side is also complex and has multiple drivers: historically low interest rates, an accelerating supply of mortgage credit, cross-border direct investment (in big well-connected global cities and in the 'global countryside', see Woods, 2016) and the rise of rentier capitalism: more people and institutions investing in land and housing as a source of rent income, perhaps through traditional 'buy to rent' or platform-based short lettings. New supply blockages and demand drivers, concentrated in the second-hand stock, come together to suppress the amount of housing available to those who really need it, pushing up house prices and rents and pushing down levels of affordability and access. Gallent (2019: 75–6) traces six pathways that have brought the United Kingdom, and particularly *southern England*, to its current housing crisis.

First, too few homes are being built in England and this is leading to rising prices and limited opportunities for people to find and access the housing they need (Bowie, 2017). Responsibility for this lies in (private sector) construction capacity, the business models and practices of developers, and in planning regulation (underpinned by the way in which land for housing is allocated and, in some instances, by popular local rejection of development: see Coelho *et al*, 2017). Second, the pattern of housing demand has changed in recent years: overseas buyers and direct investors are eating into the supply of housing, causing a crisis centred on London (and other hotspots), which is rippling out to other parts of the country (Rossall Valentine, 2015). Third, the United Kingdom is too reliant on the private sector to supply the homes it needs. Greater output, and choice, was achieved when the state was directly involved in building affordable homes, which were bureaucratically allocated and shielded from creeping privatisation in the form of the right to buy (Tunstall, 2015). Fourth, the country is also too reliant on one type of private sector output – build to sell. New models from that sector (including 'Build to Rent') and other social and collective approaches to housing provision (including 'Community Land Trusts' and greater opportunities to move away from speculative build to self-build, for example) could extend access to good housing and, in some instances, address issues arising from the private ownership of land and the private capture of land rent (Benson and Hamiduddin, 2017). Fifth, the tax treatment of housing is hindering supply (for instance the VAT liability on conversion), impeding market function (such as stamp duty adding up-front costs on purchase) and driving rising demand for housing over other assets (for example, removal of 'Schedule A' tax in the past, application of capital gains tax and inheritance tax and the structure of council tax), with implications for the wider economy (Barker, 2014; Dorling, 2014). And finally, increased credit supply and money creation (achieved through financial deregulation) has been part of an economic strategy designed to activate new housing demand and consumption in support of the 'productive economy' and also the service-based economy (particularly financial services). This has had the effect of pumping new capital into the available housing supply and pushing prices out of the reach of households on average incomes – and even higher-earners in some areas (Ryan-Collins *et al*, 2017).

These pathways cross and interact. Housebuilding (and transaction activity in the 'real estate market' – see Beauregard, 1994) responds to money (credit) supply and not simply to the need for homes. The housing crisis is a disequilibrium between the supply of money and the supply of the housing asset. For those in need, this leads to declining affordability and a crisis of access. But at the centre of this is the intentional refunction of the relationship between housing and the economy. This draws in overseas buyers, privileges the private sector and owner-occupation, functions on the basis of privileged tax treatment and is underpinned by the supply of credit/debt. What is clear from different analyses of housing crises, in the UK and elsewhere, is that the supply of new housing is part of a larger jigsaw. But it is an important part, justifying a focus, in some quarters, on ensuring that the planning system effectively facilitates rather than hinders new housebuilding.

This generalised view of the housing crisis is concerned with affordability: why house prices have accelerated far ahead of earnings over recent decades, driving a sharp fall in the rate of homeownership (which fell 10 percentage points between 2007 and 2017). As our focus is on village locations, these six drivers need some reinterpretation. First, villages are certainly one of the locations where too few homes are being built. But there is no potential to build at scale in villages, given the need to balance character and amenity objectives. Scarcity – arising from demand pressures and limited new-build potential – is key to price change but a simple supply response is neither credible nor desirable. Second, the pattern of housing demand has changed in recent years: this is certainly true in many villages, but the source of that demand is not overseas investors. Rather, counter-urbanisation has brought domestic buyers to rural areas. This was revealed during the recent COVID-19 crisis, when the flight to second homes was widely reported (Gallent and Hamiduddin, 2021). It was households from London and other big cities that sought refuge in their rural properties. Indeed, Gallent and Madeddu (2021) have suggested that the pandemic has brought many rural areas to a 'critical moment', with more people choosing to live in the countryside and with those choices risking an acceleration of rural gentrification that can only be countered by a new diversity in housing options, market and non-market. Given extant supply restrictions, these buyers are very clearly 'eating into the available stock'. Third, reliance on private housing is critical to housing outcomes in villages given the small stock of council homes, much of which was lost through discounted sales to sitting tenants from 1980 onwards (in areas not afforded special protection – see Chapter 3). Once restrictions on sales in rural areas were lifted, these proved the most popular places for 'right to buy' sales, obliterating the supply of non-market housing in villages, and – according to research in the 1990s – turning many ex-local authority properties into second homes (Chaney and Sherwood, 2000). Fourth, there are limited housing alternatives in villages, besides housing for private sale. This is clearly the case and is a challenge that has, as noted above, been accentuated through the loss of council housing. Fifth, tax impacts on housing consumption. Tax levies on investment property are less than on alternative assets (Barker, 2014), meaning that housing is a preferred asset class for many investors. Council tax valuations are outdated and do not account for the trajectory of price change over the last 30 years, meaning that many valuable rural properties (which have grown that value in recent decades) are under-taxed. For second homes, council tax is levied at the same rate as first homes (unless local councils charge a premium) and can be avoided if they are registered as 'holiday lets' and held by limited companies. Owners then become directors of those companies, pay business rates and eventually pay capital gains tax (on sale) at a lower rate. All such loopholes and limited liabilities push investment into housing. Sixth, bank lending has had a general inflationary effect on house prices over the long run (Keen, 2018). This might be seen as an aspatial driver, but it is in selected amenity areas that banks have, through their favoured mortgagees, competed against one another to generate loans on prime property. The preference for lending on land and housing, over business investment, has amplified demand and provided a critical bootstrap to house prices. This final driver, which is of universal relevance, evidences an assetisation and consequent financialisation of housing, which has become an important dimension of the housing crisis in many advanced economies (Ryan-Collins, 2021).

In the remainder of this chapter we track through five key questions and themes that shape the consumption of village housing and accentuate production barriers: these are (1) the mixed function of housing (for individuals and modern economies), linking to (2) assetisation; (3) how that assetisation shapes the choices of discrete property classes; how (4) the associational interests of dominant classes impact on the politics of rural development; and how all of the above (5) shapes the critical barriers, centred on land, planning and finance, introduced in the last chapter

The mixed function of housing (*underpins its asset status*)

Housing is a complex commodity (Quigley, 1997; Robinson, 1979; Gibb, 2009) with its consumption motivated by both *utility* (the *services* it provides to its occupants) and by *investment* (how it will support wealth accumulation). It provides services by virtue of its size, layout and location. Location is critical, determining price via commuting costs, accessibility to nearby public services and amenity, and because of proximity to environmental benefits ranging from air quality to good weather (O'Sullivan, 2012). It is also a complex commodity because of its long durability, its high level of heterogeneity, the high transaction costs associated with sale and purchase, and because of its role in personal finances. The personal decision to purchase residential property is shrouded in complex 'spatial and temporal considerations' (Maclennan, 1979: 327). The broader consumption of housing is shaped by financial and welfare considerations – not only the costs of the house today, but the benefits it will bring in the future.

The investment motive is a critical driver behind housing consumption and one that is particularly important in rural amenity areas, where many purchasers do not require the 'service' of employment proximity. General benefits are also important in rural settings, and so these are briefly unpacked here.

Homeownership, achieved with a residential mortgage, transforms a debt liability into an asset within the space of 25 years – as the mortgage is paid off. During that period, imputed rent (the income saving against the rent that would otherwise be payable if a home were rented rather than owned) increases as the mortgage debt liability (typically) shrinks relative to the growing value of the asset. Home ownership delivers the ultimate benefit of rent-free and mortgage-free occupation. House purchase can therefore act as a hedge against future uncertainties and risks: reduced income or eviction (Kemeny, 1980; 1981). But long-term financial certainty and security – as a personal welfare strategy (Lowe, 2011) – is just part of the investment motive behind ownership. More broadly, housing is a *store of wealth* that can be released, or borrowed against, to support spending (Smith and Searle, 2010). It also provides an *income supplement* (via imputed rent benefits) that enables people to live well on lower workplace earnings or smaller private pensions (Quilgars and Jones, 2010). It may also allow them to invest in private education for their children, something that non-owners can seldom afford. And with the relentless rise of housing wealth, because of the upward march of house prices, housing becomes a channel through which owners can transfer their wealth to those children, later on, with limited inheritance tax liability. The intergenerational transfer of wealth through this 'housing channel' is the primary driver of class reproduction (Saunders, 1984). What all this means is that housing wealth, or housing's 'asset function', plays a central role in determining financial well-being and life-chances, for owners and for their dependents. The ownership of housing confers significant socio-economic advantage.

Housing is therefore an asset that grows in value, supports spending, and can be passed on. There has been a general shift towards homeownership in recent decades, which has been pronounced in rural areas – for reasons that are outlined later in this chapter. The assetisation of housing, and the turn from other assets, has created a loop in which house-price rises feed housing demand: as housing becomes more expensive (relative to earnings), the necessity 'to get on the housing ladder' intensifies, being 'the only way to protect effectively against future house price rises' (Barker, 2014: 42). Instead of depending on state-managed social transfer to deflect poverty risks, individuals take greater responsibility for their own welfare plans by investing in property assets, whose value is likely to increase over time (Aalbers and Christophers, 2014: 548). Market competition intensifies, as does the defence of private equity in housing against potential threats – including from additional development, with its potential to impact negatively on the amenity that supports value or to reduce the 'scarcity' that scaffolds price.

Indeed, commodity complexity – housing's dual function – produces the perverse effect that declining housing supply (or inherent supply constraint) and rising (or high) prices act as a financial *incentive* to buy a home rather than as a *deterrent*. This reality has particular resonance in rural amenity areas where housing, by virtue of scarcity, remains a 'good investment'. And once purchased, increases in market supply (but not necessarily non-market options) are clearly against the associational interest of homeowners (see Housing conflict, below).

The assetisation, and onward financialisation, of housing (*is core to driving price inflation through credit supply*)

This assetisation of housing is fundamental to contemporary housing outcomes across urban and rural areas. It was noted above that asset-holding supports consumer spending. This is one of the reasons why governments have been keen to scaffold housing markets, thereby reorienting economies towards the extraction of income from property. This is derived not only from spending and tax on spending, but also from mortgage lending, debt securitisation, insurance and other financial services – the growth of which has been a global phenomenon since at least the 1980s. Financial extractions are achieved via a process of *financialisation* – examined more closely below – which is facilitated through the loosening of finance and lending controls, causing a rapid expansion of real estate portfolios and profits, and fuelling the inflation of house prices (Atkinson and Jacobs, 2020: 13).

'Successful' housing markets are thought to support a general uplift in incomes and spending, delivering optimal welfare and shared prosperity. But this has not been the experience of housing markets in England over the last 50 years. Rather, house-price rises have been associated with falling rates of home ownership (since the global financial crisis), barriers to personal wealth and welfare and overall negative economic effects. Indeed, as the housing stock becomes more expensive across urban and rural areas, a binary develops between those who already own property (and who benefit from rising prices, in all the ways noted above) and those who are looking to join the market, but for whom the benefits of ownership come at a spiralling cost. Advantage is often gained from inheritance, from the intergenerational transfer of wealth – causing a concentration of housing in fewer hands. This binary has been observed across many parts of the UK, where incomes have been unable to keep pace with rising asset prices. This has necessitated the issuing of longer-term mortgage advances on higher loan-to-value ratios. These increase the financial burden on borrowers, negating the benefits of homeownership and introducing increased personal and systemic risk (Atkinson and Jacobs, 2020: 14–15).

The inability to achieve market access through workplace earnings (or stretched ratios between earnings and housing costs) suggests that the market is being shaped and dominated by investment capital (Atkinson and Jacobs, 2020: 11) and the accumulation of intergenerational wealth. Besides inheritance windfalls, Barker (2014) argues that the benefits of rising prices are increasingly captured by those 'aided by parents who already have a stake in the housing market', resulting in 'sharp divergences in the distribution of wealth and the opportunity between generations, and between those living in different areas' (p. xi). This means, firstly that the number of people who cannot become homeowners, or accumulate wealth in the manner that property affords, is increasing – reinforcing and deepening already entrenched patterns of inequality (see Assetisation and housing classes, below). It also means, secondly, that the barrier to personal wealth creation acts as a drag on the general economy because of the latter's dependence on consumer confidence and spending.

One might imagine that the advantages of homeownership, and patterns of consumption and therefore advantage, are somehow natural. But the preference for, and advantages of, private housing has been crafted and magnified through successive policy interventions by governments that recognise how the 'asset function' of housing impacts on national economies.

The first significant move to bolster this asset function in the UK happened in the mid-1950s when public subsidy for homeownership was allowed to exceed funding for council housing for the first time. That subsidy took the form of exchequer advances to building societies for re-lending in the form of mortgages (Ministry of Housing and Local Government, 1958). Those advances accrued a lower interest rate than public finance for schools, roads, healthcare and (council) housing[1]. Government was therefore, in effect, subsidising homeownership at a preferential rate – using taxpayers' money to fund cheaper loan credit. Other tax reforms then followed that continued to reshape the financial benefits accruing to homeowners. Before 1963, owners were taxed on the imputed rent (see above) of owning their homes, as part of their overall income tax liability. They paid 'Schedule A' tax on property at a hypothecated rate depending on value. When this was scrapped, the incentive to invest in housing – rather than other assets – was greatly increased. Twenty years later, in 1983, government introduced 'mortgage interest tax relief at source' (MIRAS). Along with the retention of tax relief for improvement (which was available on second homes until 1974: Gallent, 1997), the arrival of MIRAS meant effectively that the cost of borrowing against, and renovating, housing was now being subsidised by the government. Homeownership, as a form of asset investment, was becoming increasingly tax efficient, bestowing income benefits that were absent from renting, which came to be seen as an inferior tenure. Government was playing a key part in the assetisation of housing (Lowe, 2011) while peddling the myth that homeownership – and asset-based welfare – derives entirely from individual effort, while state welfare, particularly in the form of public housing, is a burden on the taxpayer. The truth is that state spending was simply being redirected and this redirection, this sleight of hand, generated growing support for a withdrawal from more direct investment in council housing (Castles, 1998; Kemeny, 2005).

'Asset housing' can be financialised, and financialisation has become another way to connect residential property to economic performance – often in more abstract ways. Housing has today been caught up in a wider debate centred on the primacy of rentier capitalism in driving western economies (Christophers, 2020). At its most basic level, this is concerned with holding assets and extracting rent. There are often strong rental markets in amenity villages. The arrival of platform-based short rentals such as Airbnb has accelerated rentier capitalism in rural areas, helping it expand its influence over housing markets (see Paris, 2019). For the housing domain, the oddly named *sharing economy*, a label that suggests some sort of altruistic social enterprise, is in fact an accelerator of assetisation, helping reduce ordinary households' access to housing services while advancing capital accumulation in fewer hands. But the transformation of homes into financial assets extends well beyond this direct rental activity. Financialisation, more broadly, transforms all housing into an 'asset class' from which income can be derived through 'financial channels' (Krippner, 2005). This is primarily achieved through trading in the mortgage debt on which private housing consumption (and public housing production funded from market borrowing) depends. The expansion of mortgage finance is at once a condition for and a driver of financialisation.

By the early 1970s, the centrality of housing consumption to national prosperity, and to public revenues, was widely acknowledged – as was the part played by building societies in sustaining consumption and the housebuilding sector. 'Non-traditional' policies for building society finance, including new types of investment and mortgage facilities and 'special arrangements for tapping into the capital market for long-term funds' were the subject of regular talks between the Bank of England and the Building Societies Association (Stirling, Gallent and Purves, 2022). Those 'special arrangements' – untethering finance capital from bank and building society deposits – have since become one of the principal mechanisms of financialisation, enabling banks and building societies to draw down capital from global money markets, de-risk lending, and originate more loans on residential property at higher loan-to-value ratios, producing the credit-price feedback loop described by Ryan-Collins (2021) and thereby underwriting house-price inflation (Atkinson and Jacobs, 2020: 13).

The extensive literature on housing financialisation starts with the premise that the interest of investors lies in making otherwise *illiquid assets* liquid, thereby overcoming their 'spatial fixity' and drawing income from assets fixed to different places. Housing has obvious spatial fixity: so how can it be mobilised as a *financial asset* for investors?

Researchers in this area regularly use the work of Harvey (1974; 1978; 1981; 1982) to explain how capital 'switches' into housing and other forms of real property and, thereafter, how economies may become more reliant on the extraction of rent for their growth and for their public finances. Harvey (1978) explains that investment capital flows in three circuits, including a primary or *productive* circuit. There, it is employed in the making of things, and from that *making,* and the creation of *value,* profit is derived. But he drew attention to a tendency towards the over-accumulation, and periodic movement away, of capital from this productive circuit. Over-accumulation – 'too much capital produced in aggregate relative to the opportunities to employ that capital' (p. 106) – causes a number of issues for investors: overproduction, market glut, falling profits and 'money capital lacking opportunities for profitable employment'. In these circumstances, where there is a lull in the productive economy, the built environment (a secondary circuit comprising land, housing, infrastructure and commercial property) becomes a place to park surplus capital. That secondary circuit serves 'jointly for both production and consumption', in that 'investment in the built environment […] entails the creation of a whole physical landscape for purposes of production, exchange and consumption' (Harvey, 1978: 106).

While the primary circuit is mainly about 'making', the secondary circuit delivers profit through 'taking': command over and the extraction of land rent. But a way needs to be found to facilitate capital switch and turn fixed items – land and buildings – into commodities that can be traded on international markets (selling and trading the incomes derived from these things, rather that the physical assets).

Harvey showed that this needs to be achieved through a 'functioning capital market', by consumer credit and mortgages and other financial instruments that 'mediate' movements between the primary and secondary circuits (that is, by the 'special arrangements' being discussed and designed in England in the 1970s). Recent literature on the 'financialisation of housing' is primarily concerned with the means of 'taking' from housing – and with the centrality of housing in the trading of 'asset-backed securities' (Wainwright, 2009). Banks originate mortgages on housing, but those mortgages, particularly in sub-prime markets, are risk laden. Banks can distribute and reduce that risk by securitising debt and selling it on to third party investors – who accept the risk in return for income from the securities.

Hence housing – and mortgages – are implicated in the switch of investment capital from the productive (making) to the non-productive (taking) circuit, which has become a permanent rather than episodic practice in 'late capitalist' economies, with capital markets (and associated financial services) evolving to primarily deliver this outcome. Indeed, while Ryan-Collins and colleagues (2017) argue that this 'shadow banking' drives credit supply and fuels house prices, Aalbers (2017: 542) adds that mortgaged home ownership now exists to support financial markets rather than *vice versa*.

This 'financialisation' perspective on crises of housing affordability is rooted in the 'revived intellectual reputation of Marxist analysis in the social sciences in the 1970s' (Savage *et al*, 2003: 44). It centres on the classical distinction between capitalists (who control assets and extract profit for reinvestment, with a view to long term capital accumulation) and labourers (who control only their labour power, sold at a price determined by the market) (Harvey, 1978). It reinstates and updates an old binary, used by Engels in *The Housing Question* (1872). This perspective is unpalatable to those who ascribe housing inequalities to the softer target of land-use regulation (and its claimed impact on supply) rather than the complexities of financial markets – and their indirect impact on price and affordability at a *structural* level.

What does all this mean for our particular focus on village housing? House prices everywhere are driven up by the assetisation of housing: it is a *structural driver* of cost and affordability. There is macro-economic interest in seeing prices rise, in support of consumer spending, financial services and asset-based welfare. The emphasis placed on the promotion and protection of house prices has general implications for housing debate, and for how we might address wealth inequalities in housing without upending economic growth. Very broadly, it says that by shifting back to making (returning capital flows to productive activities), we could deliver the general benefit of increased housing affordability, by raising earnings and reducing asset prices. This thesis emphasises the centrality of credit and interest rates in price setting. But others argue that restrictions on new housing supply have a greater overall effect, and so planning reform (removing supply restrictions) will impact positively on the distribution of housing wealth (Breach, 2019). There is of course some truth in this, but local circumstances do not invalidate the structural explanations of housing inequality.

Private market housing in villages is subject to the price-setting effects of these structural drivers. The credit available to homebuyers and interest rates matter, intensifying competition for additional housing space and investment opportunity. These structural drivers then interact with local forces, including the strength of rural planning restrictions, to further corral wealth into housing and lock less advantaged 'housing classes' out of the market for homeownership and private renting. Past research has revealed how different housing classes, differentiated by wealth and income, incur relative advantage or disadvantage in the housing market. Attention to class divisions, and potential conflicts between classes, illuminates how housing is distributed through the market and how wealth inequalities are generated and reinforced.

Assetisation and housing classes
(assetisation has supercharged wealth disparities and widened the gap between homeowning and non- owning property classes)

Class is rooted in transmutable economic capital (Bourdieu, 1986). Wealth, carried forward from one generation to the next, supports the accumulation of social and embodied cultural capital – and land and property provide an important means of raising and transferring wealth. Class position is dependent not only on the ability of an individual to generate income through employment (with the capacity to do so anchored in existing class advantages), but also the capacity to generate income and grow wealth through the accumulative potential of property ownership, whether landed property or basic home ownership (Shucksmith, 1990a).

Housing wealth is now a significant factor in facilitating, contouring and perpetuating patterns of British social class. The assetisation processes examined above have resulted in uneven wealth accumulation in housing. The mix of rising asset prices and stagnating earnings has resulted in 'propertied winners' and 'working losers'. Individuals with no family history of property ownership, for instance, have struggled to keep up with rapidly rising prices in recent years, and have often remained locked in the rental sectors. They have not been in a position to benefit from the upward march of house prices. Asset holding confers a potential for wealth accumulation and distinguishes advantaged from disadvantaged property classes. Those classes come to share *associational interest,* which is often manifest in contrasting attitudes to planning and development, with the advantaged viewing planning control as a means to defend private equity in housing and the disadvantaged seeing it as a means to advance greater access. This précis of the significance of class is now briefly unpacked.

Analyses of housing market outcomes frequently build on Max Weber's notion of 'life chances in the market' (Weber, 1921) being determined by social class (Saunders, 1978: 235), thereafter developed by Saunders (1984) in his conceptualisation of 'domestic property classes'. Private property provides a framework for market action, motivated by asset and wealth accumulation. Local market outcomes – who is locked out and by whom – are determined by the property histories of different classes, and often by the intergenerational transfer of property wealth (inheritance or property-owning parents helping their children get on 'the housing ladder' with cash advances on inheritance). Accumulated capital and income at a household level are inevitable determinants of housing market advantage under capitalism. But it is property (and *tenure* divisions) rather than income poverty that fixes outcomes over time and across generations.

Saunders (1984) has underscored the primacy of tenure in the structuring of housing markets and, more generally, the key role played by domestic property ownership in the 'structuration of class' (p. 202). He argued that owner occupiers constitute a distinct domestic property class, advantaged relative to public or private renters by the releasable (and potentially mobile) equity they have accumulated through asset ownership. Similar points have been made more recently by Aalbers and Christophers (2014: 380), who argue that the owner/non-owner (or landed/landless) binary remains the most visible marker of material wealth inequality within western society.

Within a closed market (devoid of external buyers) a simple division exists between advantaged owners and disadvantaged non-owners.

But where there are *market entrants* (a global elite flying in to park wealth or domestic investors finding that they can release equity from urban homes, or borrow against that equity, to fund the purchase of additional homes in amenity areas and in 'aspirational' villages), a more complex pattern of advantage and disadvantage emerges, with the scales of advantage often tilted towards those market entrants – many of whom are investors, motivated to enter a new market by their wealth advantage, relative to local housing classes, and the expectation of capital appreciation.

The extent to which market entry accentuates existing disadvantage will depend on the housing (tenure) circumstances of existing residents. The injection of mobile capital, pushing up house prices, can make it more difficult for households aspiring to leave the private rental sector to do so. Local homeowners may also find it more difficult to 'trade up' through the market, especially if new supply options are limited. These outcomes are common to urban areas (London's housing crisis is marked by rising rents and falling levels of homeownership – see Gallent, 2019) and to rural areas, where lower income groups – lacking a family history of homeownership – are confined to a shrinking social rented sector, which is often concentrated in key settlements. Market impacts will always be greater where there is a concentration of families trying to become homeowners for the first time or where rising house prices are reflected in upward rent levels.

Past research has drawn attention to the life-stage, family history and socio-economic class divisions that further complicate domestic property classes and produce 'consumption cleavages' within rural housing markets (see Pahl, 1966; Ambrose, 1974; and Dunn *et al*, 1981). Shucksmith drew much of this work together in his studies of housing access in the Lake District (1981; 1990b) and subsequent reflections on market dynamics and social class (1990a). Broadly, he observed that 'low income and low wealth groups' were invariably outcompeted by 'more prosperous groups' (Shucksmith, 1990a: 225) but that neither class was homogenous. The most disadvantaged of the former tended to be childless singles and couples, who were not only struggling to pay private rents and purchase property, but also finding it very difficult to access social housing (which was being sold off to sitting tenants, under the 'right to buy' legislation, and was anyway more likely to be allocated to households with children). Scales of advantage were observed among the more prosperous groups: income-poor owner-occupiers enjoyed a more stable existence but could struggle to maintain their property.

Higher-income owner-occupiers, on the other hand, shared similar advantages (and 'associational interests' – Milbourne, 2006) with market entrants (moving in for retirement, second-home purchase or for lifestyle reasons – and then commuting back to city jobs), forming a more discrete property-owning class, which has since displayed shared class interest. As noted above, the *associational interest* of property owners may lie in the defence of asset value, by influencing or taking control of the governance of land policy and planning. For this reason, counter-urbanisation has been associated with an increasingly conservative rural politics and the rejection of any new housing that threatens local amenity, housing scarcity and hence stored equity in private housing. Critics of the planning system contend '[...] that allowing considerable and continuous input from existing residents disconnects housing supply from demand by ratcheting down the number of new homes that are built' (Breach, 2019: 25), as residents try to protect the amenity value of their homes by fighting any new developments. Coelho *et al* (2017) have shown that opposition to new housing development, and conflict centred on planning, is invariably greater where there are a high proportion of owner-occupiers, lending support to the argument that new housing is opposed for private reasons – to maintain the current distribution of wealth and class advantage.

Housing conflict *(centred on divergent class interest)*

Associational interest is therefore important when analysing housing stresses and solutions. Ryan-Collins and colleagues (2017) have argued that high rates of home ownership – locally and nationally – limit the range of responses to housing crises. Where a *simple majority* has faith in the status quo, the perceived aspirations and interests of that majority will guide the policy programme of a democratic government. Where owner-occupation, supporting asset-based welfare, is dominant, governments tread carefully, supporting the aspiration towards wealth creation through housing even if that wealth creation, measured in rising house prices, locks new entrants out of the market. But a tipping point can be reached, as rates of ownership fall, where government starts to give greater consideration to other housing classes – renters and aspiring ownings.

A window of opportunity arguably opened in the decade between 2007 and 2017 – a period when owner-occupation declined but house prices continued to rise, despite some fall-back after 2009. During those 10 years, government withdrew tax reliefs on private letting and introduced a Stamp Duty Land Tax (SDLT) surcharge on second homes (see Chapter 5). 2017 was the peak year for the housing market in the UK, with prices subsequently falling, in some areas, or plateauing elsewhere. This was not entirely down to tax changes: market confidence was rocked by the 2016 Brexit vote and by subsequent uncertainty over the UK's eventual trading relationship with the EU. But there is at least some evidence, nationally, that a different set of associational interests – *those of renters and aspiring owners* – came to the fore and started to influence government's housing interventions.

What happens in local markets, downstream of these big upstream debates, is of course part of this wider picture. However, local markets also have their own dynamics: different places are affected by their own peculiar challenges and dynamics. The associational interest of home owners in exchanging villages lies in, and is frequently expressed in, the defence of *local character and amenity* – including the potential overloading of village services if further development were to be accepted (Pendall, 1999: 114). Character and amenity are presented as public goods: there would be a net loss to 'the public' if they were diminished in any way. Thankfully for these owners, the public and private value attributed to, and derived from, character and amenity are difficult to untangle. This means that where the underlying motive of homeowners is the defence of stored equity, this can be presented as well-meaning public concern (Pendall, 1999: 114). But of course, divisions between different groups emerge and the public interest, to build or not to build, is contested. Homeowners are painted as NIMBYs and the case for a 'fairer distribution of housing resource', achieved by a combination of development and perhaps market closure (via occupancy restrictions – see Chapter 3), will be advanced by other interests. Pendall (1999: 115) notes that given the importance of housing in the reproduction of class, ensuing conflicts are in essence class antagonisms rooted in deep anxieties around the protection or erosion of wealth and social advantage.

The dynamics of all villages are not configured in this way. Circumstances differ and there are varying levels of acceptance of development, even in the smallest hamlets. For example, some owner-occupiers will support more housing for local needs, if this is limited and if they are able to exert control over allocations to that housing (Gallent and Robinson, 2011). Likewise, older residents may want to bring in young people, seeing this as a way of growing the services that they may need in the future. And elsewhere, there may simply be a level and type of development that is felt to be appropriate and unlikely to have any significant impact on amenity, character and stored equity. Homeowners are not a homogenous class, with life-stage and occupation (and personal linkages to the local economy) also explaining opposition to, or support for, development (Milbourne, 1997: 43). Sturzaker (2011: 567) adds that attitudes are not unshakeable: the deeper community engagement that is sometimes a feature of life in small villages can reduce opposition to development, especially if that development is seeded in governance processes that bring together a mix of groups, who share evidence and experiences, and think through the longer development trajectory and needs of a village. Indeed, intransigent rejection of development, where it occurs, is likely to be rooted in particular circumstances: for example, where there are concentrations of second homeowners who may have no interest in growing services, and wish rather to preserve seasonal amenity. But irrespective of the particular configuration, associational or dominant interest will shape local politics, impacting on land planning and development.

This happens because of the way the English planning system is constituted and how it is operated, especially in lowest-tier settlement. Principle-based plans are drawn up by local authorities and discretionary development-control decisions are made by elected council members. Through those members, the system gives direct voice to village conservatism – with local homeowners able to exert considerable influence over development. This is an over-simplification. The current system already presumes against development in rural areas, so the extent that homeowners are able to magnify that presumption is unclear. What seems certain is that there are structural constraints that are potentially reinforced by associational interest. That structural constraint is deep-seated. In 2020, government proposed sweeping reform to the planning system in England, arguing a need to move away from the case-by-case consideration of planning application to a system of automatic consent, achieved through a mix of statutory instruments (MHCLG, 2020a). But that change would apply only in growth and renewal areas. Elsewhere, including in the village locations examined here, the existing approach to development control was to be preserved and the 'protection' afforded many rural areas maintained. In short, it seems likely that planning decisions, now and in the future, will reflect the views of an existing population which, in amenity areas, is often affluent, white and middle class. These are not insurmountable barriers to development, as Sturzaker (2011) has shown, but they are an important context for village housing schemes in many areas. Further comment on the direction of change in the planning system is provided later in this book.

Linking assetisation and associational interest to land, planning and finance

Where there are identified housing needs, and the championing of a positive response by a supportive community, critical land, planning and finance barriers will need to be overcome. Land barriers (impediments to the availability of developable land) can be physical but are more likely to be political: a tightly drawn village envelope beyond which land is not 'zoned' (or allocated) for development. Those boundaries will be framed by national or strategic policy, reflecting agreed approaches to the use of rural land and the balance of priorities between community/housing use and conservation. Land within the envelope may command a high price, again impeding development for anything other than high-end use. The planning system is generally the instrument of this constraint, but planning can also introduce other barriers around siting, access and design: the relationship between new development and the rest of a village, sight lines and so forth. We can distinguish planning's general effect on land availability and costs from its specific effects on its acceptability, and compliance with detailed planning rules. Related to all of this – to constraint, land costs and planning/design strictures – is development finance: how to overcome cost barriers and secure the finance needed for development to proceed. These are all issues affecting 'low cost' (relative to market prices) development everywhere, but they are magnified in small village locations.

A pejorative view of land policy and planning is that it is allied to the defence of private value, heightening the critical barriers introduced in Chapter 1. Land is a financialised commodity, its use policed and defended by planning systems (Bradley, 2021). Planning also adds cost to development, with that cost generally borne by consumers, who pay more for housing. It has been observed many times that the land market connects to planning in many ways. Planning corrals value to preferred or planned locations. It also has a role to play as market-maker, by co-ordinating the infrastructure investments needed to open up sites for development. Therefore, a more positive view of planning is that it creates public value and is a source of development opportunity. But as well as corralling value, it limits the proportion of value that is extractable as private profit by insisting on direct or in lieu contributions to infrastructure or affordable housing. It also sets density, design and layout policies affecting what can be built and therefore the value of developable private land.

A reduction in 'planning costs' – combined with the retention of its role in land rationing and infrastructure co-ordination – is considered by many commentators as a means of accelerating land development (see Bowie, 2017: 122 for a broader discussion) in pursuit of a broader public good. But that public good conceives housing as social infrastructure rather than private asset. It was noted earlier in this chapter that housing is a complex commodity: afforded the right protections it retains its value, and indeed that value often grows over time, so consumers with the means to do so are happy to pay more for an 'asset'. Planning is a 'double-edged sword': increasing *private cost* but also, over time, increasing *private value*, through its protection of amenity, which is conceived as a public good (protected and enhanced by regulation), which is arguably 'privatised' in socially exclusive locations (the greater benefit of that good is directed to the individuals fortunate to reside in that location). So, in a sense, planning becomes 'privatised' or mobilised in the defence of mainly private interest (assetisation in villages is the privatisation of wealth, the inverse of prosperity, which denotes the pursuit of shared wealth).

Critical questions

The argument advanced in this chapter has been that the *assetisation of housing* in the twentieth century has reinforced a dominant private interest view of housing supply and consumption, which is defended by homeowners via planning, and is particularly pronounced in rural amenity areas. Private interest is a significant barrier to development in villages, generating the nexus of planning–land–finance constraints previously noted. It occasionally faces challenge and innovations break through. That happens where particular inequities are acknowledged to threaten the wider well-being of, *and* dominant private interests within, villages. So older homeowners fearing service decline or recognising the damage done by high concentrations of second homes can, for example, join a surge in support for non-market housing interventions – to 'save the village'.

In the remainder of this book, we explore an array of past, present and future housing interventions. Some are rooted in more 'systemic' approaches, driven by the public sector, while others – the contemporary ones – are breakthrough innovations that challenge current constraints in specific pressured rural places. Chapter 3 explores the principal means of addressing housing needs in the decades before the contextual changes discussed in this current chapter. It details interventions that responded to labour questions rather than consumption and market pressures, in the form of tied housing and the development and expansion of council housing.

As these more 'historic' responses to rural housing needs receded, and as the assetisation and consumption pressures outlined in this current chapter grew (driving up rural land values), a much more 'mixed' and localised economy of housing interventions took root, often on the back of experimentation and local innovation. This is the context for our contemporary cases and our reflections on the sorts of land, planning and tax reforms, detailed in Chapter 5, that could incubate and support future innovations. The discussions offered and cases presented in Chapters 4 and 6 explore different means of overcoming the nexus of key constraints introduced above. Four questions frame our examinations of current and future village housing projects. These relate to recognising the problem and providing leadership, solutions to land constraint, circumvention of planning barriers, and overcoming development costs and finance. Where cases are presented, we consider:

1. What were the *drivers* behind the response and where did the leadership come from – what was the recognised problem to be solved and who recognised it? The answer is often a mix of state, third sector and/or community action, mobilised behind a recognition that social exclusion produces externalities linked to community well-being, service levels and so forth.
2. What were the *land constraints*, how had these been generated/sustained, and what was the strategy for overcoming them? Consideration of the land question often focuses on public actions (compulsory purchase or the introduction of new flexibilities in the governing of agricultural land release); philanthropic gifting linking to community control; cross-subsidy mechanisms (releasing portions of sites for non-market housing); or other unanticipated approaches.
3. How were local planning restrictions – strictures on siting, design or access (that may limit development opportunities even where land is made available) – overcome or eased? Private enterprise has long been critical of the many ways in which design and siting prescriptions, and planning conditions – emerging from a discretionary planning process – increase uncertainty and add to development costs (Shucksmith, 1990b: 213). Left unresolved, planning prescriptions (or inflexibility) can halt development or undermine viability by adding to costs.
4. How were schemes able to overcome critical finance barriers and meet higher rural development costs? Besides land and planning

constraints, small rural housing projects must contend with potentially higher development and finance costs, which may be overcome through a range of land-subsidy or cross-subsidy mechanisms, or through charitable grants – non-market finance that does not demand the same return or dividend.

Note

1. National Archives CAB 21/4421 Housing Policy 1953–1960, 'Home Ownership' Joint Memorandum by Secretary of State for Scotland and Minister of Housing and Local Government and Minster for Welsh Affairs (July 1958).

3
Private and public responses: the past

Past responses to village housing pressure were situated in a very different socio-economic and planning context. Sectoral solutions, including the provision of housing 'tied' to rural jobs, reflected the need of landowners to maintain a supply of nearby labour. This was also the rationale of early public housing during the interwar period – support the land-based economy with a supply of housing that avoided wage inflation by keeping rents low. Later on, as tied accommodation became less common and the supply of public housing dwindled, protection for agricultural workers took the form of occupancy clauses, with access to housing dependent on engagement in farming. This chapter reviews these historic village housing models: private tied housing, council housing, the emergence of the modern voluntary sector and the use of agricultural and more general occupancy conditions. These models are linked to important transitions: in the farming economy, in strong state intervention through council housing, and then the decline of that invention and the move to private housing dominance with an element of non-market innovation. The examples used in this chapter are drawn from archival sources.

Introduction

This chapter looks back over the last 120 years of village housing intervention. It is largely concerned with private and public actions in England but also tracks the early development of third sector responses to housing needs in villages. The village housing problem looked very different at the beginning of the twentieth century. Industrialisation had triggered a drift away from the land: a shift in the locus of economic production, away from farming and towards manufacturing in the growing towns and cities. This was facilitated by the opening up of foreign grain markets and the expansion of global trade, which reduced the country's reliance on growing food at home. At the same time, the farming that stayed in England and other parts of the United Kingdom had rapidly mechanised and needed fewer labourers. The geography of rural population change is a complex one: Britain's upland areas lost population at a faster rate than lowland England and the absolute decline in population everywhere was less pronounced than the relative change between urban and rural areas. The country still needed feeding and not all foodstuffs could be sourced overseas. This meant that the population of rural areas in England and Wales grew by roughly 1.7 million between 1801 and 1911 – from nearly 5.9 million to 7.6 million (figures reported in Satsangi et al, 2010: 58, adapted from Law, 1967: 130). But much of this growth was in bigger towns located in otherwise rural areas. There was an absolute loss from areas of dispersion, low density and low 'nucleation' (Law, 1967: 130) which is not easily quantifiable, but the headline, relating to urbanisation and the increased importance of urban manufacturing, is that the population share in rural areas fell from 66.2 per cent to 21 per cent during this period.

The hollowing out of many smaller and lowest tier settlements – in Law's (1967) areas of low nucleation – meant that there was no housing supply challenge confronting villages, but rather a quality issue endured by agricultural workers. In the early years of the twentieth century, those conditions were described as a 'disgrace to the country' (Savage, 1919: 174, quoted in Satsangi et al, 2010: 33) requiring urgent resolution. They were thought to be a hangover from the unregulated and unplanned squalor of the nineteenth century, which had been remedied, in some instances, through a combination of state and philanthropic action in larger towns and cities. But in Savage's view, rural areas had fallen behind, and the needs of farm labourers had been neglected.

Those labourers were living in tied housing. Village housing was owned by large landowners or farmers, many of whom were tenants of aristocratic landlords. This pattern of paternal land ownership shifted significantly in the early years of the twentieth century. A principal cause of the shift was the introduction of estate duty – a tax on the capital value of land – in 1894. The duty replaced a raft of death duties and inheritance taxes, most of which dated from the war against Napoleon. The 1894 duty was intended to address a growing Treasury deficit. It precipitated the break-up of many estates, as landowners struggled to meet tax liabilities. Woods (2005: 31) notes that around 800,000 acres (324,000 ha) of land was sold off between 1910 and 1915. After 1919 the rate of land sales accelerated sharply: citing Beard (1989), Woods notes that 'around a quarter of the land surface of England […] changed hands between 1918 and 1922' (Woods, 2005: 31).

A significant impact was felt in landed politics and the end of the 'squirearchy'. Some aristocratic owners departed entirely from the countryside, with a few leaving Britain for the colonies where they could re-establish themselves as major landowners. However, the setting up of the National Trust – in 1895, a year after the introduction of estate duty – enabled some owners to remain on their estates, transferring their assets to the Trust as a means of shielding themselves from those liabilities. But an arguably more important process was the trimming of land holdings by landowners: the selling off of parts of their estates to their tenant farmers (Woods, 2005: 31). This resulted, according to Woods (p. 33) in the rise of a new 'agrarian elite' that came to dominate rural politics. Although many of the great estates did not survive the disruptions of the early twentieth century, the power of private landowners – now transferred from aristocrats to farmers – remained intact, leading Martin (1962) to observe that the land-based class system, and the broader social system it sustained, had remained intact by the end of the Second World War.

This chapter tracks through the transitions and major shifts that occurred in England's rural areas in the twentieth century, impacting on the nature of rural housing needs, on competition for rural homes, and ultimately shaping a variety of responses. During the land transfers at the end of the nineteenth and beginning of the twentieth centuries, *tied housing* had remained the norm in rural areas. The transfer of land title was largely invisible to farm labourers in their tied cottages, whose lives were unchanged by the break-up of the great estates. *Council housing* had arrived in the countryside during the interwar years (1919 to 1939). The vast majority of the 159,000 homes built by rural district councils before 1939 (Rowley, 2006: 200 – referenced in Boughton, 2019: 58) were outcomes of the Addison Act or later legislation detailed in this chapter. But few farm workers were able to access these homes and the majority remained in tied accommodation, sometimes in 'barbarous' conditions (Armstrong, 1993: 144). Pressure remained, therefore, on government to do more on the housing front: to give the same attention to the countryside that had been shown to towns and cities after 1919. Parliamentary debate, recorded in *Hansard*, provides a glimpse of this pressure right at the end of the Second World War:

> There is undoubtedly awareness in the countryside to-day as never before of the deficiencies of rural housing and amenities.

> The countryside looks to the government to do something to ameliorate that position, and I would urge upon them to give a fair share of government energy and attention to the problems of the countryside. The Cinderella of the countryside has waited a long time to go to the ball, and awaits anxiously the arrival of her Prince Charming in whatever unexpected and unfamiliar guise he may arrive. (Derek Walker-Smith (Hertford), *Hansard*, 17 August 1945, Volume 413, Cols 192–272)

After the war, a new commitment to public housing as part of a more comprehensive planning and welfare package had clear implications for the countryside. But the rural housing focus largely comprised the expansion of selected key settlements into new towns, alongside more targeted investment in smaller service centres not earmarked for substantial growth (Sturzaker, 2019). Emphasis was put on environmental protection and landscape enhancement while agricultural activity remained free from significant planning constraint. This allowed landowners to continue to provide tied homes for their workers, with attached *agricultural conditions*.

Planning constraints meant that the council housing revolution, which was heading for its zenith in cities, was more muted in the countryside. A general presumption against development in the open countryside and outside of the envelopes of smaller settlements was a significant brake on the provision of council homes, which were directed to rural population and service centres. This particular distribution of public development ensured a continuing role for tied accommodation – and for specialist housing providers much later on. A third of farm workers (33 per cent) were in tied accommodation in 1948 (Short, 1982). Because of new investment in the farming sector, via the subsidy regime created by the 1948 Agriculture Act, a stabilisation of labour demand combined with the limits on public housebuilding caused an increase in dependence on tied housing. By 1976, more than half of farm workers (53 per cent) were in this type of housing (Short, 1982: 218).

At the same time, public housing faced particular 'antipathy' in the countryside outside key settlements (Short, 1982: 218). The paucity of new housing opportunities in villages, either private or public, alongside continued reliance on tied accommodation, meant that rural communities would be particularly vulnerable to the stresses and potential inequities that counter-urbanisation would bring to the countryside.

That counter-urbanisation began, in earnest, from the 1960s onwards – and resulted in intense competition for the limited supply of housing available in rural amenity areas and especially in those villages that had been 'redlined' against development by the planning system. Counter-urbanisation triggered, in many ways, a deeper housing challenge for rural areas – no longer just about quality and conditions, but now focused on the absolute quantum of housing available. The imminent arrival of this pressure had been hinted at 20 years earlier.

An exchange in Parliament in 1937 had drawn attention to 'a growing tendency for town dwellers to rent or buy rural workers' cottages for occasional occupation', which was resulting in 'an acute shortage of houses' in near-urban rural areas (Hansard, 20 July 1937, quoted in Satsangi *et al*, 2010, 33–4). But that pre-war trend was only a taste of what was to come. One important sign of post-war recovery was wage growth in manufacturing and the service sectors outpacing agricultural earnings. Then, for reasons examined in the last chapter, housing became an important consumer and investment good. In many other European countries, looser planning rules and a greater stock surplus meant that rural areas could accommodate the rising tide of demand for rural homes. This was certainly the case in France, which has never faced the same rural housing shortages as England and the rest of the UK (Buller and Hoggart, 1994).

But the consumption patterns and pressures that took root in England in the 1960s, linked to wage differentials, greater accessibility to the countryside and an element of rural nostalgia, hit the barriers created by the nascent planning system. The result was a scramble to supply the lucrative demand for rural homes now being registered by urban investors and lifestyle migrants. The trend of converting workers' cottages into retirement retreats or second homes began. Such conversion represented a more profitable use for landlords keen to cash in on emergent rural tourism and the new 'consumption' of the countryside (in much the same way that the 'staycation' boom of 2020/21 resulted in the loss of long-term rented homes to platform-based short lettings).

Therefore the relative rural to urban population loss noted above was stemmed in the second half of the twentieth century. Between 1951 and the early years of the twenty-first century, the rural population share stabilised and rose slightly from 18.7 per cent to 19.9 per cent (Satsangi *et al*, 2010: 60). The repopulation of lowest tier settlements (following a period of decline) in low nucleation areas is a key feature of this change, driven not by employment growth but by the arrival of second home investors and retiring households (Gallent and Tewdwr-Jones, 2000).

Counter-urbanisation – the inversion of the 'traditional positive relationship between net migration and population size' (Buller *et al*,

2003: 8) – caused a radical shift in patterns of housing consumption. Heightened pressures on the housing resource, first noted in the 1930s, was also a land market pressure: it incentivised the sale of tied cottages and made it more costly to provide council homes. In time, that counter-urbanisation became associated with a mixed approach to addressing the housing needs of villages. The rural housing market became increasingly differentiated during this period. General arrangements for meeting the needs of a population that was generally homogenous – by, for example, supplying an element of council housing in key settlements to address longstanding quality concerns – had to give way to tactics for dealing with a much more heterogeneous set of needs and demands, set within a housing market becoming increasingly dominated by private demand for homeownership.

The purpose of this chapter is to provide a broader and longer view of England's rural housing challenges. We have already argued, in the last chapter, that it was the assetisation of housing – and consequent investment pressures – that had precipitated the transition in the rural housing market: a new heterogeneity of housing classes and intense competition for a resource increasingly limited in its supply by a planning system prioritising landscape and investment interests. But this transition in housing's broader socio-economic role interfaces, in rural areas, with specific approaches to housing *rural workers* that have been fundamentally concerned with meeting the needs of the farming economy and, more specifically, providing that economy with relatively cheap labour by suppressing housing costs. Three important *narratives* are now explored.

The first details a shift from reliance on *tied accommodation* that faced no pressure from market entrants, to a need to protect the interests of farm workers using *agricultural occupancy conditions* (later extended, from the late 1970s onwards, to 'local needs' conditions). The second looks at the jump from providing a relatively small amount of rural council housing in the interwar period, catering for the needs of retiring farmworkers, to larger public investments as a response to displacement from tied accommodation and private renting in the second half of the twentieth century. And the third introduces the move to a more 'mixed economy' of housing solutions, including both public housing and a wider array of specialist third sector responses to emergent rural needs in the context of a strengthening housing market and a reduction in private housing options.

These narratives overlap, blurring into each other. But they broadly show how governments grappled with the 'rural worker – low wage' problem in rural areas, firstly through tied housing, then through council housing, and then through a mix of third sector provision and occupancy restrictions. A hundred years ago, tied housing was central to the structure of the rural economy in England. Changes in that economy meant that tied housing played a diminishing role in rural areas: it remained important for farm workers, but as the number of farm workers declined, and tied tenancies were removed, new responses to non-farming housing needs were required. Council homes took over from tied housing. But council housing's eventual demise at the hands of roll-back neoliberalism left a vacuum in rural housing provision that is currently being filled by the work-arounds and local experiments that are detailed later in this book.

Narrative 1: Tied housing and agricultural occupancy conditions

Seen through a historical lens, tied housing is indicative of the landed–landless binary that has defined social relationships and social class in the countryside for centuries. It shares some characteristics with feudalism: serfs living in self-constructed homes under a manorial arrangement – tied to the land and bound, in service, to their landlord. Serfdom declined after the fourteenth century, but so too did any opportunity to be free from the power of landowners. The Enclosure Acts, starting in the early seventeenth century, deprived peasants of the right to forage and graze animals on common land, making them more dependent on private land for their livelihoods and increasing the power and wealth of the landed class, who controlled all civil institutions and made all laws (Woods, 2005). This arrangement held fast until the beginning of the twentieth century, after which the wealthier tenant farmers became the new landlord class (see above), taking control of much of the country's tied housing from the departing gentry. Although no longer bound in serfdom, rural labourers remained reliant on the new landlords for both their livelihoods and their homes.

In this section, we begin by elaborating the nature of tied rural housing. The aim then is to reveal the connection between *tied housing in farming* and the rise of both *council housing and occupancy restrictions* in rural areas. Both provided scaffolds for a low-wage farming economy, ensuring continuity in labour supply and a means of suppressing wage inflation.

Farming and the tied cottage

The farm sector's reliance on tied cottages ensured the survival of this type of housing well into the late twentieth century. It was not until the

1970s that significant steps were taken to move farmworkers onto tenancy rather than labour contracts, which resulted from decades of lobbying, a significant increase in 'free' (rather than tied) homes provided by local authorities and guarantees on the availability of housing for farm workers via agricultural occupancy conditions (AOC). Rural housing for those workers was viewed as a vital economic infrastructure.

During the interwar and post war periods, tied housing was intended to support the health of the farm sector during a period of global economic change, protecting the sector from potentially catastrophic wage inflation. This is revealed in the engagements between the National Union of Agricultural Workers (NUAW), the National Farmers Union (NFU) and various government departments, particularly the Ministry of Health. The NFU viewed tied housing as key to the survival and prosperity of farms, and also sought to ensure maximum flexibility for farmers in relation to the 'Rent (Restrictions) Acts'.[1] Those Acts prevented landlords, outside the tied sector, from recovering vacant possession of let properties unless they could show that alternative accommodation was available for sitting tenants.[2] Since tied housing for agricultural labourers was not *let for a rent under a tenancy contract,* but rather provided accommodation for workers under a *labour contract,* tied housing residents did not gain the benefit of the Rent (Restrictions) Acts. The NFU clarified its position in a memorandum distributed to County War Agricultural Executive Committees in England and Wales in 1947:

> A tied cottage is one in which the right to occupy is an integral part of the contract of service; this right comes to an end with the ending of the employment. When the occupier ceases to be employed by the landlord, he becomes a trespasser, and the landlord has a full right to recover possession of the cottage. It is not even necessary for the landlord to go to the Court for an Order, though most landlords do so; in this case the Court cannot refuse an Order, though its issue may be delayed.[3]

This special consideration for tied housing, conferring greater powers on landlords and curbing the rights of occupants, was deemed necessary for agricultural production. While occupants could be removed from their homes on the cessation of employment, they were protected from high rents as farmers needed to keep wages low. The NFU added that the presence of tied cottages is a major draw for workers, the majority of whom would not be able to take up labouring opportunities in the absence of homes tied to service.⁴ The General Secretary of the NFU confirmed as much in a letter to County Branch Secretaries in 1945:

> It is obvious that we shall never be able to recruit or maintain anything like the requisite labour force on the land unless we have the houses for them to occupy. At the present time most workers want their houses to be near their jobs, and are aware that they have the benefit of the occupation of the house, not at an economic rent but for a nominal deduction (if, indeed, any is made) from their wages that is permitted by law.⁵

A decade earlier, the Secretary of the National Housing and Town Planning Council had issued a memorandum on the 'rural housing problem' in which it noted that '[…] until agricultural wages are increased, it is absolutely impossible for these workers to contemplate paying an economic rent for their housing accommodation'.⁶

While different forms of tied housing were also present in cities, the structure of rural economies and the lower wages of agricultural workers, making the availability of housing below economic rent essential for agricultural production, gave tied housing particular importance in rural areas. Any change in the law, potentially granting new 'tenancy rights' to occupants and limiting the flexible use of tied housing, would pose a significant threat to the farming sector. Therefore, the farming lobby kept a close watch on political developments in this area, with the NFU flagging the importance of tied housing and the NUAW, representing workers, seeking reform and substitution.

In 1946, the NUAW addressed the following note to the Prime Minister's Office:

> Before the Royal Commission on Agriculture of 1881, Joseph Arch, who formed the first national rural trade union in the '70s, denounced the tied cottage as a 'monstrous injustice' and demanded 'cottage right' for farm workers […] Since then several resolutions demanding the abolition of tied cottages have been passed unanimously by Congress. The Labour Party conferences have been equally emphatic […] Both Arch and [Sir George] Edwards testified that tied cottages, which had not become at all prevalent until the movement for the formation of an agricultural trade union assumed some importance, were a weapon used 'to keep the labourers in check', as the Duke of Marlborough openly

advocated [...] Condemnation of the system has not been confined to Labour organisations [...] The Liberal party in their Rural Land [sic] Enquiry of 1913 and again in their 'Land and the Nation' of 1925 [made] the important observations: 'The case for tied cottages is economic. The case for freedom in the home is human'.[7]

Government was slow to address the issue. In a letter to then-Prime Minister Clement Attlee in 1950, the General Secretary of the NUAW highlighted consistent inaction on this front since 1916, adding that 'our members are bitterly disappointed'.[8] The technical issue holding up reform was the complexity of amending the Rent (Restrictions) Acts, aligning the rights of those with service and tenancy contracts. But this was not an insurmountable hurdle: the bigger picture was that government wanted to avoid bringing tied housing under the Rent (Restrictions) Acts, because this would have the effect of raising the rents charged to agricultural workers (if landowners had to meet rehousing costs and factor these into rents or deductions) and thus lead to a demand for higher agricultural wages, with knock-on effects in the rest of the economy.

The need for 'free cottages'

In short, tied housing provided a buffer against economic rents and that buffer would need replacing if tied housing were to be abolished. It was widely acknowledged that some form of non-market, low-rent housing would be required for the rural population in order to maintain agricultural production, and to avoid putting inflationary pressure on the wider economy (through higher food prices and therefore knock-on wage claims). Tied housing served a crucial economic function not only for agricultural production, but for the nation as a whole.

However, the NUAW became more forceful in its opposition to the status quo and to the injustice of tied housing, as an affront to 'human freedom', with that opposition gaining popular support and forcing government to seek solutions to the 'agricultural tied housing problem'. But rather than trying to unpick and rewrite the Rent (Restrictions) Acts, a broader solution to the problem was sought – through a substantial increase in the supply of 'free' houses in rural areas.

In 1945, The Labour Party Agricultural Committee reported Aneurin Bevan's view that 'the tied cottage problem would disappear if enough new houses were built in the villages'.[9] This would not require legislation but rather an acceleration of the building programmes of Rural District Councils.[10] A year later, Clement Attlee echoed this view to the NUAW, eventually arguing in 1950 that the council housing route, rather than a politically difficult revision of the Rent (Restrictions) Acts, was the logical way forward.[11] A bigger role for councils, and a smaller role for farmers, was offered as the means of providing the homes needed by farm workers and by the farming economy. The NUAW agreed:

> The practical solution to the 'tied' cottage problem is a sufficiency of houses to let. Rural Districts have a substantial programme in hand in the shape of some 38,000 houses completed at 31st January, 39,000 under construction and a further 12,000 in tenders approved […] The number of permanent and temporary local authority houses actually let to agricultural workers at 31st December [1948] was 7,000 and we may expect the proportion to increase as building proceeds.

Rural council housing was viewed as a scaffold for the farming economy, which would be further supported by occupancy conditions on both tied cottages and the homes being built by rural district councils. Indeed, it was argued that the conditions of occupation (of tied agricultural cottages) 'should remain undisturbed'[12] and in 1947 it was reported that the Ministry of Housing and Local Government had been 'consulting with the Ministry of Agriculture as to 'arrangements which might be made, with the co-operation of Rural District Councils, to get the maximum possible number of houses let to agricultural workers in the interest of food production'.[13]

The need to house farmworkers, and control labour costs, was the overarching objective of these developments. Indeed, the expansion of council building and the eclipse of tied housing is very much a shift in how government would simultaneously address the needs of farm workers and the needs of farms:

> The great need is for more cottages for agricultural workers. In the main, these are now being provided by local authorities, and of course they are free. The greatest service at the present time would be given by encouragement, help and stimulation of local authorities to push on with their building programmes, and to allocate appropriate numbers of cottages for occupation by agricultural workers – for which especially generous subsidies are available.[14]

This statement by the County War Agricultural Executive Committees in 1947 was followed, in the Housing Subsidies Act 1956, with special subsidies targeting council homes for farm workers.[15]

The decline of tied housing – and retention of the 'agricultural tie'

There is no neat dividing line between the rise of rural council housing and the decline of tied cottages: indeed, council housing's growth began much earlier in the twentieth century while tied cottages have retained a presence in the rural economy to the present day. But their relative significance altered drastically. After the Second World War, the *proportion* of farm workers reliant on tied housing increased, rising from 33 per cent in 1948 to 53 per cent in 1976 (Short, 1982). During this period, the *absolute* number of farm workers declined – from 843,000 (1950) to 334,000 (1980) across Great Britain[16] – but those that remained found it increasingly difficult to rent private ('free') homes in villages, many of which were now being used by holiday-makers or sold for retirement or investment. It was in that context that Newby (1977: 96) highlighted the increasing importance of sustained 'agricultural ties' on rural homes, for a dwindling labour force that was unable to compete with adventitious buyers in the open housing market.

In the next section, we track the rise of council housing from the interwar period. Towards the end of this chapter, attention turns to the general use of occupancy conditions to support rural workers' and full-time residents' access to rural homes. But an addendum to the tied housing narrative is the retention of the agricultural tie across the private and public housing sectors, as a forerunner to wider occupancy conditions.

This addendum starts with renewed attention to the abolition of tied housing in the 1970s. Because of continued reliance on such accommodation at that time, albeit for a smaller workforce, the same economic concerns were circulating: how to maintain the link between rents and rural wages so as to avoid wider inflationary pressures. A Bill brought before Parliament in 1974,[17] which aimed to end the tied cottage system in England and Wales, reignited debate on the impacts of switching from labour to tenancy contracts. First, any new security of tenure would increase the (wage) bargaining power of farmworkers. Landlords would no longer be able to replace workers as their accommodation status would no longer be linked to employment contracts. And second, workers' claims for higher wages would rest on the need to service fair or market rents, as it was anticipated that tenancy rights would be balanced by the right of landlords to charge rents rather than make deductions.

It was estimated that this change could increase the agricultural wage bill by between £50 million and £100 million[18] and contribute to local wage increases outside of the agricultural sector.[19] This would happen because the Government, 'in enacting a potential liability for fair rents [for farm workers, freed from the restrictions and benefits of the tie] would in practice be introducing a disruptive element into the future pay prospect, since all experience shows that special treatment for particular groups gives rise very quickly to demands for comparable benefits from numerous other groups throughout the economy'.[20]

The 1974 Bill failed to become law, but government continued to grapple with how to control rent costs for farm workers and therefore address the wider economic dilemma. This issue became part of a broader concern for ensuring that affordable homes were made available to farmworkers. One proposed solution, outlined in an 'agricultural tied cottage legislation' memorandum issued by the Secretary of State for the Environment and the Minister of Agriculture, Fisheries and Food, was a 'more formalised role for local authorities in rehousing former tied cottage occupants'.[21] This sought to place an even greater emphasis on the provision of council housing for existing and retired agricultural workers, but warned that:

> The effect of [such] legislation could well be that local authorities will need to increase the number of houses which they provide [resulting in] an estimated additional public expenditure burden of between £6 million annually over the first five years or so after the legislation has taken effect. [22]

The merits and drawbacks of such an approach became a point of discussion. The starting point was that 'local authorities should be obliged by the legislation to take account of farming need in deciding on an offer of council housing to a qualifying occupant of a cottage required for an incoming farmworker'.[23] But uncertainties surrounded the level of priority to be given and the dangers of 'creating a specific duty relating to a specific category of people',[24] to the detriment of others, remained. Ultimately, lettings policies continued to be occupation-neutral, but the Rent (Agriculture) Act 1976 led to the creation of 16 Agricultural Dwellings Housing Advisory Committees, charged with advising rural councils on requests to rehouse farmworkers exiting the sector.

Despite the failure of the 1974 Bill, tenancy protections were eventually won for the occupants of tied cottages (specifically, *protected occupancy* under the Rent (Agriculture) Act until 15 January 1989 and *assured agriculture occupancy* under the Housing Act 1988 after that date). These *did not* shift tenancies onto fair or market rents while workers remained employed on the farm to which a cottage was tied, but once employment ceased, the landlord could exercise the right to charge a market rent, increasing the importance of efforts, pursuant on the Rent (Agriculture) Act, to ensure viable rehousing options for those leaving the farming sector.

The potential transfer of tenancies outside of the farming sector presented a potentially bigger risk: that cottages themselves could be lost to the rising tide of market interest in rural homes from the 1960s onwards. Farmers and landlords might seek to cash in, supplementing farm income by selling homes or letting them to holiday makers. But cottages built on agricultural land and in support of farm activity after 1949 (after the provisions of the Town and Country Planning Act 1947 and Agriculture Act 1948) would themselves be 'tied' to agriculture through a planning condition, later achieved through Section 52 of the Town and Country Planning Act 1971, superseded by Section 106 of the Town and Country Planning Act 1990.

These 'agricultural' ties effectively limited the pool of people able to occupy homes, preventing farmers from achieving higher rents through, for example, holiday letting. Even where cottages are sold off and effectively separated from a farm, the agricultural tie will remain. This means that older tied housing remains available to farmworkers and, in many instances, farmers will not be able to build new homes unless a planning condition, restricting occupancy to farmworkers, is agreed. Therefore, despite the decline of tied cottages, with their many problems centred on the curtailed rights of occupants, agricultural ties continue to suppress rent costs for rural workers and therefore help farms manage labour costs. But these ties have faced a critical challenge over the last 50 years.

This has come from counter-urbanisation and investment in rural housing. A home in the country remains an attractive proposition for a great many households looking for a lifestyle change, a second home, or a retirement retreat. Homes, either in villages or open countryside, are highly sought after and command high prices if vendors can connect with buyers with 'cash to splash' (which is now easily achieved via internet sales platforms). But a great many homes remain constrained by the agricultural tie, which has become more important as the market for rural housing has expanded. Planning rules governing new development were tightened in the decades after 1947, but with exemptions and protections maintained for farm workers' cottages. DoE Circular 22/60, *New Houses in the Country*, emphasised the need to protect farmland from residential development except in cases of special need. Nearly a decade later, *Development Control Policy Note 4 – Development in Rural Areas* instructed planning authorities to consider the needs of 'farm workers who must live on the spot' (Gilg and Kelly, 1997: 81). The Note 'set out the criteria by which planners should judge whether the case [to erect a home for a farm worker] was valid, and also referenced the possibility of imposing a condition restricting occupancy of the dwelling to agriculture' (Gilg and Kelly, 1997: 81). Roll forward another four years and DoE Circular 24/73 *Agricultural Dwellings* set strict criteria on the building of such dwellings and attached conditions, stipulating that providing homes in a nearby village was to be preferred to on-farm development, although where such development was essential it should happen close to existing agricultural buildings. The intent of Circular 24/73 was to set strict conditions on the building of agricultural dwellings and further limit development in open countryside. The circular remained extant until the issuing of a general planning policy guidance note (PPG7) on *The Countryside* in 1992. New agricultural ties rely on a Section 106 planning condition. These derive from the Town and Country Planning Act 1990, which also contains a definition of agriculture in Section 336(i).

On the one hand, these ties protect a portion of rural homes for agricultural need. Rents and sale prices are suppressed by the tie, increasing affordability. But on the other hand, an industry has sprung up to help vendors (often farmers trying to release tied housing to the market) and homebuyers overcome agricultural occupancy conditions. AFA Planning Consultants, with offices across England, specialises in 'lifting AOCs'. It notes that AOCs mean that:

> [...] no one is allowed to live in the properties concerned except those specified in the restriction (usually farmers). This in turn means that the property's value is vastly diminished (often up to 40 per cent below the market value). Buyers are often very hard to find especially when it's realised that they are not allowed to live in the property unless they comply with the restriction. Mortgage providers are also notoriously reluctant to lend. (https://www.afaplanningconsultants.co.uk/agricultural-occupancy)

AFA Planning Consultants is just one example of a company (employing 'ex planning officers' able to 'spot opportunities' to free homes from AOCs) offering to remove conditions on a 'no win, no fee' basis. The key driver of this industry is to realise the 30 per cent to 50 per cent uplift in property value from the removal of conditions, allowing its clients to further profit by extending property or replacing modest workers' cottages with larger dwellings, both of which are more difficult with conditions in place. The removal of conditions may be justified in some instances, making homes accessible to a wider range of occupants, but it also reduces the supply of affordable homes for farm workers. We return to the broader issue of local needs' conditions later in this chapter, which have a different purpose and potentially very different impact from agricultural ties.

Narrative 2: Council housing

Interwar council housing

The *national* rise of interwar council housing, after the 1919 Addison Act, is bound up with the state's acceptance of a direct role in housing provision as landlord. The story of public housing is rooted in nineteenth-century urbanisation, the overcrowding and squalor of the Victorian city, and the fear of an economic and social cost of not paying attention to the housing conditions of the 'working classes' (see Cherry, 1979). For much of the nineteenth century, housing was seen as a private matter: the great landed estates had, via tenant farmers, provided for their workers (with tied housing), so why not the new urban industrialists? Many embraced the need, rooted in labour supply, to house their workers on-site, thereby removing a small proportion of the working population from reliance on the emergent private landlord class that was providing shockingly poor housing for the growing urban population (Hall, 2014: 15). But many industrialists were encouraged to go further, driven by a sense of paternal and religious responsibility for the health and moral well-being of those they employed. They were also cajoled by the leading social reformers of the day – including Octavia Hill – who lobbied for a combination of public reform and philanthropic action. Industrialists including Robert Owen, George Peabody and Arthur Guinness built model housing for their own workers and eventually for a wider spectrum of need. Together with the social reformers, they seeded the modern 'third sector' of housing associations, trusts and societies. Many in government were inclined (or wished) to believe that this model – of private and philanthropic action – could substitute for significant state action, which delayed acceptance of the fact that the scale of philanthropic endeavour was not equal to the scale of challenges arising from nineteenth-century industrialisation and urban growth. Eventually, the state was compelled to act and legislated, in 1885, for the building of council housing by local authorities. The Housing of the Working Classes Act of that year handed local councils the power to assemble land, plan and provide housing. But critically it did not provide them with funding above that available from local revenues, which meant that councils built fewer than 1,000 homes per year during the first quarter-century of direct state intervention in housing. It was not until the 1919 Addison Act that councils were provided with the exchequer subsidy (in other words, borrowing consents) needed to start building at relative volume. Over the next 20 years, a quarter of total housing output (of four million new homes) were council-built (Armstrong, 1993: 144).

Towns and cities were the obvious focus for building programmes, with council homes replacing the worst of the Victorian slums, especially after the Housing Act 1930 (see below). Indeed, the elimination of slums was the primary goal of housing policy throughout the 1930s, although only relatively small replacement schemes were delivered in inner-city locations, with the major part of council provision being concentrated at urban edges, where land costs were comparatively lower.

Much of the rural component of this interwar building programme was focused on larger towns and key service centres – places like Buxton in Derbyshire, where 273 council homes were built between 1919 and 1939 (Hulme, 2010: 239). Tied housing remained the key means of meeting workers' needs in many rural areas (see above), although small numbers of council homes were distributed across rural centres and some smaller villages, providing for workers retiring from farming or remedying the problem of poor housing conditions. Some homes were built before 1919, by civil parish councils (established by the Local Government Act 1894) which were responding to particular needs (see, for example, Townley, 2021). But more was delivered during the interwar period and comprised clusters of red-brick semis, sometimes replacing dilapidated cottages, which can be found in villages across England and the rest of the UK.

The council building programme in rural areas was intimately linked to the fate of tied housing and its role in supporting the farming economy, as noted in the previous section. Emphasis shifted towards the building programmes of rural councils as debates in Parliament drew attention to the inadequacies and injustices of tied housing, suggesting that reform of that sector was dependent on the expansion of council provision. That expansion gained momentum after 1945 under the guidance of a Labour Government. But the seeds for an expanded programme were sown in the interwar period as the subsidy regime evolved and as rural councils became more adept at building and managing council housing. In this section, we begin by looking at the subsidy regime before turning to examples that reveal the drivers behind local programmes and how councils were able to overcome critical delivery barriers.

Funding council homes for the farming population

Data from the Ministry of Health reveal that between 1919 and 1941, Rural District Councils directly built 163,025 new homes. A further 134,489 were delivered through private enterprise with state assistance. These were part of the 866,320 homes built in rural districts during this period.[25] A small number of rural council homes had been built before 1919, under the provisions of principal legislation enacted in 1885 and 1890, but this trickle did not become more substantial until after the First World War. A series of key Acts of Parliament, known by the names of their key sponsors, provided the subsidies needed, largely in the form of borrowing consents, to advance council building: these were the Housing, Town Planning, etc. Act 1919 (Addison), the Housing etc. Act 1923 (Chamberlain), the Housing (Financial Provisions) Act 1924 (Wheatley), the Housing Act 1930 (Greenwood), the Housing Act 1935 (Hilton Young) and the Housing (Financial Provisions) Act 1938 (Kingsley Wood). Several shifts in focus are apparent during this period of legislative development. The period 1919 to 1933 is one of concern for meeting 'general need' but with special provision for agricultural parishes in the Wheatley Act. Focus then shifted, between 1933 and 1938, to rehousing workers from unfit homes. Then, in 1938, the focus shifted again to the 'large scale building of new houses for agricultural workers'[26] which was prompted, in part, by parallel debates over tied housing and its support for the farming sector. However, progress was soon reported to be slow, resulting in continued concern for the supply of 'free' as opposed to 'tied' homes.

The various Acts adjusted and updated the subsidy regime, often shifting the balance between monies directed to councils and to private enterprise, via councils. The Chamberlain Act (1923) renewed the general exchequer subsidy for new houses[27] of the 'working class type', providing £6 a year for 20 years, available to both private enterprise and local authorities. The subsidy was paid to the authority which, in the case of houses built by private enterprise, passed it on, usually in the form of a capital sum of about £75. No provision was made requiring a contribution from local rates towards the cost of the houses, although in practice many authorities did in fact make a contribution. The subsidy under this act was reduced in 1927 to £4 and ceased in 1929.[28]

There was no special provision for 'agricultural areas' in the 1923 Act[29] but such provisions evolved over the next few years as governments grappled with the supply of free homes available to farm workers. The Wheatley Act (1924) established a higher rate of subsidy for houses built in agricultural parishes:[30] £12 10s per home per annum until 1927 and £11 thereafter until a new regime took over in 1934. This led to approximately 30,000 council houses being built in agricultural parishes under the 1924 Act.[31] Eventually, the need for special and comprehensive provisions for rural areas was acknowledged. The Housing (Rural Workers) Act 1926 (updated in 1931 and 1938) gave attention to the improvement of housing conditions faced by agricultural workers and others of a similar economic status in rural parishes. Higher subsidies were conditional on cottages being tenanted for the next 20 years by persons who 'would not ordinarily pay rent in excess of that paid by agricultural workers in the district or by an agricultural worker or employee of substantially the same economic condition'.[32]

Little was done in rural areas before the passing of the Greenwood Act (1930) with regard to demolition and replacement of unfit houses. The Greenwood Act, however, provided for assistance to be given to local authorities for the demolition and replacement of houses totally unfit for human habitation in the form of exchequer grants of £2 5s (£2 10s in agricultural parishes) for 40 years for each person displaced, the local authority being required to provide a supplement grant of £3 15s per house for 40 years charged to the local rates. In the case of houses intended for farm workers, the County Council was also required to assist Rural District Councils by contributing £1 per house for 40 years. There was an expectation that the stock would be improved but there would be no expansion of the current pool of available housing under the Greenwood Act.[33] Yet these, and later Acts, had the effect of growing and improving the supply of rent-restricted housing in rural areas, frequently targeting the needs of farm workers.

Slightly later legislation, from the mid-1930s onwards, sought to take stock of what had been achieved and what additional progress was needed. The Hilton Young Act (1935) directed local authorities to assess the level of overcrowding in their jurisdictions. Of the 1,447,918 'working class dwellings' located in England and Wales's rural districts, just under 42,000 (2.9 per cent) were overcrowded.[34] Three years later, and in response to the picture drawn by the many local surveys conducted, the Kingsley Wood Act (1938) prescribed special rates of exchequer subsidy for the agricultural population that would address the full combination of: rehousing persons from unfit dwellings, relieving over-crowding and meeting general needs.[35]

Hence the funding regime had evolved from a general programme, with periodic 'special attention' to agricultural areas, to a dedicated focus that placed a duty on local authorities to accelerate building activities in rural districts while giving greater attention to the abatement of over-crowding.[36] However, the outbreak of war in 1939 checked the progress being made under the Kingsley Wood Act. The expectation had been that greater emphasis would henceforth be placed on rural areas, increasing exchequer subsidies across the board, but with special measures and increased funding in those rural areas with the greatest need, generally and in terms of dwelling unfitness and overcrowding.[37] This regime also sought greater flexibility, permitting authorities to contract out building works and also make exchequer subsidies available to the 'owner of the house [of] up to £10 a year for 40 years subject to conditions that such *grant aided houses are reserved for the agricultural population* and that, if let, they should be let at the value determined by the local Agricultural Wages Committee of a cottage provided in part payment of wages'.[38]

Delivering rural council homes in the interwar period

Prior to the receipt of the subsidies noted in the last section, Rural District Councils needed to agree plans and details of the homes to be provided with the Ministry of Health, either its central office in Whitehall or its regional branch in Bristol. Details of site allocation and acquisition, architectural layouts, sources of additional funding (from local rates or County Councils) and even the choice of materials for the new builds needed to be specified by either a Parish itself or by the Rural District Council in what, for many councils, was their first foray into the business of housebuilding. Indeed, many small councils, particularly their chairmen and clerks, were 'suddenly thrust into the roles of both builder and landlord' (Claxton, 2020).

Government wanted to control costs, ensuring that 'new expenditure on housing should be used to the greatest possible advantage' and requiring that local authorities 'concentrate their efforts on the provision of a type of house which can be built at a low cost', leaving private enterprise to meet other needs and demands without subsidy.[39] To that end, the Ministry of Health sought preliminary submissions from councils, setting out the broad justification for homes, followed by definite plans and specifications.[40] Engagements between councils and the Ministry are captured

Figure 3.1 Interwar council housing, Sherston, Wiltshire. © Iqbal Hamiduddin.

Figure 3.2 Interwar council housing, Sopworth, Wiltshire. © Iqbal Hamiduddin.

in the Wiltshire cases set out below (see also Figures 3.1 and 3.2), which reveal the advocacy role played by councils, funding arrangements and the sanctioning of loans raised privately, how sites were identified and purchased, the processes of tendering for construction and detailing of design and materials. They provide an insight into the experiences of councils building for the first time.

Case 3.1: The practicalities of building interwar council housing: Staverton and Sherston, Wiltshire

Experiences at Staverton and Sherston – both in the county of Wiltshire – are drawn together here to illustrate the complexities of interwar council building.

Staverton Parish, in the rural district of Melksham (abolished in 1974), sought to build 12 houses under the provisions of the Chamberlain and Wheatley Acts. It was argued that 'according to the 1921 Census, the population of the village was 235' but the average number of employees working for 'the Nestle and Anglo-Swiss Condensed Milk Company for the past year [1932] was 274 – considerably more than the total population of the village'. Moreover, 'during the last 10 years, no new houses have been built, though three have been demolished'.[41] In a letter to the Minister of Health in 1932, the council referenced a recent speech on housebuilding by the Prime Minister, Ramsay MacDonald, arguing that '[...] the tenor of the Prime Minister's speech [...] was to the effect that he hoped people would make all endeavour to spend, so long as the expenditure was really productive: my Council feel that the provision of twelve houses would [...] be of general advantage to the locality'.[42] Eight homes were authorised and a period of correspondence ensued between the Council and the Ministry, with an initial request for a form 'A.G.61a' detailing the revised application and new subsidy request for fewer dwellings.[43] This was because the Minister of Health was 'not satisfied [...] on the information furnished that there is an urgent need for so many as 12 houses to relieve over-crowding and replace unfit houses, and he is only prepared to agree to the Council proceeding to obtain tenders for the erection of 8 houses of the type and size indicated in Circular 1238'[44] (referencing the principal 1890 legislation). The Council reiterated its request that the Ministry sanction a loan of £3,050,[45] eventually receiving the go-ahead to borrow the sums of '£2,685 and £165 for the erection of 8 houses at Staverton and works connected therewith under Part III of the Housing Act, 1925'.[46] Following the sanction of the loan amounts, these were advanced by the Trustees of the Wiltshire Working Men's Conservative Benefit Society at a rate of interest of '4 and one eighth per cent' to be repaid in half-yearly payments of principal and interest combined.[47] Just over 1 acre of land was obtained from a 'Mr Blake' for just over £204, with the Ministry sending a cheque for this purpose (although different documents refer to 'formal sanction of borrowing'[48]). The Staverton case illustrates the incredible level of detail addressed in Council–Ministry dealings: the Ministry asked the Council to look again at sewage disposal and boundary fencing arrangements with a view to trimming back the costs, eventually agreeing to a cost of just over £312 per house. It also made suggestions on the placing of gas stoves so that a 'better outlet for the gas fumes could be provided'.[49]

Five tenders were received for the building of the eight houses at Staverton: the lowest price was quoted by Messrs Bigwood and Co. from Melksham, to whom the contract was awarded. The cost was just under £2,900, with the Council going back to the Ministry for a revised loan sanction to cover architectural fees (£100) and finance and miscellaneous costs (of £57).[50] After this toing and froing, the Council secured loan sanction for just over £3,000. It purchased an acre of land, with land cost amounting to less than 7% of total development cost. The homes built were delivered by a local contractor. These were each 760 square feet and comprised concrete block homes built with 11-inch cavity walls and tiled roofs.

The second example is that of *Sherston Parish* in the north-west of Wiltshire, bordering Gloucestershire and now within the Cotswolds AONB, where it was proposed to build 16 homes at Sherston (under the Housing Act 1936) and acquire a third of an acre at Sopworth, demolish an array of derelict buildings and unfit cottages (under the Housing Act 1930) and build a 'block of three-bedroomed non-parlour type houses to provide re-housing accommodation for 20 persons'.[51] Significant detail was provided on the Sopworth proposal: '[…] The Council propose to demolish six old stone cottages which are unfit for human habitation and/or derelict and erect two storied workmen dwellings, built in a block of four constructed on front and end elevations of face stone work on brickwork and the rear elevation of 11½ inch cavity brickwork cement rendered. The roof to be covered with stone tiles on front and Marley concrete tiles on rear […] the accommodation to be of five rooms, comprising of Living

Room, scullery and three bedrooms with larder, bathroom and entrance hall in main building [...] the water supply will be from the West Gloucestershire Water Company's main with existing service on to the site [...] drainage from each house will be to a septic tank and filter bed and effluent disposed of through land drains [...] The superficial area of houses no. 1 & 4 will be 756 square feet and houses no. 2 & 3 will be 798 feet'.[52] In its response, the Ministry questioned the sizes of bedrooms, which 'were less than those recommended in Circular 1539' and suggested that landing arrangements appeared 'wasteful'. A sketch of an alternative configuration was provided by Ministry staff who concluded that 'subject to the willingness of the Council to amend the plan they may now proceed to obtain tenders for the erection of the houses'.[53] The council agreed and the Sopworth site was handed over to contractors at the beginning of April 1938. Demolition commenced in June and building works later that month. The main building work finished in September 1938 and all ancillary works by March 1939.[54] The lag between main work completion and final completion was attributed to labour shortages, especially carpenters, plumbers and masons. This was reported back to the Ministry: '[...] in the end we had, at considerable expense, to fetch men from long distance to rectify this trouble'.[55] That trouble translated into an annual loss for the Council of £6 as the homes were not completed by the end of December 1938. The Ministry sought clarification, asking the Council to state the capital value of such annual loss of £6 for a period of 40 years at 3⅝ per cent. The Council came back with the answer of almost £128.[56] Delays added to cost overrun, for which the council sought additional loan sanction.

These interwar cases illustrate the level of detail required by the Ministry of Health before exchequer subsidies, in the form of sanctioned borrowing, was permitted. Engagements with the Ministry reveal that Councils were called upon to fully investigate development opportunities, setting out the minutiae of schemes, while the Ministry, for its part, had the skills needed to intervene in plans at a very detailed level. There was concern for the quality of homes being built and for their utility. The object, in many instances, was to substitute unfit dwellings with modern homes: hence, a concern for compliance with Ministry standards, set out in circulars, and value for money. Land deals were done locally, with land cost representing a small part of overall development cost – in villages where speculative development had yet to gain any foothold.

Council housing after 1945

Building by councils was given new impetus after 1945. Slum clearance, urban renewal and the development of new towns was part of a post-war welfare and economic development package that saw council housing enjoy more than 30 years of uninterrupted growth. Local authorities and development corporations led large-scale development in renewal areas and on green-field sites. Most of the housing provided was at scale. But this was also a period in which generally good quality council housing was built in rural settlements of various sizes: in market towns and in villages (Boughton, 2019: 58). The rural housing market experienced rapid change in those 30 years, coinciding with post-war economic recovery and growth. The first waves of counter-urbanisation arrived in rural areas, facilitated by centrally planned new towns and the expansion of satellite market towns in metropolitan fringes, especially around London. The 1960s was the period of 'urbs in rure' (Pahl, 1965): the arrival of hitherto urban people into rural areas, facilitated by a mix of private speculative development and public housebuilding, often but not exclusively in over-spill new towns. All of this was also grounded in the development of a comprehensive planning system and the nationalisation of development rights. It made sense to decentralise population away from bomb-damaged inner-urban areas. As with the 1930s slum-clearance, renewal areas could not accommodate the total population displaced from overcrowded housing – and those areas could not be expanded because of higher land and development costs. Therefore the development of public housing nearer the urban edge, or in overspill sites, was cheaper and easier. Agricultural land beside towns and villages earmarked for expansion could be acquired cheaply by New Town Development Corporations (NTDC). In the years immediately after the Second World War, demand for that land – for anything other than farming use – was low, allowing the NTDCs to assemble sites at close to agricultural value. It was only later on, with rising interest in rural property, that land costs rose and rules on compensation following public acquisition needed to be clarified in law, via the Land Compensation Act 1961.

Indeed, flat rural land prices after the war – and illustrated in the interwar period in Case 3.1 – provided the context in which New Towns and edge-of-town public developments were possible. These forms of development were a significant part of council housing's post war golden age. We now look in greater detail at three important themes: the evolving policy context for rural council building, in the context of a continuing supply shortage; land assembly for post-war council housing, including in villages; and the pattern of post-war provision in villages, revealed through specific examples.

Continuation of low supply and evolving policy

Despite many local successes in interwar building by Rural District Councils, the overall supply situation in many parts of the country remained bleak. In the absence of private building, councils were alone in addressing the acute need for good quality, affordable and below-market rent housing in villages. Government conceded that the subsidy regime was not generous enough to deliver genuinely affordable housing in some rural settings. In 1946, a House of Commons report into agriculture and the farming economy observed that while the rural districts hosted nearly one-fifth of the national population, fewer than one-seventh of council houses were being built in those districts. The reason for this was that until 1938, exchequer subsidies for rural housing made insufficient allowance for the very low 'rent-paying capacity' of the agricultural population.[57] This meant that more subsidy had been expended on fewer homes in many villages.

Immediately after the war, the 1945 Housing White Paper set out ambitions to broaden and expand the subsidy regime, creating a framework for 'housebuilding both by local authorities and by private enterprise' (HM Government, 1945: Para. 26). In an earlier draft of the White Paper, the division of responsibilities between these different sectors is unspecified but the goal of ramping up supply is clear:

> After the last war, the average price of houses in England and Wales increased (between May 1919, when the first tenders were invited, and September 1920) by 50%. Local authorities had been allowed to invite tenders far beyond the real capacity of the building industry. This time the government will exercise control over the volume of contracts let by local authorities, over the building and repair work done on private account, and over the prices of building materials and of standardised components and fitments. By these methods, and with the co-operation of employers and labour, they intend to reduce building costs, as quickly as possible, to the level at which the building industry and its ancillary trades can be fully employed, and houses can be made available for sale or rent at reasonable prices, without the need of subsidies

from the Exchequer. The Government recognise however, that subsidies will at first be needed, while building costs are, in consequence of the war, abnormally high; and they propose to provide them for house-building both by local authorities and by private enterprise. The necessary legislation will be introduced, after consultation about the amount of subsidies required with the interests chiefly concerned.[58]

The 'necessary legislation' arrived in the form of the Housing (Financial and Miscellaneous Provisions) Act 1946 (amended in the Housing Act 1952, the Housing (Review of Contributions) Order 1954, the Housing Subsidies Act 1956 and the Housing Subsidies Order 1956). For rural areas, a '[…] special subsidy for housing for the agricultural population built in groups of not more than eight [dwellings] in isolated sites' was created. That subsidy from the exchequer was 'intended to assist towards the higher cost of such building, and is payable at the discretion of the Minister of Housing and Local Government.'[59] This regime enabled Rural District Councils to increase building, matching the one-fifth fraction of population share with one-fifth of total council building (see Table 3.1):

Table 3.1 Houses completed by Local Authorities, 1947 to 1959[a]

Period	All local authorities	Rural District Councils	Proportion granted by RDCs
1947	86,567	15,861	18%
1948	170,821	32,656	19%
1949	141,766	30,239	21%
1950	139,356	32,240	23%
1951	141,589	20,391	21%
1952	165,637	34,091	21%
1953	202,891	43,914	21%
1954	199,642	44,637	22%
1955	162,525	32,823	20%
1956	139,977	27,174	19%
1957	137,584	25,051	18%
1958	113,146	18,205	16%
1959	99,456	14,603	15%
Totals	1,900,955	380,885	20%

[a]TNA: MAF 186/86

Land assembly for post-war council building

In response to the continuation and expansion of exchequer subsidy, rural councils drew up plans for housebuilding in towns and villages. Land assembly, through single purchases, was negotiated between the Rural District Councils and the Ministry of Health, which was consulted on all sites, their suitability and cost, and which sanctioned each individual application for a loan for the purchase of land. This is illustrated by the case of Bradford and Melksham Rural District Council, formed by the amalgamation of two separate councils in 1934 (Case 3.2 and Figure 3.3).

Figure 3.3 Post-war council housing, Semington, Wiltshire. © Iqbal Hamiduddin.

Case 3.2: Land assembly for council building: Bradford and Melksham Rural District Council, Wiltshire

The Ministry of Health designed and co-ordinated an application process to be used by all councils seeking loan sanctions. The Ministry asked that Local Authorities submit 'house plans' to its regional office, adding that 'such submissions [should] in all instances be accompanied by information referred to in Circular 128/44'.[60] That Circular included an appended form that required the name of the site, its acreage, the number of houses to be built on the site, whether the site was already in the possession of the Council, whether development works were completed or still required, layout plans of houses agreed with the Local Planning Authority and Highways Authority, and other details of proposed houses: detailed plans, dwelling types and floor areas.

Bradford and Melksham RDC made an application to build homes in a number of its parishes in 1945 and 1946. Following applications to the Ministry late in 1945, formal borrowing consent was granted by the Ministry to the RDC, allowing it to raise 'the sum of £615 for the purchase of 3.098 acres of land at Semington and 1.1 acres at South Wraxall'.[61] Further correspondence from the Council confirmed that a decision was taken to proceed 'with the site at Semington (OS 97)[62] and the remaining site at South Wraxall (OS 110)'. The correspondence details site issues that were discussed directly with the Ministry: 'In connection with the Semington site, at the suggestion of the Regional Architect, a footpath access to the main road is being provided, and strips of land [OS 89 and OS 96] are being purchased for [that] purpose […] Land for a sewage disposal plant is required in OS 96. Negotiations with the owner of OS 89 are completed, and the transaction is included in this application; negotiations with the owner of OS 96 are not completed, but no difficulty is anticipated, as he has indicated his readiness to sell'.[63]

Also in 1945, a loan sanction for £1,080 was agreed for further sites at the parishes of Broughton Gifford and Holt. Not all of the cost could be met from 'available internal resources', necessitating a loan of £135 from the Public Works Loan Board.[64] A longer list of sites was drawn up by the RDC in support of its post-war housing programme, to which the Minister of Health raised no objection 'to negotiations proceeding for the acquisition of the sites'.[65] The specified sites totalled almost 45 acres across 14 separate parishes, on which 216 new homes were planned and received loan sanctions.[66]

The Ministry then became involved in the detail of schemes: in the design of elevations, the mix of house sizes, the positioning of coal fires and back boilers, window and door detailing, bathroom furnishings (down to the inclusion of soap trays), the positioning of airing cupboards, and the standardisation or embellishment of external features such as gabled roofs. These discussions involved not only RDCs and the Ministry: other groups were invited to offer their views.

At Bradford and Melksham, the Women's Institute was asked to comment on plans.[67] Applications were often revised and re-revised after input, with Councils expending an extraordinary amount of effort on accommodating diverse views and tastes.

Land assembly, in contrast, was greatly simplified by the absence of private demand and therefore the lack of speculative build. There were no competitors for the land being sought by RDCs, whose bids therefore represented the best offers to landowners. This situation changed during the decades after the war, but in the 1940s and 1950s, it was key factor driving the expansion post-war housing programmes in towns and villages.

While land assembly appeared straight forward, getting homes built presented some challenges. In the case of Bradford and Melksham RDC, these challenges were the topic of a local conference in November 1946[68] and were thought to centre on the relationship between the Council, the Ministry of Health ('in the shape of Mr Bevan') and the local building trade. The position of the Council was presented as follows: the Minister of Health 'blames us for the slowness of [building] houses [but] we are doing our best to get houses put up [...] 'Suggestions have been made from time to time that we are not getting all the help we need from the building industry'. The position of the 'building trade', represented by two local builders at the conference, appeared rooted in a dislike of the 'instructions imposed on us by the high-ups' (that is, by the Ministry). Micro-management by civil servants ran contrary to usual practice, and went against the preference of one of the builders 'to put something of [him]self in the house'. The Council responded that the problem lay in flexibility, in the freedom of contractors to deploy labour as they wished, in a mix of public and private projects, but with a preference for the latter. The dislike of micro-management was viewed as a partial explanation: being tied to a highly prescriptive contract prevented builders from realising higher profits. And with limited available labour, they clearly preferred to focus on private projects. But the Council had been slow with the permissioning of private builds, knowing this would divert labour from its own projects. The Council agreed that while 'it is perfectly natural that any builder would prefer to work for himself as against putting up Council Houses [...], it is no good railing against not liking to build Council Houses – it is that or nothing'.

The conclusion from the Bradford and Melksham conference was that labour shortages – especially a shortage of bricklayers[69] – stood in the way of accelerated new build. The Ministry of Health was pushing for only 1 in 4 homes to be 'private enterprise' in 1946. Labour issues in this RDC had shifted the ratio to 1 in 3. The Council concluded that 'we will try the one in three ratio, but Mr Aneurin Bevan is my boss'.[70] Labour and not land was the major impediment to rural housebuilding in the immediate post-war period. But this impediment gradually eased, allowing the rural programme to gather pace through the 1940s and into the 1950s.

The loss of rural council housing through the right to buy

It was noted in the beginning of this chapter that council housing's golden age after 1945 was rooted in low land values. The absence of a strong private housing market in villages in the years after the war, with the potential to drive up land values and prompt landowners to seek higher returns, meant that it was only public bodies that had any interest in replacing squalid cottages with new rented housing. That housing was viewed as a necessary economic infrastructure that could only be provided with subsidy. But this began to change, after a decade or so, for reasons set out in Chapters 1 and 2. First, economic recovery measured in wage growth seeded a new appetite for private housing consumption; second, the private market for housing was incentivised and facilitated in the 1960s by tax breaks for homeownership (including the scrapping of the 'Schedule A' element of income tax) and the arrival of new mortgage products; third, road-building – another part of the post-war infrastructure package – was opening up rural areas to the urban population; fourth, a surfeit of old housing, in need of renovation, was targeted by second home investors (who could access government renovation grants until 1974 – see Gallent, 1997); and finally, county-level structure planning eventually responded to counter-urbanisation by tightening rules on further development in lowest-tier settlements, increasing scarcity of housing supply in villages and hence changing the trajectory of land values.

Shifting land economics in rural amenity areas was a result of the assetisation of housing noted in Chapter 2. It eventually meant a more inhospitable and challenging environment for council housing – and for other forms of non-profit provision. Therefore the decline of rural council housing had already begun before the election of a Conservative government in 1979, which initiated a more direct ideological assault on local government's developer and landlord role.

The 'right to buy' introduced through Part III of the Housing Act 1980 gave the sitting tenants of council homes the right to purchase those homes at significant discount, calculated according to the length of time they had been tenants. It precipitated the 'residualisation' of council housing in the

UK (Forrest and Murie, 1983). Better-off tenants, assisted by specialist mortgage providers, purchased the best housing – often traditional brick-built family homes in small town, urban fringe and rural locations – leaving less well-off tenants, unable to secure necessary finance, in the worst – 'residual' – inner city housing. There were of course exceptions to this general pattern, with housing on some London estates selling quickly – the Barbican for example (see Gallent and Tewdwr-Jones, 2007).

The popularity of rural right to buy was a significant challenge for rural authorities and communities. In the decade after the 1980 Housing Act, more than a million council homes were sold to sitting tenants in England – a reduction of 27 per cent against the 1981 stock total. Rural areas lost similar amounts to urban areas: more than 61,000 homes in 'extreme rural districts' and a further 86,000 in 'intermediate rural districts' (Chaney and Sherwood, 2000: 80). The number of sales in all rural areas between 1981 and 1991 was oddly similar to the number of council homes built during the interwar period and had significant repercussions for the 'longer term re-composition of the rural housing market' (Chaney and Sherwood, 2000: 80). The authors of the 1980 Act knew that the release of council homes onto the open market (a market that had heated up during the previous 20 years) could produce significant social and demographic impacts in rural communities. For that reason, some protections were afforded 'pressured rural areas': Section 19 placed conditions on resales in National Parks, but other amenity areas were left unprotected.

Data revealed that rural districts were already exercising discretionary powers to dispose of council homes in the run-up to the Housing Act 1980. A total of 1,581 homes were sold across 63 rural districts between 1974 and 1978.[71] Following the introduction of right to buy, the housing charity Shelter warned that the 116,964 second homes across England and Wales (a growing sign of investment interest) were concentrated in rural districts with relatively few council homes. There was a risk that those few council homes would be attractive to investors and quickly bought from former tenants and converted to second home use.[72] Part of that risk had been factored into the development of right to buy policy for rural areas, in the form of the Section 19 provisions, but the protections it offered were limited.[73]

Debates in 1980 indicate a minor shift in the government's position but also an overriding concern to not geographically limit the right to buy:

> We recognise that there is a need for safeguards in some rural areas. On the other hand, in view of our clear commitment at the General

> Election to give council tenants the right to buy their homes we consider it would be wrong to exclude certain tenants simply because they live in a rural area.[74]
>
> We believe it is important that the right to buy should be as universal – and subject to as few restrictions – as possible. On the other hand, we recognise that problems may arise in some rural areas.[75]
>
> Section 19 of the Act enables local authorities and housing associations to place a limitation ('locality covenant') in conveyances or grants of leases under the right to buy in respect of dwelling-houses situated in National Parks, Areas of Outstanding Natural Beauty, or areas designated by order of the Secretary of state as 'rural areas'. Section 104C of the Housing Act 1957 (as substituted by the 1980 Act) does the same for voluntary disposals. […] The locality covenant would restrict further disposal of a dwelling-house only to a person who had lived or worked for 3 years in a region designated by the Secretary of State.[76]

The extended definition of 'rural areas' arrived in Section 157 of the Housing Act 1985. However, Williams and Twine (1994) showed how many former council homes in Scotland were sold on to second home investors, driving a process of gentrification and displacement. That process was accentuated by restrictions on the replacement of council homes by local authorities. There was an effective bar on the recycling of receipts (directed into Housing Revenue Accounts, HRA) from sales into new council-led housebuilding: a bar that remained in place for almost 40 years and was only lifted in 2018. Margaret Thatcher did not conceal her disdain for the 'inefficiencies' of local authorities, particularly in respect of their direct role in housing provision. She believed that authorities should be 'enabling' alternative forms of provision by other bodies, including housing associations, which could mix grant funding with commercial finance raised from banks and, later on, contributions extracted from the land development process through the planning system. The role of this 'third sector' in rural areas is briefly introduced below. Despite an expansion of protections to rural areas, the 'right to buy' caused a catastrophic loss of 'affordable housing' and contributed to a social reconfiguration of rural areas that housing associations have frequently been unable to counter.

In much the same way as the *tied housing problem* seeded the acceleration of council building in the interwar period, the *sale of council housing* and the rolling back of council building seeded the expansion of the third sector in rural areas. Big response shifts have periodically emerged to fill new vacuums. The third sector's emergence predates the policy shifts of the 1980s, but its growth accelerated during that decade – with housing associations, eventually rebadged 'registered providers' – becoming part of a 'mixed economy' of housing solutions that evolved to fill the void left by the retreat from state welfare. It is that mixed economy that is examined in later chapters.

Narrative 3: Towards a mixed economy of housing solutions

The third sector in villages

The 'third sector', not private and not state, has had a sustained and prolonged presence in rural areas. In the next chapter, we will look at the development of *community land trusts* and the projects they promote in villages. Here, concern is with the larger charities and (community benefit) societies that have played important roles in many rural areas but are not necessarily rooted in community-based actions (Satsangi *et al*, 2010: 215). The 'alms houses' (funded with 'alms' for the poor – charitable giving) built hundreds of years ago are now managed as charities (trusts) with housing provided to specific target groups, including retired members of the armed forces. The philanthropic actions of nineteenth-century industrialists – housing provided by Peabody, Guinness and others – have given rise to the societies bearing the names of those industrialists. These are among the modern 'housing associations' that continue to develop new social housing today, often drawing upon an element of direct government grant. The legal constitution of third sector 'registered providers' is as charities/*trusts* (where the legal title of property or assets is entrusted to a legal entity with a fiduciary duty to hold and use it for another party's benefit) or, more commonly today, *community benefit societies* (comprising share-holding members who conduct business for the benefit of a wider community). These charities and societies must be run democratically and according to principles set out by the Financial Conduct Authority (FCA). Other providers (not registered with the regulator) can be co-operatives, but these are constituted to work for the benefit of members only 'as autonomous association[s] of persons united voluntarily to meet their common economic, social, and cultural needs and aspirations through jointly owned and democratically controlled enterprise'.[77] The Regulator of Social Housing (2015) in England lists the current role of registered providers as protecting social housing assets; ensuring that providers are financially viable and properly governed; maintaining confidence of lenders to invest into the sector; encouraging and supporting the supply of social housing; ensuring that tenants are protected and have opportunities to be involved in the management of their housing; and ensuring value for money in service delivery.

A mix of large national and regional registered providers operate alongside smaller housing associations in rural England. Their strategic focus is set by trustees or boards comprising society members, all of whom are unpaid volunteers (hence 'voluntary sector'). The day-to-day operation of the providers is the responsibility of chief executives and other professionals with experience and training in residential development and housing management. The longer history of the sector is recounted by Cope (1999), but this book – charting the diverse origins of housing associations – does not cover recent development.

In February 2021, there were 1,626 registered providers in England, but not all were traditional housing associations or non-profit. Of this national total, 211 were listed as 'local authorities' presumably either local housing companies (see Chapters 4 and 6), established to engage in council-led housebuilding outside of the Housing Revenue Account (a mechanism for local authorities to build homes that are not funded from past sales receipts and not subject to right-to-buy rules) or arms-length transfer associations managing LA stock. Another 102 were for-profit companies registered with the regulator to directly provide an element of social housing as part of their business models. Of the 1,313 traditional housing associations, 512 were charitable companies or charities (including trusts) managing existing housing assets (including alms houses), 12 were community interest companies (CIC), 10 were charitable incorporated organisations (CIO), two were limited liability partnerships (LLP), and the remainder, 777, were registered societies. Excluding local authority registered providers, housing associations manage more than 1.9 million homes in England (Regulator of Social Housing, 2020). While the larger part of the housing association stock is located in urban authorities, there has been a recent increase in new supply in rural areas. Recent data on 'affordable housing supply' from MHCLG (2020b: 6–7) reveals that nearly 26,000 new units were provided in rural authorities in 2019/20 compared with 32,000 in urban authorities. This is not only homes provided by housing associations, but includes affordable housing of all types and from all sources, including low-cost home ownership projects and local authority direct-build.

Official data do not give a clear picture of the contribution of particular providers to net housing supply in rural areas, and the pattern of provision – between larger and smaller settlements – is equally difficult to discern. A major part of the problem is that data are disaggregated according to DEFRA's broad urban–rural classification and no mapping has been undertaken of accumulated supply in different types of settlements across rural authorities. Despite some important developments in the sector during the nineteenth century, housing associations spent much of the twentieth century in the shadow of mass council housing. This led many, especially associations operating in small towns and away from the cities, to become specialist providers – catering for very specific sets of need. But this changed with the turn away from local authority provision, and associations have, over the last half a century, become much more important providers of non-profit affordable housing.

After the setting up of the Housing Corporation in 1964 – the original regulator and registration body – rules were put in place for the regulation, governance and constitution of third sector providers. The 1974 Housing Act then established a system of grant support for associations that wished to build additional homes. This precipitated the third sector's own 'golden age'. A regulated and more professional third sector presented Thatcher with an opportunity to end the state's role in direct housing provision – because that sector was now providing a wider 'safety net' for households unable to meet their needs through private renting or home ownership. The 1974 grant regime continued until 1988, after which rates were reduced year-on-year in order to bring 'market discipline' to the sector and encourage a shift to mixed sources of funding. The previous year's Housing White Paper (HM Government, 1987) pledged that '[…] the future role of local authorities will essentially be a strategic one identifying housing needs and demands, encouraging *innovative methods* of provision by *other bodies* to meet such needs, maximising the use of private finance, and encouraging the new interest in the revival of the independent rented sector'. The 'other bodies' mentioned were the housing associations, which would henceforth be supported through private debt funding (from the banks), a declining portion of public funding (eventually 'social housing grant') and through 'planning and affordable housing' mechanisms, which the government issued guidance on in 1991 and 1992.

The detail of these planning mechanisms is examined in the next chapter. But what sorts of third sector schemes were being brought forward during this latter part of the twentieth century? And what sort of contributions were housing associations – properly called registered providers, RPs – making to housing supply and affordability in small village locations? Little can be gleaned from national data (see above) and there have been few recent studies of housing association activity in villages. But the associations themselves are keen to illustrate the ways in which they have been developing new homes in rural areas, through exceptions schemes (examined in the next chapter), grant funded provision, or a mix of the two. Contemporary examples of registered providers working with partners in rural areas are offered in Chapter 4. The more historic example of the *National Agricultural Centre Housing Association* (NACHA) is presented here, as Case 3.3, as a bridge to the discussion of tied housing presented earlier in this chapter, with housing associations seeking to fill a void left by both demise of tied housing, resulting from new tenancy protections in the middle of the 1970s, and the cessation of council build just five years later.

Case 3.3: The evolution of the third sector: National Agricultural Centre Housing Association

An important debate took place in the 1970s over the effectiveness of rural housing associations in the context of policy affecting both tied and council housing. Rural associations were often small and seeking to bring forward small schemes. They faced similar challenges to Rural District Councils after 1945, rooted in a grant regime – and cost yardsticks – unsuited to rural contexts with their higher development costs. At the same time, associations often faced detailed negotiations with Parish councils; many schemes were aborted at a late stage with associations left to foot legal costs; and they were forced into 'no scheme, no fee' professional fee arrangements, but these were more costly if a scheme went ahead. It was also the case that associations encountered significant duplication in their dealings with the Housing Corporation (HC) and the Department of the Environment (DoE), with regional HC officers often inconsistent in their interpretation of policy.

Land availability was seldom a barrier to development, but where land was gifted, any acquisition grant that they would otherwise have been awarded could not be rolled into a development grant. Associations were frustrated by this, as it would enable them to up the quality of rural schemes. When bidding for local authority land, councils frequently dragged their feet and often insisted on a new valuation (from the District Valuer) after a number of months. The prospect of housing use on the land would cause the value to rise, with associations viewing this practice as a form of 'gazumping'. The DoE acknowledged that rural associations faced challenges and at a meeting with NACHA in 1979, committed to reviewing yardstick flexibility, the recycling of acquisition grants into development grants and the duplication of compliance checks, but added that public money needed to be safeguarded.[78]

The NACHA had been established in 1975, alongside the Rural Trust, to provide rented housing for retiring agricultural workers. The purpose of the Trust was to fundraise for its partner association, with those funds used to meet any capital costs not eligible for loan or subsidy and also to provide ancillary care and welfare support for those being housing. NACHA was registered with the Housing Corporation in 1976, becoming eligible for grant support under the provisions of the Housing Act 1974. It quickly became apparent that the extension of its social purpose to meet general rural needs, rather than just the needs of those retiring from farming, would allow it to develop larger and more viable housing schemes. It enjoyed strong support from landowners, with gifted land enabling it to address dispersed, but locally severe, housing needs. At the same time, the Housing Corporation's policy of distributing 10 per cent of its grant allocation to rural schemes enabled an annual development programme of 100 units, albeit more concentrated (in service centres) than the association had wished, given the need to achieve viable scales of development. NACHA aspired to operate nationally. The Corporation's view, however, was that a single association trying to roll out smaller schemes would not, at that time, be viable, since the 'scattered nature of its operation was bound to make it an uneconomic proposition'.[79]

The National Agricultural Centre Housing Association was operating in an emergent grant context in the 1970s. It was able to access relatively cheap or gifted land for its developments but faced complications from a funding regime calibrated to deal with urban settings. These forced the association to focus on larger schemes in higher-tier centres. While this continues to be a reality for *registered providers*, mechanisms have evolved to drive down the costs of developing smaller sites in villages. As land costs rose in many rural areas, some associations started experimenting in the 1980s with development site exceptions on farmland and, at the same time, won concessions on the application of grant yardsticks for rural sites. The 'site exceptions' approach, and funding arrangements, are explored later in this book.

Occupancy conditions – affecting private, third sector and council homes

Since the 1970s, rural housing associations have become a key part of a 'mixed economy' of rural housing interventions. With the fade-out of tied housing and the near-cessation of council build, a range of different mechanisms and approaches to providing affordable homes for working rural households have emerged. The remainder of this book explores this mixed economy and how, through land, planning, tax and finance reforms, it might be possible to resolve persistent rural housing inequalities. One remaining issue for this chapter relates to the rising tide of speculative housing demand in rural areas, introduced in the last chapter, and the attempt to 'protect' rural homes, across different sectors, from those market forces that might make them unavailable to local families.

Two types of occupancy condition have been used to restrict who can reside in rural homes: general conditions stipulating a 'local' connection (and/or full-time occupancy) and occupational conditions that usually require someone to be engaged in agriculture or a related activity. Agricultural Occupancy Conditions – or 'agricultural ties' – were examined earlier in this chapter. The focus now is on the use of more general conditions, used to ensure that homes can only be occupied by those deemed 'local' or intending to live 'full time' in a village. Planning permission is *conditional* on subsequent occupation by someone meeting the condition, irrespective of the intended tenure of the home being built (Satsangi et al, 2010: 141). Conditions (at planning stage) can be attached to homes for rent, shared ownership or purchase. They have been used, for example, to guarantee that only specified target groups can occupy homes built with a planning exception (see Chapter 4). That sort of condition, linked to affordable rented housing, has seldom proved controversial. Conditions attached to general market housing have, however, been a source of considerable debate – and these are examined in this section.

Section 52 Agreements (Town and Country Planning Act 1971) before 1990 and Section 106 Agreements (Town and Country Planning Act 1990) afterwards have been used to impose conditions on the occupancy of new housing. For reasons of greater market intrusion and increased pressure on a limited housing stock, general conditions came to be seen as a means of giving local priority to new housing where additional building, at a scale required to satiate wider demand *and* meet local need, would have adverse landscape and character impact.

This type of prioritisation means, in theory, that all new build housing is reserved for local need (thereby limiting the level of building activity). Arguments against this degree of control centre on undue 'interference' in the operation of the housing market (on the grounds that it should be markets that allocate, not bureaucrats, although bureaucratic allocation has been shown to deliver a fairer distribution of housing resource (Tunstall, 2015)), on the difficulties of enforcing conditions over the longer term (as homes are sold on) and uncertainties over what it means to be 'local' or what constitutes a local connection. The uncertainties of localness have led to greater emphasis on full-time occupancy, which nevertheless remains difficult to enforce. The case in favour of using general conditions is that, in theory, they limit the consumption of land for new housing (only that which is needed gets built) and they are a means of winning local support for development: communities want to see housing built for young people living and working in the area, for local families, or for older residents retiring to homes more suited to their needs.

So general use of conditions has intrinsic appeal in some quarters, because of its potential to ease development pressure while ensuring that a community's needs are prioritised. But in practice, such general use has been shown to have numerous unintended consequences. One important study of their use, in the Lake District in the late 1970s, was conducted by Shucksmith and published in two books (Shucksmith, 1981; 1990b). He looked at the housing market and development activity impacts of using conditions to prioritise the needs of 'low income, low wealth' groups above 'more prosperous groups' looking to retire or purchase second homes in the National Park (distinctly different housing classes – see Chapter 2). The Lake District Special Planning Board's 1977 draft plan sought to 'restrict completely all new development to that which can be shown to satisfy local need' and applied Section 52 conditions on *all* new development to that end. The same policy found its way into the Cumbria and Lake District Joint Structure Plan three years later (LDSP and CCC, 1980), but broadened the definition of local need to all 'full-time residents'.

The policy met with immediate criticism: the report on the Examination in Public of the Joint Structure Plan concluded that it was 'unreasonable' to use 'planning powers to attempt to ensure that houses should only be occupied by persons who are already living in the locality', adding that planning should be 'concerned with the manner of the use of land, not the identity or merits of the occupier' (DoE, 1981). While the policy was eventually deleted by the Secretary of State, it remained in force – first in the Draft National Park Plan and then the Joint Structure Plan – for a full seven years between 1977 and 1984, giving Shucksmith the opportunity to study its operation and impacts. He made a number of important observations.

First, more prosperous groups seeking second homes in the Lake District were undeterred by the restriction. They had always preferred secondhand property (older village homes with 'character' rather than characterless new build) but now demand from them became entirely focused in that segment of the market. Second, although new-build housing was now targeted at full-time (that is, 'local') residents, the supply of that housing reduced: 'builders ceased speculative residential development, partly because of the uncertainties raised by the new policy, but principally because of the greater difficulty of acquiring suitable land with planning permission' (Shucksmith, 1990b: 122). Third, the aggregate impact across the entire housing market – comprising secondhand housing and a declining quantity of new build – was a slightly faster rate of house-price inflation. This, combined with the restriction on non-local purchase in the market for new build, choked off some of the external demand. Some aspiring second home buyers found the Lake District suddenly too expensive and shifted their attention elsewhere, outside the area of restriction. But fourth, price adjustments for secondhand and new-build property were largely balanced out across the market. Excess external demand refocused entirely on secondhand property, benefiting existing owners. That same demand was removed from the new-build segment, but prices there were largely unaffected owing to changes in land values, development activity and therefore reduced supply.

Shucksmith concluded that, overall, 'local people who could afford to buy new housing will have found prices roughly the same as before, once the shifts in the demand and supply schedules had worked through' (p. 123). 'Low income, low wealth' groups unable to access home ownership before were not assisted greatly by the policy.

Despite these findings, faith in the potential of land-use planning to engineer different housing outcomes has never completely disappeared (see Brooks, 2021). The basic problem that planning faces is its inability to control the occupancy of existing homes, built without any restrictive condition. If it sets conditions on new build, the supply

Figure 3.4 St Ives town, Cornwall. © Herry Lawford. CC BY 2.0.

of that housing dwindles (to the detriment of local people looking for homes), while the queue of buyers for existing housing lengthens. The combined effect of falling supply and concentrating demand is rising house values, which benefit existing owners. In fact, general occupancy restrictions accentuate the pressures that rural amenity areas already face. They have an amplifying effect. But still, the debate rumbles on, largely because a community's need for more 'affordable housing' has become a material planning consideration. The much-cited 'Mitchell' case, brought to the Court of Appeal in 1993, confirmed that local authorities can give consideration to the characteristics of intended occupants when determining applications for residential development, overruling the view of the Secretary of State from 1981. Legal precedent has, therefore, given a green light to repeats of the Lake District experiment, although research and analysis cautions against this sort of intervention across general housing markets. One recent example of general occupancy condition use is provided by St Ives, Cornwall (Cornwall Council, 2015).

Reflections

In this chapter, we have painted a broad picture of rural housing interventions in the twentieth century. Those interventions track a number of trends: significant rural employment in farming at the beginning, far

Case 3.4: Using general occupancy restrictions in St Ives, Cornwall

Cornwall, with its pristine coastline and pretty fishing villages, has long been a focus of second home and retirement housing demand. About a quarter of homes in St Ives – a town on Cornwall's north coast, with around 12,000 residents – are owned by seasonal residents. Analysis by Cornwall Council (2015) suggests that house prices in towns like St Ives, with this level of second home ownership, are inflated by roughly 50 per cent (compared to what they would have been without second homes). In May 2016, residents of the town voted to adopt a Neighbourhood Development Plan (NDP) containing policy 'H2', restricting the occupancy of new built housing to 'full time residents' (St Ives Town Council, 2016). A study into the policy then looked at the drivers and logic of the restriction as well as early evidence of its impacts (Gallent *et al*, 2019a).

Political pressure to tackle St Ives's second home dilemma – and a view that new housing development was not serving local needs – had been growing for several years. A housing survey conducted in 2013 revealed the desire of residents to ensure that new housing was affordable, but also protect the character of the town from additional development. They wanted the Town Council to 'square the circle' of increasing the affordability of housing while curbing the pace and quantity of housebuilding. A Housing Topic Group (HTG) was established to examine options and quickly concluded that occupancy restrictions offered a mechanism to prevent new housing being used seasonally. This was not about meeting 'local' needs, but ensuring that full time residents were prioritised. A policy was developed and consulted upon. That consultation revealed 'possibly more support from people who are brought up here for things like holiday lets that [bring] an economic benefit to the area than there was from newcomers' (HTG member). 'Locals' prioritised jobs while newcomers prioritised town character, with the latter supporting occupancy restrictions as a means of slowing the pace of housing development. St Ives estate agents saw clear associational interest in the split of opinion, believing that wealthier home owners wanted to protect their investments against potentially damaging change. HTG members, on the other hand, believed that they were running an experiment, to see if restrictions might limit second home use.

The logic, from their point of view, was to increase levels of year-round housing occupancy. Delivering affordable homes was the goal of a parallel policy, H1, which sought Section 106 contributions from new development. But the closure of the new-build market from non-resident buyers could depress house prices (it was conjectured), and reduce the capacity of development sites to deliver planning gain. Worst case scenario – sites would not come forward; best case scenario – they would come forward without affordable housing. Estate agents estimated that two-thirds of homebuyers were non-local. Most, but not all, were buying secondhand housing. Some were looking to relocate to St Ives and others were seeking second homes. If this demand transferred entirely to the secondhand market, the combination of continued demand and reduced development activity (meaning higher prices), alongside fewer Section 106 contributions, could leave lower-income local households in a worse predicament.

The HTG view was that such a scenario was unlikely given that their experiment had arrived at the mid-point in the delivery of the current Local Plan and would therefore affect a relatively small proportion of new development. The County Council planning team added that greater emphasis should be placed on developing rural exception sites around nearby villages, if any compensation were needed. Local developers, however, were unhappy with H2 and claimed that it had already (early in 2017) hit market confidence. Developers seeking land were making lower offers in light of the policy (and gross development value expectations) but landowners had been slow to change their price expectations. They could choose to develop at higher densities, but feared refusal at the planning stage. They also feared that homes would be more difficult to market given the 'burden on title' created by the occupancy condition and possible limits on mortgage advances. HTG members rejected such claims, but developers displayed a clear nervousness over the policy.

It was too early, in 2017, to conduct a full investigation of impacts arising from St Ives's general use of occupancy restrictions. However, there were already signs of suppressed market confidence and reduced development activity. Housing markets are formed of new build and secondhand segments. A reduction in new build will not affect the overall demand for homes in a popular rural amenity area: that demand will simply transfer to the secondhand segment. This may produce an outcome – reduced levels of new development and rising prices – that is of greater benefit to existing homeowners than people struggling to rent or buy homes.

less at the end; zero investment interest in rural housing for much of the twentieth century, accelerating investment interest in the final few decades; consolidated private ownership of land in the early part, a greater distribution later on, but still in the hands of farmers – Woods's 'agrarian elites' (Woods, 2005). Housing interventions were initially centred on the private sector, with great estates providing tied housing for workers, via their tenant farmers. There was then some intrusion of state provision, which only accelerated after 1945 as the need to provide an alternative source of low-rent housing for the farming economy gathered pace. But by the 1970s, the housing scene was becoming more mixed: private enterprise bidding for land and catering for buyers joining the urban exodus, and housing associations starting to eclipse local councils in the provision of affordable rural homes. The 1970s heralded the beginning of a period of change, when 'tied' housing and 'free' council housing would be substituted by a more mixed economy of housing intervention across different sectors. We start to explore this new diversity in the next chapter and also examine local planning's shift from intervening in the occupancy of housing to levering replacement affordable homes through mechanisms, including site exceptions, that are examined in the next chapter.

The twentieth century saw rural housing in transition: it went from being something surplus, unwanted and of little value for anyone outside the farming sector, to being an increasingly scarce investment commodity, prized for status conferred and for amenity. Rural housing, like housing elsewhere, went from being a service required by local workers to an asset desired by mobile capital. It is that latter role that foregrounds our examination of the present situation in the next chapter.

The past also holds lessons for the future – a subject that we return to in Chapter 6. Restrictive interventions in the private housing market are difficult to execute effectively and risk unintended consequences. But removing housing from the market, or decoupling land from private interest, provides a means of *re*presenting housing as a public or community infrastructure (as it was for much of the twentieth century) rather than an investment asset. Past council building did exactly that, as have the programmes of housing associations. In the next chapter, we explore the power of community action to restore the social role of housing. But all such removals and restorations work counter to the role of housing in modern economies: as sources of private wealth that can be accessed for personal spending and that support growth. Any general interventions that restrict the growth in housing value in rural areas will have implications for the distribution of wealth, bringing a levelling down rather than a levelling up; and any interventions that separate groups into (unrestrained) market and non-market housing risk perpetuating wealth inequalities. This is a major challenge for future policy.

Notes

1. The first of these Acts (Increase of Rent and Mortgage Interest (War Restrictions Act 1915) was intended to prevent profiteering from a housing shortage experienced during the First World War. Updates followed in 1917, 1918 and 1919. Consolidating legislation was provided by the Increase of Rent and Mortgage Interest (Restrictions) Act 1920 (see Wilson, 2017: 4–5).
2. TNA: MAF 228/63
3. TNA: MAF 228/63
4. TNA: MAF 228/63
5. TNA: MAF 228/63
6. Museum of English Rural Life: SR 3NUAW H/5/3
7. TNA: PREM 8/402
8. TNA: MAF 228/63
9. TNA: HLG 40/50
10. TNA: MAF 228/63
11. TNA: HLG 40/50
12. TNA: MAF 228/63
13. TNA HLG 40/57
14. TNA: MAF 228/63
15. TNA: MAF 186/86
16. Figures from Zayed and Loft (2019) who note that the 1950 figure includes Women's Land Army and Prisoners of War. The 1940 figure, of 712,000, suggest that these groups may have added 100,000 to the farm workforce reported in 1950.
17. This was a private member's bill brought forward by Bob Cryer, Member of Parliament for Keighley.
18. TNA: LAB 112/226
19. TNA: LAB 112/226
20. TNA: LAB 112/226
21. TNA: LAB 112/226
22. TNA: LAB 112/226
23. TNA: HLG 118/2410/2411
24. TNA: HLG 118/2411
25. TNA: MAF 228/63
26. TNA: PRO 57/929
27. TNA: MAF 228/63
28. TNA: MAF 228/63
29. TNA: MAF 228/63
30. TNA: MAF 228/63

31. TNA: MAF 228/63
32. TNA: MAF 228/63
33. TNA: MAF 228/63
34. TNA: MAF 228/63
35. TNA: MAF 228/63
36. TNA: MAF 228/63
37. TNA: MAF 228/63
38. TNA: MAF 228/63
39. Wiltshire archives G2/132/17: Circular 1238, Ministry of Health: Housing of the Working Classes, 12 January 1932
40. Wiltshire archives G2/132/17: Circular 1238, Ministry of Health: Housing of the Working Classes, 12 January 1932
41. Wiltshire archives G2/132/17: Letter to the Secretary of the Minister of Health, 24 March 1932
42. Wiltshire archives G2/132/17: Letter to the Secretary of the Minister of Health, 24 March 1932
43. Wiltshire archives G2/132/17: Letter to the Secretary of the Minister of Health, regarding Housing (Financial Provisions) Act 1924, Parish of Staverton, 1932
44. Wiltshire archives G2/132/17: Letter dated 7 May 1932
45. Wiltshire archives G2/132/17: Letter to the Secretary of the Minister of Health, 12 September 1932
46. Wiltshire archives G2/132/17: Letter to the Clerk to the Rural District Council of Melksham, from the Ministry of Health in Whitehall, 10 October 1932
47. Wiltshire archives G2/132/17: Letter to the Clerk of the Rural District Council of Melksham, from the Chief Secretary, 30 July 1932
48. Wiltshire archives G2/132/17: Letter from the Ministry of Health to the Clerk to the Rural District Council of Melksham, 10 June 1932
49. Wiltshire archives G2/132/17: Letter dated 19 July 1932
50. Wiltshire archives G2/132/17: Extract from Minutes of a meeting of the Melksham Rural District Council held on 2 June 1932
51. Wiltshire archives G7/132/15: Letter from Malmesbury Rural District Council – Housing of the Working Classes – to the Secretary of the Minister of Health, 8 May 1937
52. Wiltshire archives G7/132/15: Letter from Malmesbury Rural District Council – description of proposed block of four non-parlour type dwelling houses to be erected at Sopworth
53. Wiltshire archives G7/132/15: Letter to the Clerk to the Malmesbury Rural District Council, from the Ministry of Health, 1 July 1937
54. Wiltshire archives G7/132/15: Letter from the building surveyor of Malmesbury
55. Wiltshire archives G7/132/15: Letter from the Building and Public Works Construction Co to Chas Campbell, Malmesbury surveyor, 18 February 1939
56. Wiltshire archives G7/132/15: Financial query, 6 January 1940
57. TNA: HLG 40/50
58. National Archives 315/45 'The Office for the Minister of Reconstruction – Draft White Paper on Housing': Draft White Paper, section of text removed from the final version.
59. TNA: MAF 186/86
60. Note from the Ministry of Health, 3 July 1945
61. Wiltshire archives G2/132/14: Letter from the Ministry of Health to the Clerk to Bradford and Melksham Rural District Council, 2 January 1946
62. Ordnance Survey (OS) site references
63. Wiltshire archives G2/132/14: Letter dated 27 November 1945
64. Wiltshire archives G2/132/14: Letter from the Secretary of the Ministry of Health, regional office in Bristol
65. Wiltshire archives G2/132/14: Letter from the Ministry of Health, 7 March 1945
66. Wiltshire archives G2/132/14: Review of sites for the two-year programme, 10 November 1944
67. Wiltshire archives G2/132/14
68. Wiltshire archives G2/132/14: Letter dated 16 November 1946
69. Wiltshire archives G2/132/14: Letter from Carter & Co building contractors to Bradford-on-Avon and Melksham Rural District Council, 13 December 1946
70. Wiltshire archives G2/132/14: Builders conference [with the council] 28 November 1946
71. NA HLG 29/1729
72. NA HLG 29/1729: Shelter pamphlet

73. NA HLG 29/1729: Shelter pamphlet: figures on the numbers of second homes and council dwellings were mainly taken from the 1980/81 Housing Investment Programmes submitted by each local council to central government.
74. NA HLG 29/1729: Letter from the Department of the Environment, 16 May 1980
75. NA HLG 29/1729: Letter from Michael Heseltine, 17 March 1980
76. NA HLG 29/1729: Housing Act 1980: Section 19: Dwellings in National Parks or Areas of Outstanding Natural Beauty: Designated Regions Order
77. International Co-operative Alliance's *Statement on the Co-operative Identity, Values and Principles*
78. TNA: HLG 118/3340: Meeting with representatives of the National Agricultural Centre, 22 November 1979
79. TNA: HLG 118/3340: Meeting with representatives of the National Agricultural Centre, 22 November 1979

4
Planning, community action and neighbourhood planning: the present

The curtailment of council building in the 1980s, along with the private disposal of council homes, foregrounded a shift to a greater mix of non-market housing models. This chapter looks at the support provided by the planning system to the provision of 'affordable housing' in rural areas – through planning gain and through the granting of exceptional permissions to develop homes on non-housing land. Planning mechanisms have also been an important part of the support package available to community land trusts, other community projects and a set of possibilities that eventually came together under the umbrella of neighbourhood development planning. In this chapter, we illustrate the 'present' of village housing delivery, drawing on a range of project examples. Planning and community-based interventions are, in a sense, 'downstream' disruptions that try to circumvent 'upstream' game rules for the benefit of rural households. The open market for private housing allocates on an ability-to-pay basis. Discussions and examples in this chapter provide cues for a broader reappraisal of extant game rules, relating to land and housing taxes, in Chapter 5.

Introduction

Planning systems corral land value into locations earmarked for development – where housing and other land use changes will be permitted. This is true of all systems, whether land is zoned for development (and then proceeds 'by right') or principles are laid out to guide discretionary decision-making. Planning does not generate value but it creates opportunity (for others to develop land in profitable ways) and, in return, usually has a facility to capture some of that value for public purpose, rooted in an acknowledgement that land values are elevated by public investments in infrastructure that make land developable. In Chapter 2, we noted that planning may reduce the supply of developable land, often in places where demand is greatest. Villages may be such locations, where amenity and scarcity cause prices to spike. In those locations, 'the market' (formed by interactions between willing landowners, developers and homebuyers) would like to unlock and extract that value through development; but at the same time, the interest of existing homeowners lies in protecting the value of their own homes through the preservation of scarcity and therefore the prevention of development. But in many instances, they will support the delivery of a controlled and small amount of housing that targets 'local' need. Planning creates and sustains scarcity in high amenity areas but can also be used to deliver opportunities for non-market housing.

In this chapter, we look at a number of linked issues: first, how the planning system can support the delivery of non-market housing through site exceptions; second, how communities sometimes take the lead on small housing projects, through community-interest companies or trusts; third, how a wider range of community initiatives are now evolving, some linked to formalised 'neighbourhood' planning structures; and fourth, what impediments remain to the expansion of community-led responses. The planning system operated in England and in other parts of the United Kingdom is an outlier internationally. It is not a regulatory system, with fixed rules, but 'principle based'. This means that local authorities have significant discretion over development control decisions, drawing up principle-based plans against which to judge and grant development applications on a case-by-case basis. It is not the purpose of this chapter to unpack the mechanics of England's planning system, but the way it operates and how it might be reformed (and potentially deliver different housing outcomes) is picked up again in Chapter 5.

Land-use planning – 'rural exception sites' in villages

Research into rural needs – whether for housing, essential services or broader development – regularly argues that rural areas fall into a gap between public investment and market interest. The argument goes like this: rural markets are thin, in the sense that demand for services is lower given population sparsity. This means that if public intervention costs more *per capita*, and the returns on private investment are far lower than in dense and thicker urban markets, then both public intervention and private investment will head to towns and cities, leaving rural communities to do more for themselves.

This is a very general argument that does not always stand up to scrutiny. The presence of affluent households can be a magnet to some forms of private investment, especially high-end retail or housing. In those situations (the 'exchanging areas' introduced in Chapter 1), private investment may be present, serving the needs of wealthier households, but public intervention may still be lacking – in transport and key services for less well-off households. The presence of those affluent households can therefore mask rural poverty. In depleting areas, a lack of external support and interest may well trigger community self-help: people fending for themselves in a context of indifference. In the exchanging areas, the displacement of needs has the potential to 'weaken the case' for action (the needs appear more pressing elsewhere); but at the same time, middle class communities find themselves in an array of situations: there will still be vulnerable community members to assist, including the young, the old and those delivering key services. Those middle-class communities, rich in resource and human capital, may be highly motivated towards self-help.

In essence, there is thought to be a 'natural leaning' towards communitarianism as the producer of social goods, which is encouraged by more limited support from outside interests. This means that the focus of rural planning is seldom *delivering for* rural communities but rather *supporting* communities looking to meet their own needs (Gkartzios *et al*, 2022).

The planning system can do this by exceptionally circumventing its own rules. It generates scarcity (of housing), but can then support non-market housing by exploiting its own impact on land price: granting exceptional planning permission on (lower value) farmland (and other land not allocated for housing use) or requiring developers to build 'affordable homes' on (higher value) housing land as a condition of planning consent. The latter mechanism – 'Section 106 contributions' in England – works where bigger schemes are planned, so often in key service centres. In villages, planning can support communities by granting exceptional permissions (on 'rural exception sites', RES) or by allowing community-interest companies, or land trusts, to convert buildings for residential use that would not normally be permitted.

Many studies have focused on Section 106 contributions and the factors, land market and skills, that result in bigger or smaller contributions (Gallent *et al*, 2002; Farthing and Ashley, 2002; Crook *et al*, 2015). Less has been written on 'site exceptions' in recent years, although a number of early studies focused on this issue. The aim here is to bring the narrative of village-level planning innovation up to date with recent case studies. Barlow and Chambers (1992) charted the story of planning innovation in housing delivery from the 1970s onwards. They noted the use of conditions (using Section 52 agreements under the 1971 Act) requiring contributions to council building and also experimentation with 'exceptional' permissions in the New Forest in the early 1980s. The early use of exceptions was also the subject of a study by Williams *et al* (1991) who flagged the proliferation of the exceptions approach across England and Wales before the issuing of formal guidance to planning authorities in 1991 (DoE Circular 7/91 in England and Welsh Office Circular 31/91 in Wales). Gallent (1995) surveyed planning authorities in Wales and was able to estimate the small number of new homes delivered via site exceptions immediately after that guidance appeared (see Gallent, 1998). He also identified growing support for the initiative, among local authorities and associations, but also an appetite amongst local authority officers to reclaim their direct housing role (Gallent, 1998: 73). However, exceptional planning permission on farmland, and other sites not allocated for housing use, adjoining village development envelopes marked the start of a more flexible response to meeting housing needs in lowest tier settlements, with planning authorities, rural enablers, community councils and landowners coming together to overcome the critical planning–land–finance nexus of barriers.

Site exceptions are a formal response to the barriers confronting housing development for local need in villages (Gallent and Bell, 2000: 376). Exceptional permission for housing can be granted on farmland – or other land not allocated for housing use – where there is evidence of clear local need and the exception is supported by the community (represented by a community or parish council), a landowner (who is willing to either gift the land to the community (a rare occurrence) or sell it at at a discounted price, less than full development value, in order to support the delivery of affordable homes) and a body willing to undertake the development and manage the housing in perpetuity (either a housing association or a community vehicle, perhaps a land trust). These parties are often brought together by a 'rural housing enabler' whose remit is to identify these opportunities and broker deals between key partners. An enabler can be a local authority officer with time allocated for this function. Alternatively, they may be employed by a housing association or by the ACRE (Action with Communities in Rural England) network. Webb *et al* (2019: 14) have examined the work of enablers in Wales, flagging their importance in undertaking local needs work, promoting important interactions and in general advocating for affordable housing. Baxter and

Murphy (2018: 23) note that many parish councils in England are also good at developing the outreach strategies needed to promote affordable housing schemes, often with the support of enablers.

Broadly, the process leading up to the granting of an exception has the following steps. First, there will be general awareness of the mismatch between new housing supply and the patterning of rural needs. The existence of enablers, who will be in regular contact with parish council clerks, form part of a network of interests that possesses the social and cultural capital needed to stimulate rural development (Yarwood, 2002: 277). Second, the community (with the support of, or encouraged by) an enabler conducts a targeted study and identifies an unmet need for affordable housing that cannot be provided through the general market – there are too few new homes, and those that do get built are beyond the price range of local households. Third, the enabler and/or the community are aware of local plan restrictions on development outside of the village envelope. They are also aware of who owns adjoining land (perhaps the owner is a member of, or connected to, the Parish Council). Fourth, the granting of a planning exception emerges as a possible response and, through the enabler or because of existing Parish Council links, a conversation ensues with the local authority and one or more landowners – testing the idea that land might be sold at a price that would support the development of affordable homes. And then fifth, a registered provider (see Chapter 3) is found to take forward the development and manage any homes built via the exception in perpetuity. In practice, the sequencing of conversations need not follow these steps. The landowner may propose the site exception or the enabler may work for a housing association, and may have been tasked to scout opportunities that advance the association's charitable mission. In no particular order, there has to be a community assessing and thinking about meeting local needs, a local authority looking to facilitate the delivery of affordable homes, a landowner with (accessible) land to either gift (or perhaps lease at a peppercorn rent) or sell at a discount, and a registered provider who can build and manage homes (and is willing and able to do so given the management costs of having a dispersed portfolio of small schemes). It is also possible that a community might decide to develop the scheme itself, through a community land trust.

With all these partners in place, and proactively talking about a site exception scheme, the progression of that scheme can be a fairly simple undertaking. The impediments to development – planning, land cost and finance – are all addressed, or at least circumvented. The evidence provided by the community supports the granting of an exceptional permission; the landowner is willing to sell a plot of land at discount (against full development value); and there is a provider willing to develop a scheme of four or five homes that will be rented to households on its waiting list. The affordability of the housing built will depend on land price, build cost (including finance cost) and the developer's required return. Ideally the land cost would be zero (although English Rural Housing Association is currently paying at least £10,000 per plot in southern England,[1] which is well above agricultural value, but significantly below the cost of land within a village's development envelope), the required return for a non-profit would also be zero, and build cost could be covered by grant (resulting in a zero finance cost). In that case, the rent could be set to cover the overheads and maintenance costs of the provider. But in reality, there are likely to be build and finance costs that are incurred by the provider. But land in very 'exclusive' and expensive village locations will represent the biggest part of development cost, so significantly reducing that element provides an important means of delivering affordable homes.

However, research has revealed regular and significant barriers to the delivery of housing on exception sites. As well as facilitating exceptions, planning can also impede their progress. The land on which a development is proposed may be set back, requiring the insertion of an access road that presents 'highways difficulties', often relating to site access. *Highway Authorities* – the top-level local authority, often the county in rural areas unless a village sits within a unitary authority – have responsibility, defined by the 1980 Highways Act, for public roads apart from trunk roads and motorways. A proposed access road to an exception site can sometimes raise road safety concerns, which can only be allayed by a different and potentially more expensive routing. A scheme might also be impeded by design prescriptions, which can impact on cost or make it difficult to deliver homes in locations where land is available. For example, village design rules may require new homes to be within a fixed distance of existing buildings (and not appear to be 'development in the open countryside'). But the land being made available for development may be beyond paddocks or private gardens, causing a gap that contravenes planning rules. In the recent past, Neighbourhood Planning has provided communities with a new framework for thinking about exceptions as a response to local housing needs. Fixed distance and siting prescriptions can be removed within Neighbourhood Plans – see the Upper Eden discussion, below. Communities can therefore adjust policy to suit local circumstances, potentially increasing the contribution of this mechanism to supplying additional village housing.

Another problem that some schemes encounter is intransigent landowners who, on hearing that there is a need for additional housing in the village, may hold out in the *hope* of a local plan and boundary

Figure 4.1 Cannomede Cottages, South Tawton, Dartmoor. © Hastoe Housing Association.

Case 4.1: Site exception in a national park: South Tawton, Dartmoor National Park

Dartmoor National Park Authority (DNPA) notes that '[…] the village of South Tawton is situated on the northern fringe of the National Park, on a knoll in the valley below Cawsand Beacon. It was recorded in the Domesday Book as one of the wealthiest parishes in Devon. The foundation of the new town of South Zeal in 1298, just 1 mile to the south, probably suppressed the growth of South Tawton and it stayed as an agricultural settlement'. The modern parish covers South Tawton, South Zeal and Taw Green and had a resident population of 912 at the 2011 Census (DNPA, 2019: 3). South Tawton Parish Council undertook a local housing needs survey in 2014, which confirmed the need for affordable housing in the parish, and particularly in South Tawton village where Land Registry data showed that the average sale price of a home in 2016 was just over £300,000 – more than £50,000 more than in neighbouring South Zeal and well out the range of families on local incomes. Prices across the National Park have risen in recent years, pushed upwards by the purchasing of second homes (Kime, 2019). Prices in Dartmoor were 25 per cent higher than the regional average in 2019 and although less afflicted than other national parks, the number of Airbnb listings in Dartmoor rose from 76 in August 2016 to 261 exactly three years later (Kime, 2019). The parks are nationally important amenity areas, which is reflected in patterns of housing consumption and price inflation.

The Parish Council had previously worked with Hastoe Housing Association on a rural exception site in the early 1990s. Four homes were completed in 1992 on land donated by a local farmer. Because of increasing pressures on the housing stock and signs of growing local need, evidenced in the 2014 survey and in Land Registry data, the council resumed its relationship with Hastoe and sought to deliver additional homes on the site developed in the 1990s. Work commenced on site in June 2017 and six homes for rent to people with a connection to South Tawton were completed in September 2018. The 'Cannomede Cottages' scheme (see Figure 4.1) comprised six houses for rent – bringing the on-site unit total to 10. The new homes have air source heat pumps, mechanical ventilation and heat recovery systems that reduce fuel costs. The total build cost was close to £1.2 million. A large proportion of the cost, £905,000, was met from borrowing by Hastoe Housing Association. Homes England provided a grant of £178,000 and West Devon Borough Council – the local housing authority – contributed £100,000 from its own resources. But it was the development partnership between Hastoe, Dartmoor National Park Authority (as the planning authority) and South Tawton Parish Council that got the scheme off the ground, on land donated at zero cost to the partnership.

Given the level of demand for new homes in the National Park, housing land commands a significant price premium. There is immense pressure in the park to extend existing houses, convert agricultural buildings to residential use and allow infill development within village envelopes. Without some means of reducing land costs, it is impossible to deliver affordable housing. In nearby South Zeal, a proposal for an affordable self-build scheme comprising four homes went before DNPA's development management committee in January 2019. In that instance, agricultural land for the scheme was provided by a family member of one of the self-builders. And because the occupancy of homes would be restricted in perpetuity by a Section 106 agreement, officers advised that the scheme be approved as another site exception on agricultural land. Neither the South Zeal nor South Tawton exceptions provoked any great policy debate. The Highways comment at South Zeal was that 'the proposed access is adequate in respect of geometry and visibility to serve the proposed development so there are no objections from a highway safety point of view.' Both schemes needed to be compliant with a suite of DNPA policies relating to sustainable development, limited new housing for local needs, settlement strategies, sustainable transport, protecting special environmental qualities and national park purposes, sustainable design, conserving plant and animal life, biodiversity and geological conservation, place quality, access onto the highway, protecting local amenity, parking and landscape and built environment safeguards. Given the clear need for affordable housing in national parks, there was considerable support and enthusiasm for these exceptions. Policies relating to housing for local needs took precedence, with careful site planning and conditions – 18 in the case of South Zeal – addressing other policy considerations. But in both cases, land was the vital ingredient, reducing development costs and making homes affordable to those on local incomes.

Sources: Dartmoor NPA: https://www.dartmoor.gov.uk/__data/assets/pdf_file/0028/77419/Settlement-Profile-South-Tawton.pdf
Dartmoor NPA: https://www.dartmoor.gov.uk/__data/assets/pdf_file/0033/88476/20190111-DM-Reports.pdf
Financial Times: https://www.ft.com/content/bb3977d4-f5bf-11e9-bbe1-4db3476c5ff0
Hastoe HA: https://www.hastoe.com/about-us/building-homes/recently-completed-homes/south-tawton-devon/

amendment that reallocates their land for market development (Gallent and Bell, 2000: 378). But while the prospect of a windfall profit may seduce some owners, many others are willing to support exceptions through discounted sale (or leasing at a nominal ground rent – as in the case of Kinlet), often because they have a long association with the village and community. Where that is not the case, the enabler will be able to explain to a reticent landowner that the reallocation of land for market development, if this were to happen, would not be a means of addressing *local needs*. Depending on market conditions, land value (now for housing rather than agricultural use) would soar and any development would be high-end but not of a scale, in small village locations, to support Section 106 contributions in the form of on-site affordable housing – although a high-value development could generate cash *in lieu* of that contribution, to be spent on the provision of affordable homes elsewhere.

Based on that information – and in a context of clear planning policy and consistent decision-making – an otherwise reticent landowner may be persuaded to part with land at a price that enables affordable homes to be built, or may ultimately decide that there is benefit in gifting the land (Gallent and Bell, 2000: 381). One final challenge will be to find

Figure 4.2 Little Stocks Close, Kinlet, Shropshire. © Shropshire Rural HA.

a registered provider to build and manage homes, if one was not involved in the exception from the start. For some housing associations, having a portfolio of homes distributed across a number of villages can present a management challenge – bigger schemes in market towns are easier to service – although specialist rural providers recognise the dispersed nature of rural housing need and are used to dealing with this issue. In the absence of a registered provider, the community might choose to set up a land trust – or even its own registered society.

> Case 4.2: Site exception on private land involving off-site manufacture: Kinlet, Shropshire
>
> Kinlet parish is in south-east Shropshire and contains three small hamlets – Kinlet Village, Button Bridge and Button Oak. The parish had just over 900 residents at the 2011 Census and most of its services, including a church, small school, village hall and pub, are in Kinlet Village. A Parish Plan was produced in 2006 and updated in 2021. This is not a Neighbourhood Development Plan, but simply a one-page list of core priorities for the Parish. Under the 'housing' header, the standing priority has been to work with partners – Shropshire

Council (a unitary authority) and Mawley Hall Estate (a major local landowner) – on the development of affordable homes in Kinlet Village. The plan notes that approval has been given for 15 dwellings at 'Little Stocks'.

Those homes, when developed, will be available for rent by people with a local connection and will join existing phases of development on this rural exception site. The first phase of development at Little Stocks Close was completed in 2000 on land provided by Mawley Hall Estate (see Figure 4.2). This 'landed estate [...] has long established ties with the local community' and because of this connection, 'the landowner is motivated by philanthropic intentions and was willing to provide land for a social purpose at a modest ground rate' (Rural Coalition, 2017: 6). Land was leased to Shropshire Rural Housing Association and because of continuing growth in local need, identified in partnership with Kinlet Parish Council, the Association approached Mawley Hall to discuss a second phase. That second phase was completed and opened at the beginning of 2016. It comprised six semi-detached houses and two detached bungalows, all provided at affordable rent.

The ground rent, management and maintenance costs are recovered from rental income. Capital costs (totalling just £900,000 for the eight units following the planning exception) were met from a combination of borrowing (by Shropshire Rural Housing Association), an £80,000 community-led housing grant from Shropshire Council and £132,000 from the Homes and Communities Agency. The Rural Housing Alliance reported that the scheme responded to the high costs of purchasing or renting homes privately in the parish. The cheapest home for sale in the previous year had been on the market for £235,000 – well beyond the means of households on average Shropshire incomes. Private rents were also at least £65 pcm above housing association rents, with private tenants enduring the added burdens of agents' fees and hefty security deposits. The expansion of the Little Stocks Close development was viewed as an opportunity to help sustain the community. The chief executive of the National Housing Federation was present at the opening of the scheme and commented that 'Kinlet is lucky in that it still retains a school and a pub. Many other villages are not so lucky and one of the reasons is that affordable two- and three-bedroom homes for young families were not built in time to sustain the community and its facilities. Housing associations identify need and act on it, and at the heart of that ethos is the building of quality affordable homes for rent. Anyone who says building new houses destroys villages needs to see this example in Kinlet.'

One of the stand-out features of the Little Stocks Close development was its use of Off-Site Manufacture (OSM). The homes were produced by Accord Group less than 30 miles away. So-called 'LoCal Homes', these highly insulated closed-panel timber dwellings are heated by ground source heat pumps as Kinlet is not connected to mains gas. They are said to deliver 'affordable warmth' to occupants. And because the scheme is also served by a dedicated bio-disc sewage treatment plant, which delivers bacterial digestion of sewage pollutants that allows discharges into local watercourses, its green and community-led credentials provided an opportunity for engagement with Kinlet Primary School. The School faces the development and during the construction phase, children made multiple site visits and worked on 'eco-projects' linked to the national curriculum. In this way, the scheme helped foster broader engagement.

But the key message at Kinlet relates to the delivery of a site exception in the context of a willing landowner. Shropshire Council has sanctioned exceptional planning permission on a slightly larger site because the housing provided can meet the needs of families across this scattered parish, including the neighbouring hamlets. A wealthy private landowner has been willing to lease land for affordable housing, to be made available for families with strong local connections. Overall, a combination of the planning exception, landowner participation, and innovative off-site manufacture ensured that the scheme overcame critical planning, land cost and finance barriers.

Sources: Kinlet Parish Council: https://www.kinlet-parish.org.uk/wp-content/uploads/2021/02/2021-parish-plan.pdf
Rural Coalition: https://www.nfuonline.com/rural-coalition-2017-statement-case-studies/
Shropshire Live: https://www.shropshirelive.com/news/2016/02/12/innovative-rural-housing-development-in-kinlet-officially-opened/
Rural Housing Alliance: https://ruralhousingalliance.net/wp-content/uploads/2016/06/Shropshire-Rural.pdf

A further twist in the story of planning exceptions in England is the recent debate on the use of 'Entry Level Exception Sites', which has now become 'First Homes Exceptions'. The former was proposed by government ahead of the 2018 revision of the National Planning Policy Framework (NPPF). The basic idea was that landowners and developers would lead on the development of mixed schemes (with market housing supporting the delivery of affordable homes) on edge of village (or town) sites not allocated for housing. These sites were to be no larger than one hectare or five per cent of the size of the existing settlement. The removal of community leadership was criticised, as was the enlarged role for cross-subsidy via market development (an element of cross-subsidy was already permissible, but strictly limited). Hence, the approach was amended, with government conceding that homes on 'entry-level exception sites' needed to be 100 per cent 'affordable'. This policy was maintained in the June 2019 revision of NPPF (Para. 71). Annex 2 of NPPF specified the housing to be permitted on these sites: that is, all forms of 'affordable housing' including occupancy-restricted 'entry level' starter homes for sale, which would be used to cross-subsidize other tenures.

Although government appeared to backtrack, in 2019, from development sector and landowner leadership, and also from less regulated tenure mixing, debates around future exceptions models did not go away. Communities and registered providers remained resolute in their view that landowner-led mixed schemes would struggle to win support in many villages – and risked being seen as back-door attempts to foist development upon communities. On the other hand, there was some support for these sorts of exceptions on the edges of service centres, where local authorities might be able to secure more affordable housing than has hitherto been possible on market sites using Section 106 mechanisms. But the very critical issue with Entry Level Exceptions was their potential to disrupt, or even halt, traditional site exceptions by shifting landowners' price expectations for the release of land. Agreeing the sale of land for discounted market homes, possibly with an element of full-price sale housing for cross-subsidy purposes, is a more lucrative proposition than selling for social rented housing, which requires a substantially bigger land subsidy.

A Written Ministerial Statement on 24 May 2021 replaced *Entry Level Exception Sites* with *First Homes Exception Sites*, aligning the policy with government's focus on 'First Homes' (for first-time buyers, with a discount of at least 30 per cent against open market value). These exceptions will not be possible in rural areas designated under Section 157 of the Housing Act 1985 (see Chapter 3) or in National Parks, where only traditional site exceptions will be permitted. But the rebranding to First Homes Exceptions overrides many concerns aired since 2018 relating to community leadership, an expanded role for sale housing versus social renting, and shifting land price expectations.

Rural housing providers are still digesting the implications of this shift. They have welcomed not having to provide First Homes on traditional exception sites but are deeply concerned with many other aspects of the First Homes approach. There is a belief that the focus on First Homes will drive land owners' land price expectations, squeezing out other tenures. In theory, local authorities can seek to increase the 30 per cent minimum discount, but this is likely to be resisted by landowners, who will look to maximise land value, meaning that First Homes could be unaffordable to a great many rural households. Local authorities can apply local connection eligibility criteria to First Homes, but if a home is not sold within 3 months there is a default to national eligibility criteria, which simply stipulate that homes are for first time buyers with a maximum household income of £80,000 outside London. But the major concern remains the potential impact on traditional exception sites. Landowners will simply switch to the newer mechanism – making it more difficult than ever for registered providers and community land trusts (see the next section) to meet the need for social rented housing.

Nearly two-thirds of rural areas in England are outside National Parks and / or lack Section 157 designation. In those areas, landowner-led First Homes Exceptions could become the norm, with land prices driven up and the supply of social rented housing (for households earning a lot less than £80,000) driven down. Government has committed to monitor the impacts of this initiative, but the ideological predilection towards favouring private over community interest seems clear from the unfolding story of Entry Level and First Homes Exceptions. It presents a major threat to community-led housing at a time when community action is demonstrating its worth across rural England.

Community action – introduction

Traditional site exceptions are one example of communities leading responses to rural housing need. They also show how land-use planning can loosen restriction in support of local projects. But community action can do much more in terms of housing. The incubation of such action in village settings was introduced above. In the absence of public intervention and private investment, community responses tend to take root and are strongest where there is a requisite store of social and cultural capital – skills, resources and know-how. Those responses grow from a communitarian production of social goods: neighbourly interactions that lead to the identification of important (and trivial) challenges, conversations focused on possible remedies, the planning of those remedies, and structured responses. There are countless examples of 'community action' in response to rural challenges around the world (see Gallent and Ciaffi, 2014). The closure of shops and key services sometimes prompts people to come together to ensure the viability of their communities (Gkartzios *et al*, 2022). A number of charitable foundations and agencies exist to support communities looking to set up community ventures, including 'community interest companies', to buy and run those services. In Finland, communities have been digging trenches to support the installation of broadband services; in Australia, co-operatives have been created to run service stations and hotels, where owners have retired and no new buyers have been found (Gkartzios *et al*, 2022); and England is replete with examples of community pubs, shops, cafes and buses.

Housing projects are a bit more complicated than the takeover of existing facilities. New development or conversion presents planning and finance challenges. Communities looking to build housing for local need or convert the use of non-residential buildings need to secure finance to acquire land or built assets; they need development finance and they need to be able to fairly allocate and manage the homes they build in the public (or more specifically the community) interest. One option is to work with an external body, perhaps in the hope of securing public finance through a registered provider – as happens in the case of planning exceptions. Another is to establish their own delivery and management vehicle – often a Community Land Trust.

Land trusts

> Community land trusts (CLTs) are set up and run by ordinary people to develop and manage homes as well as other assets important to that community, like community enterprises, food growing or workspaces. CLTs act as long-term stewards of housing, ensuring that it remains genuinely affordable, based on what people actually earn in their area, not just for now but for every future occupier. (National Community Land Trust Network, 2020)

Trusts are entities that can be established by groups of residents: they are 'three party fiduciary' arrangements between a 'settlor' (transferring or gifting something, either land or property), a 'trustee' (bringing that land or property into trust) and a 'beneficiary' (who receives a benefit or service). In the case of Community Land Trusts, they must be established for the benefit of a defined community – a village or a neighbourhood (and people within that village or neighbourhood must have the opportunity to join the Trust, through open elections). They are non-profit but can generate a surplus that is recycled for social purpose. Where a trust has a mission to deliver housing, it can do so in the following way. First, the trust is established. Second, land (or property for conversion or renovation) needs to be gifted to, or purchased by, the trust. Third, that land or property needs to be developed (either directly by the trust as a self-build, or on behalf of the trust by a sub-contractor). The trust will seek to minimise development costs so as not to jeopardise the affordability of the project. Fourth, that property (or the land on which it sits) is held in perpetuity by the trust, which manages it for community benefit. That can mean directly managing rented or leased housing, or asking a specialist non-profit housing provider to manage it on behalf of the trust.

The National Community Land Trust Network notes (at the beginning of 2022) that there are currently almost 550 CLTs in existence or being formed in England and Wales. They have built 1,100 homes to date and there are another 7,100 in the process of being delivered. 17,000 people are members of trusts.

The CLT model has mixed origins. In the United States, it is rooted in the work of Robert Swann. Swann was a community activist, pacifist and decentralisation advocate. With the help of Ralph Borsodi – an agrarian theorist who was influenced by the ideas of Henry George and the notion of collective control over, and benefit from, land – Swann developed the idea of *stewardship over land*, for the long-term benefit of mankind, as being achievable through trust-based ownership for the common good (International Independence Institute, 1972: 1). He developed his ideas through practical experimentation. In 1968, Swann and six colleagues – including Charles Sherrod and Slater King, the latter being a cousin of Martin Luther King and also a real estate broker – travelled to Israel to review how the Jewish National Fund leased land for community use:

> Drawing on the Moshav communities [found in Israel], Sherrod and his colleagues proposed to create a co-operatively managed agricultural settlement that combined community ownership of land with individual ownership of houses – the precursor of what

came to be known as a 'community land trust'. (https://www.new communitiesinc.com)

A year later, the group – which had now become New Communities Inc. (NCI) – purchased 5,735 acres of land in Lee County, Georgia. The plan was to provide home ownership and employment opportunities for African American farmers. However, finance costs and tax liabilities absorbed most of the income generated from farming, making it difficult to build homes. Funding for the planning of a new settlement had been secured from the Office of Economic Opportunity (OEO), which opened the door to the possibility of more substantial federal funding. Hundreds of families expressed a desire to move to the New Communities site in Lee County, but the plan was fiercely contested by the Governor of the State of Georgia who vetoed the OEO grant. A long legal battle ensued against the US Department of Agriculture (USDA) and others, at the end of which – in 1985 – the land was lost and sold 'at the Court House steps in Lee County' for a quarter of its market value (https://www.newcommuni tiesinc.com). Fourteen years later, New Communities began legal action against the USDA. This time, the Courts found in its favour, awarded a substantial settlement, and New Communities went on to purchase the Cypress Pond Plantation in Georgia in 2011, enabling it to continue the development of its community land trust.

Figure 4.3 Church Hall Cottage, Chapel Stile, Lake District.
© Skelwith and Langdale CLT.

Case 4.3: Saving a single home from private sale:
Chapel Stile, South Lakeland

Chapel Stile is a small hamlet five miles to the north-west of Ambleside. The hamlet has roughly 190 full-time residents, but a 2011 local housing trust survey found that 70 per cent of its housing stock comprised second homes and holiday lets (Kime, 2019). In 2014, the headteacher of Chapel Stile's primary school (Langdale C of E Primary School) asked his 44 pupils to map the occupancy of homes in the hamlet. They found that one row of 10 cottages had no full-time residents and only one of another group of 21 was permanently lived in. While the many holiday lets in the hamlet are an important source of local income, the headteacher reflected that it would be nice if at least half the homes were lived in, so that local services – including the school – could remain viable (Pidd, 2014). But South Lakeland – and the wider Lake District National Park – is a honeypot for tourists and investors. Chapel Stile itself is an important access point for walkers and climbers. It gives access to the Langdale Pikes. Other popular fells nearby include Pavey Ark, Bowfell and Pike o' Blisco. Nestling between these peaks, the hamlet offers significant scenic and recreational amenity, making it an attractive second home destination. A home on the hillside had, at the time of Pidd's 2014 Guardian article, fetched £700,000 on the open market. Competition for what Chapel Stile has to offer is intense and very few parents of the school's 44 pupils owned their own homes, with many being forced out of the hamlet to nearby Ambleside.

It was in that context that Skelwith and Langdale Community Land Trust was established in 2010 by a group of residents concerned that local people were being priced out and forced out of their communities by the weight of second home demand. It was intended that the CLT would cover an area running north-west from Skelwith Bridge to Great Langdale and extend to nearby villages and hamlets in this part of South Lakeland, basically covering the catchment area of Langdale C of E Primary School in Chapel Stile, thereby stressing the link between affordable housing and the sustainability of small schools and other services. Although calling itself a CLT, the new group had no immediate resources on which to draw and was constituted as a Community Interest Company (CIC) with its set-up legal costs covered by the Tudor Trust, a national body supporting voluntary and community groups across the UK, South Lakeland District Council and the Lake District National Park Authority. The group set itself the task of increasing the number of affordable homes for occupancy by local people in the area, advertising its arrival at the Langdale Gala in July 2011. In the same year, it conducted a postal survey of housing needs in the Langdale area and also toured potential development sites with officers of the National Park Authority. A site at Skelwith Bridge (a village that had not been included in the survey) was identified and because that site was highly unlikely to achieve planning permission for anything other than affordable and occupancy-restricted housing, its value was significantly lower than other sites in the area. The Trust therefore purchased the site at a 'low cost' using a grant from South Lakeland District Council.

However, before developing homes at Skelwith Bridge, attention returned to Chapel Stile. A cottage in the hamlet, owned by the Diocese of Carlisle, had lain empty for two years and was in need of modernisation. The Diocese wanted to offload the property and had considered putting it up for sale. In 2013, the Trust negotiated a 21-year lease on the cottage and secured grant support from government's Empty Homes Community Grant Programme and from its local partners, South Lakeland District Council and the LDNPA, for its refurbishment. Church Hall Cottage (see Figure 4.3) became the Trust's first asset, since let on a locally affordable rent by a local agent that operates an allocation policy fixed by the Trust. Back in Skelwith Bridge, a consultation 'drop-in' was held at the community centre in July 2015 when members of the Trust detailed plans to build four affordable homes in the village – on roughly 1,300 sqm of land to the west of Neaum Hurst Cottages (that land was owned partly by the Lakeland Housing Trust, which had been bequeathed the Neaum Hurst Cottages in 1955, and partly by a private owner, Skelwith Bridge Ltd). Discussions were subsequently held with several registered providers and Two Castles Housing Association (since rebranded Castles and Coasts) came forward as a development partner. The association commenced work on three three-bedroom and one one-bedroom homes in September 2016, completing a year later. The essence of this scheme was that members of the local community formed a CIC with the purpose of providing affordable homes. Agricultural land was purchased with local authority support and that land was subsequently leased to a registered provider, which now lets and manages those homes. The Trust has been flexible in pursuit of its goals, sometimes directly managing its assets (in the case of Church Hall Cottage) and sometimes relinquishing control to a trusted partner (in the case of its four homes at Skelwith Bridge). It was the catalyst for these village housing schemes, working with donors and planning partners (including a housing trust that happened to own part of the development site), to secure land and assets – essentially doing the groundwork needed to seed very small-scale local solutions. Ultimately it was Castles and Coasts that built and managed homes on the second of the Trust's local initiatives, drawing funds from the usual channels available to registered providers.

Sources: The Financial Times: https://www.ft.com/content/bb3977d4-f5bf-11e9-bbe1-4db3476c5ff0
The Guardian: https://www.theguardian.com/uk-news/2014/jul/09/lake-district-homeowners-local-residents
Cumbria Action: https://www.cumbriaaction.org.uk/resources/case-studies/cs052-act-cs-skelwith-and-langdale-clt.pdf
Community Housing: https://www.communityhousingprojectdevelopment.uk/index.php/case-studies

Such trust arrangements offer a means of protecting local communities and land from speculative development, landowner abandonment or farm foreclosure (Gray, 2008: 70–3). These were all risks recognised by the progenitors of New Communities Inc. in the United States. In the UK, the earliest community land ownership arrangements took root in Scotland, where similar risks were perceived and where the landlord class had a long history of mistreating tenant farmers (see Satsangi et al, 2010). Indeed, the injustices borne of the landed/landless binary in Scotland – including mass evictions during the period of the enclosures – left a significant imprint on land politics, precipitating important land reforms that are reviewed in Chapter 5. The first community buy-out of private land in Scotland happened in 1908, although it was not until England's 2008 Housing and Regeneration Act that community land ownership was legally defined (Moore and McKee, 2012: 281–2). In England itself, the trust model was used to support the delivery of the original Garden Cities – Letchworth and Welwyn – and also Hampstead Garden Suburb in London. Trusts were set up, attracted investors, purchased land, and built housing on a leasehold basis. The Trusts remained the freeholders and collected ground rent for the maintenance of public spaces. However, they did not control housing in perpetuity, the price of which was bid-up through successive transactions. Leasehold reform in the 1960s also saw much of the housing transferred to freehold, weakening the power of the Trusts (Miller, 2010: 94) and altering the land stewardship arrangements.[2] Original Garden City or Suburb housing now commands a premium within its respective local markets, given its design attributes, its association with neighbourhood greenery and the exclusivity it has acquired in recent years.

Figure 4.4 Affordable homes at Conksbury Lane, Youlgrave. © Peak District Rural HA/Youlgrave CLT.

Case 4.4: CLT delivering through a registered provider: Youlgrave, Derbyshire

Youlgrave (or Youlgreave) is a village a few miles south of Bakewell in Derbyshire Dales District. It had a resident population of 1,099 in 2001, which has since fallen to 1,002 (2019 mid-year estimate). It is one of the Peak District National Park's larger villages and has three pubs. The village is popular with hikers and with second home buyers, with external demand for traditional stone cottages pushing up prices in recent years. Three-bedroom cottages in Youlgrave sell for more than £300,000. Indeed, the recent fall in full-time population is related to second home buying in the village. In response to widely acknowledged housing market pressures, the Parish Council began holding regular public meetings from 2009 onwards. These were intended to track priorities and formulate responses. The number one priority was said to be the need for extra affordable housing.

Members of the parish council therefore reviewed the options for delivering affordable housing in Youlgrave. A site of around 500 sqm straddling Conksbury Lane – a minor road leading north-west out of the village – was identified as having development potential (see Figure 4.4). Although in agricultural use, as pasture, the site was considered to offer an infill opportunity as it was bounded by existing housing. An application to erect a single bungalow on the site in 1993 was rejected on the grounds of there being no identified local need. The Local Plan requires such need to be demonstrated for projects to gain approval – '[…] Core Strategy policy HC1 states that provision will not be made for open market housing but exceptionally new housing can be accepted where it addresses eligible local needs for homes that remain affordable with occupation restricted to local people in perpetuity.' The Parish Council applied to develop affordable housing on the site in 2010 after its initial round of public meetings, but withdrew the application following concerns over neighbour impacts. A new application, again from the Parish Council, was submitted in 2011. This incorporated design changes to mitigate impacts and the planning committee was resolved to approve subject to a Section 106 agreement being signed. But in the meantime, a boundary issue arose with an adjoining bungalow. Ownership of a small sliver of land belonged to the bungalow rather than the owner of the development site. This meant that the access alignment would need to be reconfigured, requiring a revised planning application.

While that application was being prepared, objectors to the development sought to scupper it entirely by claiming that the pasture at Conksbury Lane had been used, for the past 20 years, for sport and leisure, and therefore submitted an application to the County Council to have it designated a 'Village Green'. Objectors never previously noted this past use. Letters of objection questioned the 'need' for affordable housing and noted that many homes in the village were already empty (possibly second homes), which suggested a lack of need for *new housing*. They also mentioned parking concerns and loss of amenity for neighbouring homeowners. When plans were amended, in light of these concerns, a smaller number of objectors maintained that neighbour impacts would still be negative and that new homes should not be built while others remain empty. At that point, the number of supportive letters outnumbered objections, with people pointing to the need for affordable homes for young families, thorough resident consultation, and the challenge posed by second homes.

The attempt to get the land designated a village green was a last-ditch blocking action that was rejected following an inquiry in June 2012. Less than a year later, early in 2013, a new application was submitted but this time from Youlgrave Community Land

Trust. During the hiatus of the village green debacle, the Parish Council had turned its attention to the implementation of the permission and the letting and management of affordable homes. In previous discussions with officers, the issue had been raised of lettings and management practices and retaining homes for community use in perpetuity. This led to the decision to establish a CLT that would take ownership of this site, accessing grant support for that purpose, and then work with a registered provider to deliver the homes.

The CLT was set up as a Community Benefit Society at the beginning of 2013 with its board comprising 12 residents. Youlgrave CLT did not want the responsibility of building and managing homes itself – but wished to ensure that the community had a direct stake in what was built and could derive an income from land. For these reasons, it used grant funding to purchase the freehold of the land (from a local owner who knew that permission for open market housing would not be granted) and then partnered Peak District Rural Housing Association, which accessed funding from the Homes and Communities Agency and Derbyshire Dales District Council to build the six rented and two shared ownership homes. The CLT has leased the land to the housing association for 100 years and derives ground rent as freeholder, which it uses to fund other projects including a community orchard on part of what is now the 'Hannah Bowman Way' site.

Broadly, the project came about because the community, initially in the form of the Parish Council, took the lead. It worked with the rural housing enabler to demonstrate the need for affordable homes (the enabler was able to show that 11 empty homes in the village would not be affordable to local people in need even if they were made available for private renting), with planning officers on the detailing of the scheme, and with the housing association on project delivery. The case reveals the importance of 'community leadership' in winning support for new homes. There were obstacles on the way, including tenacious objection from local homeowners who, for whatever reason, did not wish to see affordable homes built in the village. The strength of Policy HC1 is also noteworthy, ensuring that housing land remained affordable and available only for local needs.

Sources: Peak District Planning Portal: https://portal.peakdistrict.gov.uk/05100464
Youlgrave CLT: http://www.youlgravecommunitylandtrust.org/
Youlgrave Parish Council: http://www.youlgrave.org.uk/community/youlgrave-community-land-trust/

Despite these shortcomings, small local trusts building affordable homes for *rent* offer a different model. There is no chance that housing will be lost to 'the market' (unless a future government decides to extend the right to buy for public tenants to the occupants of trust housing – which seems unlikely as it would fundamentally undermine the social purpose of trusts). At the same time, the CLT model can provide aspiring homeowners with affordable forms of shared ownership. The trust retains a percentage of the equity – a 'golden share' – enabling it to control the onward sale price and therefore ensure that the property remains affordable to the next purchaser (Moore and McKee, 2012: 281). At the same time, shared owners enjoy the security and benefits of homeownership while communities secure important community development outcomes. The stake that communities take in land, and individuals in housing, means that land speculation is eliminated and whole communities – rather than a few private individuals – share in the value of that land (Gray, 2008: 74–5).

But the great challenge confronting community land trusts is the acquisition of land within a private market (Baxter and Murphy, 2018: 19). 'High entry costs' make it difficult for parish councils, and the community-led housing organisations that they sometimes sponsor, to build homes for themselves (Baxter and Murphy, 2018: 19). The cases listed above and below show how well-sited farmland (and other land not allocated for housing use in a local plan) can provide development opportunities for CLTs where local authorities are willing to grant exceptional permission for development, where landowners accept that purchase of land for affordable homes provides 'best consideration' (as it did when RDCs began building council homes in the interwar era) and that no higher price will be achievable, and where registered providers take responsibility for building and managing homes. At Youlgrave, a community orchard was also developed on the rural exception site. But the same CLT is struggling to find sites for other community projects. It wants to build an anaerobic digester as a source of income that can be recycled into other projects but is struggling to do so because of a lack of accessible land. Site exceptions are a really useful tool for CLT-led community housing projects, but eligible sites need to be well positioned and accessible. Broader land market challenges remain. Back in the United States, it took New Communities Inc. 43 years from inception to secure ownership of the Cypress Pond Plantation, which was only made possible by a landmark decision on a legal case of national importance. Trusts are reliant on securing the support of a settlor – an entity or individual willing to gift land or fund its private purchase, including where rural exceptions are not possible. This basic challenge has been examined by Moore (2021), who draws attention to the shared 'place attachment', between different parties, that is often crucial to successful trust arrangements (p. 27). We look more closely at this challenge towards the end of this chapter – under 'impediments to community-led housing'.

Figure 4.5 Sustainable homes at Worth Matravers, Dorset. © ARCO2.

Case 4.5: Delivering sustainable homes on a challenging site: Worth Matravers, Dorset

Worth Matravers is a village and civil parish in Dorset. The village stretches northwards from the limestone cliffs of the Jurassic Coast World Heritage Park along the A351. The parish covers the nearby village of Harman's Cross and had a resident population of 638 in 2011, split across almost 300 households. Before 2019, the parish was part of Purbeck District but has since come under the jurisdiction of Dorset County Council, now a unitary authority. Worth Matravers is a picturesque village with its limestone cottages set around a central pond. It often features on postcards sent from the Isle of Purbeck.

In the early 2000s, concern was growing for the affordability of homes in the area and the large number of cottages – around 50 per cent of the total – being used as second homes. Changes in the occupancy of homes and the sense of rural decline, as shops and services struggled through the winter months, catalysed support for the establishment of a 'community property trust'. The set-up of the Trust, in 2005, was facilitated by Wessex Community Assets (WCA), which supports the development of community-led housing projects across Devon, Somerset and Dorset. It provides technical advice on the legal constitution of trusts, for example as *community benefit societies,* and on land, planning and finance issues. Over the last decade, it has supported the delivery of around 200 homes by CLTs. In Worth Matravers, it carried out a local needs survey that revealed a requirement for about 20 affordable homes in the village.

Land for development had previously been identified adjacent to Newfoundland Close (known as the 'football field') and was purchased by Signpost Housing Association in 2002. An application to develop the site, as a rural exception, was made in the following year. However, this registered provider pulled out when it became clear that substantial archaeological investigations – comprising 'archaeological field work together with post-excavation work and publication of the results' – would be required ahead of development, adding substantially to the cost of developing the site. Following the creation of Worth Community Property Trust (WCPT) – as an Industrial and Provident Society in this case rather than a Community Benefit Society, which has since become the norm – a new outline application to develop five affordable homes on the site was submitted, which identified the applicant (submitting on behalf of WCPT) as also being the landowner. Sources suggest that the applicant, acting on behalf of WCPT, had purchased the land from Signpost Housing Association in 2007, although he was already listed as the owner when the outline application was received in December 2006. Following approval of the outline, consent for reserved matters was sought in 2008 and eventually received, after further modifications to the proposal, in 2011.

The consent sought was for sustainable affordable homes, achieving Code for Sustainable Homes Level 4, designed by architects ARCO2, based in Cornwall. These were to have mono-pitched green roofs, very different from the village's limestone cottages but still 'in keeping' with the wider rural landscape. The Trust faced a number of challenges and questions. The immediate challenge, particular to this site, was how to deal with the archaeological condition. Another more general challenge was antipathy towards affordable housing from some village residents. And the broader development question was who should be involved in developing the site and managing the affordable homes.

The Trust partnered with the East Dorset Antiquarian Society on issues of archaeology. The Society made a submission to the British Archaeological Awards in 2012 in which it thanked the landowner (who became the development applicant) for providing 'unlimited' access to the site for several years and for the use of nearby facilities. That submission also notes the huge input of volunteers, including from several universities, into various stages of excavation. The National Community Land Trust Network subsequently noted that the Society had leveraged 5,000 hours of volunteer time, reducing the cost of archaeological works from an estimated £200,000 (the sort of figure that had caused Signpost Housing Association to withdraw) to a much more manageable £25,000.

Ahead of the development application, a survey by Worth Matravers Parish Council had revealed that 80 per cent of residents were in favour of building affordable housing in the village. But a 'highly vocal and aggressive' minority had opposed the development. The Trust engaged another partner – the County Council's Affordable Housing Group – and was successful in changing local perceptions of what it would mean to build affordable housing locally. Rather than serving the needs of people brought into the community from elsewhere in Purbeck, local control would ensure that only local needs were met in the new housing. Knowing that the scheme would be *community-led* assuaged concerns and helped build support for the development.

The Trust took a direct role in the above, working with the following partners: with Wessex Community Assets on verifying need and developing the Trust model); with the East Dorset Antiquarian Society on dealing with the challenge of on-site archaeology, and with the county council on building the case for affordable homes within the community. It also wanted to play a direct role in developing the site but found it 'impossible to develop a rural exception site without Homes and Communities Agency (HCA) funding' and to navigate government funding strictures. This caused it to change tack. The capital cost of building the homes was estimated at £840,000. The Trust leased the site to Synergy Housing Group, which was able to cover the costs from a mix of borrowing and support from the HCA. The lease to Synergy (which merged with Aster Group in 2012) was for 125 years, meaning that the Trust retains freehold interest and receives income, in the form of ground rent, from the site. At the time, the lease agreement with Synergy was considered innovative, providing a means of unlocking government finance and taking forward the development of affordable housing on land under CLT control. This partnering arrangement with a registered provider has now become more commonplace (see earlier cases). For this scheme, it provided a means of taking forward the development when alternative funding arrangements could not be found and accessing grant funding proved impossible. The affordable homes were completed in 2012 (see Figure 4.5).

Other community-led projects have followed, including the building of a community hall in Harman's Cross and the acquisition and management of other community assets.

Sources: Planning Portal: https://planning.dorsetcouncil.gov.uk/plandisp.aspx?recno=269509
East Dorset Antiquarian Society: http://www.dorset-archaeology.org.uk/excavations/worth_baa.pdf
University of Salford (CLTs report): https://usir.salford.ac.uk/id/eprint/19312/2/Proof_of_Concept_Final.pdf

Neighbourhood planning in England

Community land trusts are a potential delivery vehicle for some aspects of neighbourhood planning – a means of realising the type of development envisaged in the plan. Those plans are frameworks that, in recent years, have focused attention on housing demands and needs at a community level, or a village level in rural areas. Neighbourhood planning in England, one outcome of the Localism Act 2011, is rooted in community action: a practice that evolved within communities and was eventually picked up by government and plugged into the formal land-use planning system. Its roots and evolution have been examined at length by Parker (2014). Before looking at the village housing dimension of neighbourhood planning, some basic history and context is needed.

In its current form 'neighbourhood development planning' in England – that is, the drawing up of neighbourhood development plans and the use of associated tools: see below – is rooted in resident activism in urban areas and in the practice of village or 'parish planning'. The practice of neighbourhood planning has much in common with the village planning that developed in rural England during the latter half of the twentieth century and which was undertaken by civil parish councils or by voluntary groups linked to those councils (Owen and Moseley,

2003: 445). Informal village planning morphed into formalised post-2011 neighbourhood planning in three steps.

Step one involved the mainstreaming of so-called 'village appraisals': in the post-war period (and before), rural community representatives collected information on their village and presented it to local authorities in the hope of prompting a response. That information might pertain to litter on the streets, the state of local roads, the housing needs of agricultural workers or questions of policing or other forms of service provision. By the 1970s, enough interest had accumulated in how 'local evidence' might be assimilated into local planning practice (broadly defined) to trigger attempts to regularise and systematise this local practice. To that end, a toolkit was developed by researchers from Gloucestershire College of Art and Technology (which later became the University of Gloucestershire) who then provided an analytical service to communities using their 'village appraisals approach' (Owen, 2002). The village 'health checks' provided evidence to underpin community action (Owen, 2002: 47).

Step two was triggered by some discontent with the appraisals approach. Communities reported feeling constrained by the statistical analysis that was becoming a common feature of the health-checks; they started to produce more open-ended 'Parish Plans' that quickly became expressions of future aspiration (in the form of 'wish lists') rather than simply analyses of key data (Gallent, 2013). Government recognised that these more open plans could act as guides for local service delivery, providing local authorities with the cues they needed to respond to a diversity of situations and needs. They seemed to fit with the then Labour government's pledge to devolve resources and power to communities (later derided as inadequate by the Conservatives), set out in its first Local Government White Paper (DTLR, 1998). Two years later, specific reference to the drawing up of parish and town plans was included in a Rural White Paper, which proposed that Parish Plans should '[…] set out a vision of what is important, how new development can be best fitted in, the design and quality standards [they] should meet, how to preserve valued local features and map out the facilities which the community needs to safeguard for the future' (DETR and MAFF, 2000: 150). The hope was that plans could be steered into a common format, addressing similar concerns for place design, preservation and local needs; in that way, they would provide part of the evidence base for statutory planning at the local scale. Small grants became available for parishes wishing to produce 'better' plans (Countryside Agency, 2004: 6): these were intended to support wider engagement and help build the evidence base for spatial planning, thereby supporting 'local distinctiveness' in policy response, new local partnerships, and increased public understanding of planning (Countryside Agency, 2004: 16). But a key dilemma remained: the parish plans being produced varied greatly in content and quality, despite the funding and steer provided by government. And this undermined the evidence they provided for higher-level planning – and made them difficult to connect with formal plan-making.

Two possible remedies were outlined: first, accept parish plans for what they were – an outcome of community-level deliberations on the future – and seek no direct 'land-use' planning link; or second, push communities through a more formalised 'community planning' process and arrive at useable land-use plans that would be connectable to higher tiers (Gallent and Robinson, 2012).

Step three – taken following the change of government in 2010 – was to formalise the process and product of parish planning, transforming it into a new tier of regularised planning at the community scale. In the run-up to the 2010 General Election, the Conservative Party pledged to extend the part played by communities in the planning process. After 2010, a framework of neighbourhood planning was outlined by the Coalition government, led by the Conservatives, and eventually legislated for in the Localism Act 2011. That legislation empowered urban communities to come together in a 'neighbourhood forum' comprising no fewer than 21 individuals (living locally or representing local business interests), self-define their own neighbourhoods and begin drawing up a neighbourhood development plan. In rural areas, the expectation was that parish or town councils would be equivalent to the forum and produce a plan for either its own jurisdiction or join forces with neighbouring councils to plan for a wider area. Once plans had been judged sound (compliant with legal requirements) in a light touch examination, they would be put to a referendum. If more than 50 per cent of residents voted in favour of the plan then it would become legally binding (Field and Layard, 2017: 106).

The stated purpose of introducing this system was not only to extend local participation in planning but also achieve greater acceptance of planning decisions by altering the manner in which those decisions were taken – to turn a generation of NIMBYs into a generation of IMBYs according to the government minister with oversight of the programme (Matheson, 2010). Through the formalisation of plan-making at a community level, there seemed to be space for a more 'transactive' (Friedmann, 1973) style of planning in which non-expert actors would have greater say (Parker, 2014), which would result in greater understanding of change drivers and therefore of the need for development responses.

The idea that communities should be producing plans that looked very much like formal development plans was rooted in the *rural experience* of community action. There was of course a rich history of activism and campaigning in urban areas (see Wates, 1976 or Sendra and Fitzpatrick, 2020), but that often took the form of protest – particularly protest against urban renewal programmes dominated by private corporate interest and from which community benefits seemed, at best, questionable (Sendra and Fitzpatrick, 2020; Watt, 2021). Loud and angry urban protest perhaps contrasted with quiet but persistent rural activism, which tracked through the episodes noted above, eventually reaching a point in the early 2000s when 'parish planning' looked very much like a dry run for the neighbourhood planning that was soon to follow. It was also the case that rural boroughs and districts already possessed the apparatus to take forward neighbourhood planning: they already had their parish and town councils, unlike urban areas, which needed to set up forums and define their jurisdictions (Sturzaker and Shaw, 2015: 598). And as noted above, parishes had already been doing something akin to neighbourhood planning for a number of years: it was easier for them to hit the ground running, embrace the localism agenda and quickly turn their parish plans into neighbourhood plans (Sturzaker and Shaw, 2015: 603). But although some of those parish plans provided blue-prints for neighbourhood development plans, being thematic and similarly structured, neighbourhood planning also introduced mechanisms and community powers that are potential 'game changers' for communities looking to intervene in the housing market. The Localism Act 2011 introduced a number of 'community rights', providing parish councils with a toolkit of options for influencing local housing outcomes. The most significant of these are Neighbourhood Development Orders (Sturzaker and Shaw, 2015: 603).

These are a derivative of Local Development Orders. LDOs can be brought forward by local authorities and used to provide *permitted development rights* for specified types of development in defined locations. Their use is encouraged in the National Planning Policy Framework (NPPF), as a means of accelerating desired development (the consultation on revisions of the NPPF in 2021 stressed the importance of NDOs, pointing out that they can also be used in areas of statutory green belt). Neighbourhood Development Orders (NDOs) work in the same way as LDOs. Surrey Heath Borough Council gives the example of a village shop: 'the [neighbourhood] plan could identify the need for a new village shop and a broad location. The NDO could then apply a planning permission [a permitted development right] to a particular site or existing building where the shop will be built' (SHBC, 2022). The NDO can be used for housing in the same way, either attaching a permitted development right to a piece of land or to the conversion or renovation of a building for housing use. Through this mechanism, parish councils in rural areas have the power to amend a local restriction, potentially granting itself the permission to bring forward a site for housing.

Community Right to Build Orders (CRtBO) can also be used to deliver a project for community benefit. A community right to build order, examined and voted on separately from the neighbourhood development plan, can be used to support the delivery of community goals, including those of a Parish Council or of a CLT if one has been established. Parish councils, for example, can draw up orders for the purpose of gaining planning consent and incentivising private development (on permissioned sites) that they believe will deliver community benefit. Orders provide communities with a means of taking control of the planning process, but few have delivered outcomes on the ground since their introduction via the Localism Act 2011. The Ferring case, detailed below, shows how they work and what they may be able to deliver in the future.

Case 4.6: Incentivising the delivery of 'downsizer' housing through a CRtBO – Ferring, Arun District

There are very few examples of delivering housing in rural areas using development orders, either NDO or Community Right to Build Orders (CRtBO). Many communities proposed and drew up orders after the 2011 Localism Act, but few were taken forward and those that were frequently failed to achieve compliance with national policy. Parish councils, or other constituted community groups, can define areas where orders will apply, engage their communities to win support for the orders, prepare detailed proposals or development briefs (that become the meat of the orders), submit their orders to their local authority for technical examination (this is where many failed), and then seek approval for the order at a local referendum organised by their authority.

One village that cleared all of these hurdles is Ferring in Arun District. It drew up three CRtBOs in 2014: two of those orders proposed the construction of homes for older residents looking to 'downsize' but remain in the village (the logic being that family homes would then be freed up) while another looked to replace the current community centre with a much larger two-storey structure that would deliver additional community facilities (funded by returns from the housing projects). The housing-related orders proposed, firstly, the development of 14 downsizer homes on publicly owned allotments and a privately owned yard behind a pub (0.366 ha), with access to the development to be shared with the pub (using its existing car-park access) and secondly, 10 further downsizer homes on a site currently occupied by Ferring village hall (0.121 ha).

Ferring is a large village on the south coast – much larger than any of the other case study villages. It had a resident population of almost 4,500 in 2011. Evidence presented for the Neighbourhood Plan revealed the need for a new type of housing in the parish – for 'down-sizers'. This would serve the needs of local people looking to move to smaller homes but remain in the village. The sites were selected for their proximity to amenities and because of the element of community or public control (over the allotments and the village hall). This raised the expectation of being able to deliver community benefit on these sites. Because the privately owned yard is only accessible through the publicly owned allotments, an agreement was reached to purchase that land 'pursuant to delivering the order'.

All the homes proposed in the orders were open market, but designed with adaptability in mind, providing an 'option for local people who would otherwise have to move away from the village making it more difficult to maintain social contact with friends and family'. Each of the CRtBO documents provides a development brief, site analysis, design concept and detailed design proposals for elderly downsizers. These were prepared by the consultants ONeill Homer, which works 'for local communities and developers to plan, design and deliver development through neighbourhood plans, masterplans and regeneration schemes'. In short, each order covers the details and information needed for a full planning application.

The three CRtBOs and the Neighbourhood Development plan were produced in tandem (and subsequently examined as a batch in August 2014). The orders were subject to pre-submission consultation between February and April 2014. Following submission, they were publicised until June. During this period, Arun District Council commented on each CRtBO and on the NDP. Comments were short, with the council stating its support for the use of orders on all three sites. It noted that the purpose of open market development on the two housing sites was to generate profits that would then support the upgrading of the community centre. However, because the costs of relocating allotments were not yet known, the details of any planning conditions (and hence contributions towards the centre) could not yet be stated as full development costs were yet to be determined. The independent examiner, reporting in August, reiterated the relationship between the open market housing and funding for the community centre. She noted, however, that no Section 106 agreement would be required on the housing sites as community control of the scheme guaranteed the retention of monies raised for community benefit. The Parish Council was said to comprise an 'appropriate body for managing and directing the monies received'. The inspector sought the following modifications: remove any mention of Section 106 agreements, fix a time limit on the permission created by the CRtBO (15 years), and make provision for replacement allotments before commencement (to be paid for from development profits), plus miscellaneous design and drainage modifications. The inspector concluded that the CRtBO met legal requirements and could proceed to referendum. Before that happened, three post-examination revisions of the orders were issued and publicised, highlighting the required modifications. Referendums were held in December 2014. All three orders passed, each gaining more than 70 per cent voter support, and hence came into force.

This case illustrates the *potential* offered by development orders, which allow communities to take control of planning, to deliberate on the best way to use their own assets, and to shape private development outcomes. The Ferring CRtBOs won support from the inspector because they were well constructed. The Parish Council had the support of consultants with considerable experience of design and development projects and of neighbourhood planning. However, the success in putting the orders in place has not been matched by development outcomes. None of the sites has been progressed. The Parish Council reported, in February 2021, that the allotment site had not moved forward because no replacement sites for new allotments had been found (they were therefore unable to clear the hurdle set by the inspector). The Village Hall project has fizzled out as the Village Hall Committee appears to have withdrawn from engagement around Ferring Neighbourhood Plan. And the Community Centre project – the centre piece of the CRtBOs – now suffers from a lack of engagement with West Sussex County Council, the site's owner. But although things in Ferring have ground to a halt, the case shows how communities can successfully make their own plans and potentially work with private interest to deliver community benefit. The major impediment, between planning and implementation, has been the availability and control of land, with complexities around public ownership and a lack of private sites available to compensate for the loss of allotments.

Sources: Links to all CRtBO documents and Inspector's Reports: https://www.arun.gov.uk/local-development-orders-ldo-and-community-right-to-build-order-crtbo/
Ferring Parish Council (minutes): https://www.ferringparishcouncil.org.uk/wp-content/uploads/2021/02/Minutes_-15th_February_2021.pdf
ONeill Homer: https://www.oneillhomer.co.uk

Development rights can only be directly exercised by the community where land or a building is owned by that community (unless the existing owner is a willing partner in the community's plans, perhaps a local authority or another public body). The Localism Act therefore established another important right: the Community Right to Bid. Communities are able to nominate land or buildings as 'assets of community value' (ACV). These must have the potential to further the social well-being or interests of the local community. This means, for example, that a shop or café that is about to close could be nominated as an ACV, or a dilapidated building or vacant land on which new affordable housing might be built. If the nomination is accepted by the Local Authority – that is, the asset is clearly of community value – and if, during the next five years (the nominating period), the asset is put up for sale, the community will have six months (the moratorium period) to try to raise the money to acquire the asset for community use. Private homes (which a community might wish to acquire for community use) cannot be nominated as assets of community value, as the nomination would conflict with the right of an owner to sell their home at a market price in a timescale of their own choosing: but land or businesses can be listed. This right, which stems from the 2011 Localism Act, is a watered-down version of a similar right arising from Land Reform in Scotland. But in Scotland, as we will see in the next chapter, designated types of community can seek to *compulsorily purchase* listed assets (even where a landowner does not wish to sell) and all communities can draw on grant support for the purchase of those assets.

A key difficulty in England has been that even if communities are able to raise money to bid for an asset, the landowner is likely to ignore that bid, wait for the end of the moratorium period and seek private bids on intended rather than current use value. A report from the Department for Communities and Local Government in 2015 noted that 122 community groups had triggered the moratorium period but only 11 assets had been purchased; a figure later lowered to *nine* (DCLG, 2015a). Imprecision in the figures, and the need to keep track of listings and sales, was noted in a 2021 House of Commons Briefing Paper (Sandford, 2021: 9) that also references voluntary efforts to maintain a database of ACV.[3] The small number of successful purchases suggests that communities struggle to secure funding and even where funding is found, bids fall short of market expectation. Prospective community buyers can seek the support of numerous charities, but charity grants never stretch to market value, necessitating a combination of grant support and local fundraising. In an attempt to increase the number of successful transfers to community ownership, government announced in March 2021 that it would create a £150 million Community Ownership Fund, providing local groups with match-funding of up to £250,000 for community assets and £1 million for sports related assets (MHCLG, 2021a). In theory, the fund will make community bids potentially more competitive relative to those from private buyers (although parish and town councils will be unable to access the Fund, necessitating the formation of CLTs or similar).

Despite their shortcomings relative to powers that exist elsewhere (and irrespective of the case for extending and strengthening powers), the community right to bid and development orders provide a *potentially* useful combination of tools for parish councils or CLTs looking to advance new village housing projects for local needs. The Localism Act introduced a further right – the Community Right to Challenge – which allows a council or trust to express an interest in running a service (for example, a bus service) which is currently the responsibility of another provider. But it is the combination of bid and build rights that offers clear opportunities on the housing front. These rights form critical parts of an overall Neighbourhood Development Planning package.

Local authorities, for their part, are legally obliged to adopt plans that are approved by community referendum as long as they 'respect the overall national presumption in favour of sustainable development, as well as other local strategic priorities such as the positioning of transport

Figure 4.6   Peek Close, Lavenham. © Bryan Panton.

links and meeting housing need' (DBIS, 2010: 24). As noted above, the compliance of NDPs is tested in a light touch inspection. By December 2020, 998 neighbourhood plans had been 'made' following their approval at referendum in England. This figure is changing all the time, but MHCLG collate regular updates from local authorities. Research by Parker and colleagues (2020) has underscored the critical role played by local authorities in neighbourhood planning – how they become a vessel for the institutional memory needed to advance better plans that draw on accumulated local experience (p. 20). Co-ordination between authorities and neighbourhood groups is also crucial, with the best neighbourhood plans following on from local plan adoption (p. 5). On the housing side, local-neighbourhood co-operation can foster greater support for development. But the converse is also true: if plan production is not co-ordinated, and if there is little or no local authority support for neighbourhood planning, the potential to support housing delivery will be limited (p. 21). The consultants Lichfields conducted a general review of housing delivery through neighbourhood plans in May 2018 ('Local Choices', Lichfields, 2018) but focused largely on general deviation from local plans measured in terms of land allocations and target housing numbers. It did not focus on community-led housing framed by neighbourhood planning, although examples do exist of communities using NDP to take a greater degree of control of housing outcomes and to incubate specific community-led projects. Lavenham in Suffolk did exactly this, adopting a mixed approach to supporting the delivery of additional affordable homes (see Case 4.7).

Case 4.7: 'Pro development' neighbourhood planning catalyses mixed approach to development: Lavenham, Babergh District

The historic village of Lavenham is five miles north of Sudbury in the south of the county of Suffolk. It is just over 70 miles from London, and its many heritage buildings, including its Guildhall (dating from 1529) and grand parish church (1525), make it popular with visitors. Its relatively opulent buildings date from a period when the village prospered as a centre of the wool trade. The village has continued to prosper into the twenty-first century, bringing development pressures that risked the character and social balance of the community. It was these risks that led the Parish Council to develop a Neighbourhood Development Plan (NDP) that it hoped would return some control, over future development, to local people. Lavenham has been held up as a rare example of a village that wants development – on its own terms.

Lavenham Parish Council's journey towards the development of its NDP began in 2012. Once designated as a neighbourhood planning area, in September 2013, the council began building the evidence base for its plan, with the support of Babergh District Council's community planning team and Planning Aid England (funded via government's Supporting Communities in Neighbourhood Planning programme). Historic England also advised on design policies. Early surveys and deliberations pointed to a number of critical challenges: the need for affordable homes and also smaller homes for downsizers; resistance to larger 'estate-style' developments; and the past failure of private housing schemes to deliver sufficient contributions of affordable homes or help expand overloaded infrastructure (including the village's primary school).

The NDP process presented the Parish Council with an opportunity to work with district planners and Planning Aid England, to better understand the planning context, and to understand options and ways to shape housing outcomes for the village. A pre-submission consultation on the plan was held between July and September 2015. Submission in December of that year was followed by examination, referendum and adoption by September 2016.

The deliberations underpinning the plan-making process kept returning to three major themes: affordable housing, levering additional contributions from private development (in the form of affordable housing and infrastructure), and building homes for downsizers. An overall expansion of the village was envisaged in the 2016 NDP, which was supported by 91 per cent of those voting in the plan referendum. In the five years since adoption, Lavenham has been hailed as the 'village building homes for young families': it has seen a mixed approach to development – new private schemes, council-led housebuilding, and community-led housing taken forward by a CLT (with the neighbourhood planning process viewed as an incubator for the Trust). Its NDP was informed by regular housing needs surveys conducted by Community Action Suffolk. The last survey, ahead of plan adoption, pointed to a need for 55 additional affordable homes in the NDP area, which the Parish Council believed could be largely delivered through a mixed approach.

During the year of the NDP adoption, the developer Hartog Hutton held talks with the Parish Council on its proposal to develop 25 homes on land off Norman Way, bounded by a disused railway. The officer's report (7 September 2021) on the application noted that 'the Lavenham Neighbourhood Plan (LNP) is now considered to have significant weight as it has now been subject to independent examination and the inspector's report has been published. The plan is subject to referendum on 8 September 2016 when residents of Lavenham will decide if the Lavenham NDP should become part of the Development Plan for the Lavenham Parish Area.' The report further noted that the Parish Council supported the scheme, and that it was largely aligned with the LNDP. Hartog Hutton flagged that support in its own publicity, saying that it 'only received positive responses' from the parish and gained planning permission at the September planning committee held at Babergh District Council. The developer went on to laud the 'pro-development attitude' of the parish, noting that Lavenham's 'population is ageing with a third of residents over 65 years old. There are few affordable homes, the village school is stretched, and many young people are earning the minimum wage. These factors have led to an urgent need for new homes, including affordable homes to ensure that the village maintains a dynamic and growing population'. Eight of the Hartog Hutton homes are to be affordable, procured via a Section 106 agreement. Parish council minutes from February 2020 show that outstanding conditions, concerning archaeological works, lighting and allotments, need to be discharged before the development can commence. In the meantime, two further similar schemes – at Indigo Fields and Bear Lane – have been completed, with the parish council claiming that the NDP has 'protected' Lavenham from schemes exceeding 25 units.

The NDP also notes Babergh District Council's own plans to redevelop council-owned garages at the Meadow Close Estate, creating a further 12 affordable homes. These one-bedroom, two person flats were designed by Infinity Architects and built by local firm Brooks and Wood Ltd, based in Ipswich. The Meadow Close development, completed in April 2017, comprised the first affordable council homes built in the district for 30 years.

The final homes supported by the NDP were provided by the Parish's own CLT in partnership with a registered provider. During deliberations on the plan, attention focused on how to deliver additional affordable homes in Lavenham. It was in that context that a CLT was 'conceived' and created in April 2015 as a community benefit society. Another trigger for its creation was the existence of a redundant Suffolk County Council Highways maintenance depot within the parish. Following discussions with the county council, an agreement was reached on the sale of the site to the CLT. At that point the CLT conceded that it had 'neither the management capacity to develop the site, nor the necessary skills to identify the risks associated with property development. Thus […] it was decided to partner with a registered provider that had expertise in delivering housing schemes in a rural setting and one that had some experience of our village'. That registered provider was Hastoe Housing Association, which had a history of working in Babergh District and had also partnered other CLTs. In July 2017, the county council granted a 125-year lease to Hastoe. Shortly afterwards, the freehold of the land was sold to the Trust for £1. A few months earlier, full planning permission was granted for the development of 18 affordable homes for local people. Hastoe secured funding from Homes England and the district council, meeting the rest of the costs from its own resources. The first tenants moved into Peek Close at the end of 2019 (see Figure 4.6).

Lavenham is a larger village, providing services for a wider hinterland and for lower tier settlements. It had been a focus of district growth plans for a number of years. But the neighbourhood planning process was used to reframe growth in a way considered appropriate, in terms of scale and mix, to the particular needs and character of the village. Lavenham's NDP was viewed as being both a source of protection and a signal of the village's pro-development stance, reflected in its relationships with developers and the creation of the CLT, which was presented as a delivery vehicle for the NDP. More generally, the case illustrates how NDP goals can be pursued via a mixed approach, with Lavenham also working with the district to secure appropriate CIL contributions from the private developments (almost £100,000 from the Norman Way development) to upgrade key infrastructure, including primary school provision.

Sources: Lavenham NDP: https://www.babergh.gov.uk/assets/Neighbourhood-Planning/Lavenham-NP-July16.pdf
Brooks and Wood Ltd: http://www.brooksandwood.co.uk/Projects/Residential/New-Affordable-Housing-in-Lavenham
Hartog Hutton: https://www.hartoghutton.co.uk/picturesque-village-welcomes-new-development-open-arms/
Lavenham CLT: http://lavenhamclt.onesuffolk.net/assets/March-20/Development-Story-v08.pdf
Lavenham Parish Council: http://lavenham.onesuffolk.net/assets/2020-02-February/Feb1min20.pdf

There have also been case studies of this wider framing in the extant literature, notably in the work of Sturzaker and Shaw (2015), who have looked at the Upper Eden Neighbourhood Plan. Rooted in a 2008 community plan, the NDP advanced four key policies that amended policies contained in the district plan. The first altered the approach to rural exception sites. The District's Local Plan stipulated that exceptional permission for affordable homes could only be given on sites close to existing dwellings. This rule had previously limited the number of suitable sites in small villages. Upper Eden's NDP amended this rule, saying that site suitability should be judged only on visual impact. Moreover, the possibility of converting outbuildings to residential use was opened up by the same policy – but only to meet local needs. The second policy allowed new housing on farms, for use by 'family members, holiday letting or renting to local people' (Sturzaker and Shaw, 2015: 16). In supporting the policy, it was argued that Eden District Council's own plan was 'silent' on the 'flexible use' of farm dwellings, and it was the intention of the NDP to create a framework in which the farming economy, and those reliant on it, would be supported. The third policy was concerned with older residents, requiring affordable homes in named villages to be reserved for local older people and designed appropriately. The fourth policy addressed the key concern in rural settlement planning noted in earlier chapters, acknowledging that non-key settlements can be starved of vital development (Gallent *et al*, 2015; Sturzaker, 2019) and essentially 'written off' (Taylor, 2008) by conventional planning approaches. The NDP noted that Eden District's Core Strategy contained an LSC (Local Service Centre) *de-designation policy*: the

Figure 4.7 Affordable homes at Bradwell Springs, Derbyshire. © Bradwell CLT.

local authority committed to review its settlement hierarchy every two years, potentially removing LSCs on the basis of their judged sustainability.

The direction of travel of the NDP could not have been more different from that of the District Plan. It contended that top-down assessments of sustainability are flawed, ignoring the needs of communities while prioritising amenity, landscape and character goals. It sought an increased housing allocation across the district (Sturzaker and Shaw, 2015: 597), widening the distribution to smaller settlements and de-designated LSCs. In those de-designated centres, the NDP promotes exception sites to meet local housing need. In effect, Upper Eden's Neighbourhood Development challenged prevailing planning orthodoxy, creating a framework that provided villages with the opportunity to tackle their own needs.

There are numerous examples of neighbourhood plans *framing* community-led housing in England. They shine a light on the different ways in which those plans can frame community action or can change basic 'game rules', allowing communities to take charge of aspects of local planning and adapt it to their own particular circumstances. The incubation of land trusts, viewed as a critical delivery vehicle for the aspirations frequently articulated in NDPs, is a very common theme. This also happened in Bradwell, Derbyshire, as Case 4.8 illustrates.

Figure 4.8 CGI of Bradwell Springs development, Derbyshire. © Camstead Homes.

Case 4.8: CLTs as a Neighbourhood Plan delivery vehicle: Bradwell, Derbyshire

Bradwell is a village of roughly 1,400 residents located to the south of the Hope Valley in the Peak District National Park. The village's neighbourhood plan, 2015 to 2030, acknowledges strong demand for housing, and acute need for affordable housing, across the area of the national park. The Park Authority has been encouraging parishes to undertake local needs surveys at least every five years to better understand local requirements and to be better placed to respond should opportunities arise. The drawing up of a neighbourhood plan after 2011 (the plan was submitted in May 2015 and approved by referendum later that year) gave the parish the impetus needed to set up a community land trust, which was viewed as the principal mechanism for delivering against the plan's ambitions. The intention to set up a CLT – Bradwell Community Land Trust – was noted in the referendum version of the plan: 'The CLT would administer monies gained via a legal agreement attached to a planning permission to ensure a phased delivery of local needs affordable housing. The CLT would also be able to receive bequests and donations, including gifts of land, and would manage these on behalf of the community. These monies or land would be used by the CLT to develop housing in the village' (p. 11). The CLT – which was set up as a community benefit society and acts as a delivery vehicle for the plan – was established with the assistance of East Midlands Community-led Housing (EMCLH), an organisation constituted to help communities bring local assets under their stewardship and operating across Derbyshire and neighbouring East Midlands counties. Consultations on the plan, and the subsequent referendum, confirmed the priority of finding ways to deliver affordable housing for local families, ensuring that Bradwell remained a living and working community. Of particular concern in that consultation was the future of the 'Newburgh' industrial site (roughly 1 ha).

Because Bradwell is a larger village, with a history of local employment, it was fortunate to have the Newburgh site available for redevelopment. Consultation with residents revealed a preference for new employment uses to be placed on the old industrial site. But it was also widely recognised that this might not be possible. An ambition to deliver a mix of uses therefore emerged and, given the size of the available site and the goals of the private landowner, it was inevitable that market housing would be used to subsidise affordable homes – through a Section 106 agreement. Bradwell did not face the land constraint seen in other Derbyshire villages, and because its ambitions centred on a brownfield site, it did not face significant planning restrictions. Rather, there was a broadly shared aim of reusing the site for a mix of general and affordable housing.

In consultation with the community, the Peak District National Park Authority gave permission for 55 houses on the former industrial site (see Figure 4.8), together with a new purpose-built factory for the continuation of light industrial uses. Forty-three larger homes of three to five bedrooms for open market sale are being built, but as a result of a Section 106 agreement and the 'work by the Bradwell Community Land Trust (BCLT), 12 three-bedroom houses on the site have been secured as affordable homes, for rent to local residents [see Figure 4.7]. Ordinarily a developer is not allowed to build open market houses in the Peak [District] Park, but by making 12 units available to BCLT the local community benefits and the developer can offset the open market houses. This is a major gain for the community' (BCLT, 2020).

The affordable homes were built by Camstead Homes. They are owned by the Community Land Trust (which hopes to use rent revenues to support future projects) and will be managed by Peak District Rural Housing Association on behalf of the Trust, which will allocate homes on the basis of local connection to the Parish of Bradwell or adjoining parishes.

This case is perhaps an outlier – focused on a larger windfall site, now renamed Bradwell Springs – but it illustrates the catalyst for community control provided by neighbourhood planning. Leadership has been provided by the community, via the trust, which has worked closely with the planning authority, the landowner and the developer, and with a housing association focused on the Peak District. Funding came from planning gain, with the case illustrating what is possible on bigger sites, although these are not the norm in many villages. And because it was a brownfield site, planning strictures were less onerous, with the Park Authority willing to allow market housing for the cross-subsidy of affordable homes.

Sources: EMCLH: https://emclh.co.uk/case-study-clts-and-neighbourhood-plans-bradwell/
Bradwell CLT: http://www.bradwellclt.org/Projects/Bradwell-Springs/
Bradwell NDP: https://www.peakdistrict.gov.uk/__data/assets/pdf_file/0020/66422/Bradwell-Neighbourhood-Plan-REFERENDUM-VERSION.pdf

Impediments to community-led housing

There are two significant impediments to community-led housing. The first is local leadership and capacity. And the second is finance: securing the resources needed to fund a community purchase of either land or buildings.

Social capital and local leadership

In recent years, *social capital* has become a shorthand descriptor for the *capacity* of communities to progress local projects. Those projects are anchored in everyday interactions: people coming together, because of shared concerns or the perceived inaction of external agencies, to identify something that needs their attention. This might be the impending closure of a pub (120 have been bought by communities according to *Locality*) or a local shop, school or post office. Housing problems can be less visible, especially in relatively affluent rural communities where stresses affecting certain groups can be masked by outward shows of wealth (Cox, 1998; Haynes and Gale, 2000), including an abundance of high-end homes. But there is a chance that local awareness of 'hidden needs' – a lack of housing suited to older residents, or young people working in key services but struggling to rent homes in the community – will trigger a community response.

Social capital has become a key focus for rural development debates in recent years (Woods, 2010), being seen as a capacity and energy that communities possess and can harness, especially in the absence of a paternal state (Gkartzios *et al*, 2022). It is an endogenous resource that stands in contrast to past reliance on exogenous development levers. But it is not a concept without critics. Fine (2001) has a particular dislike for the use of social capital as a substitute for social theory, arguing that it seeks to supplant any deeper understanding of the processes at work in urban and rural places. He has gone so far as to claim that its asocial and ahistorical use – disconnected from Bourdieu's (1986) idea of the transmutability of economic capital into cultural forms and into social energy rooted in networks – amounts to a 'degradation of scholarship' (Fine, 2001: 799).

Those who buy into the social capital descriptor need perhaps to be clearer about how leaders emerge in the process of 'mobilising' that capital. This requires greater attention to the institutions, actors and networks that give life to community action at different scales. Local networks, in particular, may concentrate energies around issues that are important to people. They have a potential to incubate a critical discourse that seeds ideas and from which achievable responses might eventually emerge (Shucksmith, 2018: 169). But there is a tendency to see social capital as a matter of fact, embodied in local institutions such as parish councils: they *exist* and therefore they *do*. But many councils are inert, or rather confine themselves to everyday issues rather than leading on big projects (and some may expend energy on blocking actions rather than leading change, see Yarwood, 2002). The jump from *existing* to *doing* can be a big one for some communities. *Leading* on projects can mean 'boundary crossing': brokering conversations with external actors, working out finance issues, and getting projects off the ground. This is why site exception projects tend to rely on a dedicated boundary crosser in the form of a rural housing enabler. In the absence of that enabler, someone (or a group) will need to take on that role. They may not be employed to do that, but will instead be volunteers, facing the barriers of apathy, time and energy.

All community-led projects face this difficulty, but some face it more acutely. Recent data on neighbourhood planning reveal that less deprived neighbourhoods are much more likely to make plans than more deprived ones. Fewer than three per cent of NDPs have been made in the two most deprived area deciles; this compares to 35 per cent in the two least deprived deciles (Lichfields, 2018). Research by Parker and Salter (2016; 2017) confirms the link between affluence and participation in neighbourhood planning, with 'uptake [continuing] to be uneven across the country and […] disproportionately skewed towards rural, parished and affluent communities' (Parker *et al*, 2020: 22). There could be many explanations for this, but the most popular is that wealthy, educated, and retired middle-class people, concentrated in amenity villages, are the ones with the greatest capacity – rooted in time, money and skills – to support neighbourhood planning. Another explanation is that more deprived and 'depleting' areas have other, more immediate, priorities: taking direct actions *now* against pressing challenges rather than investing time in formalised planning processes that appear to lack the same urgency. Local capacity differences, whatever their underlying causes, suggest a need for technical, financial and legal support to be directed to communities that have hitherto struggled to take advantage of neighbourhood planning (Baxter and Murphy, 2018: 25).

The first impediment to community-led housing, *capacity and leadership*, has a geographical patterning: and that patterning, because of the importance of skills and know-how, is also likely to affect the second impediment – that of securing necessary *finance*.

Finance for community-led housing

For some projects, finance comes from the partnership with landowners and registered providers brokered by rural enablers. A land subsidy is generated from the purchase of land, by a housing association or land trust, at a price lower than full development value, that will therefore support the delivery of affordable homes. But it is usually the case that some resource will need to be found to buy the land (even cheaply) and build the housing or undertake the renovation. In Scotland, the Scottish Land Fund – supported with UK Lottery Funding – was established to help communities acquire land, providing support for the development of the business plans required to unlock the grants and loans needed for land purchases (Shucksmith, 2018: 165). The Scottish experience is reviewed in the next chapter. In England, the various rights introduced by the Localism Act have not been hitherto accompanied with any direct grant support (although this is set to change with the creation of a *Community Ownership Fund*, see above). Responsibility for raising the finance needed for land or property purchase lies squarely with the community (and will continue to do so given the match-funding requirement of the Community Ownership Fund). Depending on the cost of acquisition, it may be possible to fundraise locally. Pubs, for example, can be bought through local subscription: people contributing cash to the purchase. On the other hand, local shops are sometimes reopened using grants from charitable foundations, although a portion of the cost may still need to be covered locally.

The basic reality is that the land and assets that communities need will have to be bought from private owners, unless there is a transfer of public land into community ownership (which happened in some of the cases outlined in this chapter). Sometimes those private owners may gift assets (or provide long leases on nominal ground rents) or leave them to the community in wills. And this is how some land trusts are seeded. But in many instances, the community must find the money itself to purchase the asset. In Loxley, Warwickshire, the local pub – The Fox – was put up for sale a couple of years ago. The property comprises the pub itself, situated opposite the village school, and a rear car park. It attracted much private interest, but only from buyers wanting to de-license the pub and convert the building, and car park, to housing use. The community did not want to see this happen. They had previously lost the post office and village shop in this way. The pub was an important public asset – the only one remaining apart from a small Saxon church and the primary school. The local authority considered the pub a viable enterprise and so would have resisted de-licensing and conversion to residential use. The community, in the guise of the parish council, nominated it as an asset of community value and purchased it. The pub's owner – Brewery Ei Group – wanted £345,000 for the property but agreed to sell it to the 'pub action group' for £290,000. £250,000 was raised from local donations and the selling of shares. The £40,000 shortfall was made up with a grant from the Plunkett Foundation – which is constituted to 'help communities to take control of their challenges and overcome them together'. It provides 'early stage' and 'established business' support for community enterprises.[4]

Stories of 'whip rounds' to purchase community assets (see examples from Australia noted in Gkartzios *et al*, 2022) are not far from the truth. But this sort of *ad hoc* approach to community buyout tends to favour communities whose residents have cash to spare (economic capital that transmutes into social capital). It can result in an uneven geography of successful community action. It is also the case that 'whip rounds' to buy the local pub, from which donors directly benefit, may be more successful than those raising funds for housing projects. Direct community action in the area of affordable housing requires more consistent sources of funding. We explore solutions to that challenge in the next chapter, drawing some inspiration from the Scottish experience, where the Land Fund has facilitated numerous land purchases – including in the Western Isles, in which 50 per cent of land has been brought into community ownership (Shucksmith, 2018: 165). Significant political will is needed to drive land reform, underpinned by a belief in the benefits of community stewardship rather than the privileging of private landed interest.

Conclusions

In this chapter, we have examined *current* approaches to delivering village housing – through planning-based mechanisms, through community-land trusts, and through the exercise of new rights framed by neighbourhood planning. These current approaches battle against important structural challenges that shape, firstly, what local planning correctives can achieve relative to the overall thrust of the planning system (which aims to prioritise amenity and restrict development to larger settlements); secondly, what community land trusts can achieve given the way that planning corrals value, reflected in high land prices, in villages (assigning hope and scarcity value to land); and thirdly, what can practically be achieved through neighbourhood planning relative to the rhetoric of neighbourhood empowerment.

Current approaches are hindered by the nexus of planning–land–finance barriers identified in earlier chapters. In the next two chapters, we consider the sorts of game-changing reforms that might be needed to better support the models explored in this chapter and also emergent approaches to delivering village housing. To that end, Chapter 5 looks again at the planning–land–finance nexus and Chapter 6 follows that up with an examination of self-build housing (currently impeded by the entire nexus of barriers), off-grid low impact development (supporting new ways of living in the countryside), and new models of council-led housebuilding in villages and elsewhere.

Notes

1. The average per-plot cost for recent schemes has been roughly £15,000, with land making up just over 5% of total scheme costs. English Rural HA forecast that total scheme costs will be £263,000 in 2022/23, rising to £271,000 in 2023/24 and £275,000 in 2024/25. Rising construction costs, due to inflation, plus higher per-unit on-costs for small schemes (consultation, needs surveys, ecology, drainage, archaeology etc.) and landowner price expectations, are all making it more expensive to deliver genuinely affordable homes on rural exception sites.
2. The Leasehold Reform Act 1967 enabled home owners to buy their freehold, nullifying leasehold covenants. Section 19 of the Act, however, allowed the Trusts to set up Schemes of Management (SoM) for the purpose of maintaining 'well managed' estates (Miller, 2010: 94).
3. In 2015, DCLG noted that *MySociety* (www.mysociety.org) was working on a database of Assets of Community Value that would fill the data gap in tracking the listing of assets, the triggering of moratoriums and successful purchases. This project encountered numerous difficulties gathering these data, but launched the Keep it in the Community (KIITC) database in 2018 (www.keepitinthecommunity.org). That database lists, as of May 2021, just over 4,000 ACVs. There are still very few triggered moratoriums, but the database relies on self-reporting rather than public data-crawling.
4. See: https://plunkett.co.uk/

5
Planning, land, tax and finance

This chapter draws attention to the ways that planning, land rights, tax and finance might be mobilised in support of non-profit and community-led housing projects in England. Across the United Kingdom, but especially in England, private property – and supports for the accumulation of wealth in housing – is presented as a natural state, and one that sits uncomfortably with the artificial intrusion of planning or restrictions on property rights. This view of the natural and the artificial corresponds with the priority afforded the right to private profit versus the capture of value for public benefit. It was responsible for the decline of council housing in the twentieth century and for the assetisation of housing, underpinned by a concentration of wealth in private land. But in the light of gross inequalities, there is significant benefit in seeing housing as a public infrastructure: land and tax reforms can create opportunities for communities to take control of land, calm speculation pressures and pave the way for planning and finance approaches that prioritise broader community interest in rural areas. Such reforms can also challenge production orthodoxies, creating spaces for alternative housing models or increasing the effectiveness of community and council-led delivery.

Introduction

Planning and tax systems are subject to regular review and reform in many countries. Finance arrangements for development also shift occasionally. But the rights of land ownership and the private use of land are far more static. Why should this be the case? The answer lies in the view, embedded in the liberal tradition, that property rights are a bedrock of modern democracies: respect of private property is a point of contrast between 'stable democracies' in which the individual enjoys a plethora of rights, property rights amongst them, and authoritarian regimes, that regularly infringe upon all sorts of rights in pursuit of a 'public good' that often boils down to the good of a political elite. That being the case, 'artificial structures' should bend, but land and property rights should remain a point of stability. Property rights are central to planning and housing challenges in many countries, but particularly in England, where those rights are centuries old and have become unassailable. They limit the extent to which broader public goods can be pursued and, at the same time, restrict the furthering of community interest. But they are important in a market economy because risk to property would limit investment and impede the flow of capital (and of value), which can occasionally be tapped for wider benefit.

The fundamentals of private property and its use, rooted in the writings of Locke (1689) and, later on, Henry George (1879), are not the concern of this chapter. Our more prosaic goal is to look, right now, at the way four structures impact on village housing projects. In previous chapters, these have been presented as a nexus of planning–land–finance constraints, but the intention later in this chapter is to unpack the 'finance' component into tax (and its impact on costs) and sources of funding, mainly for community-led projects. The reasons why planning (as currently constituted), patterns of land ownership, and tax/finance present difficulties for small scale housing projects in rural areas have been discussed at various points in this book. But the intention now is to take each of these in turn, briefly recap the challenges each presents, and then focus in greater depth on the sorts of reforms that might support new housing delivery opportunities in villages.

Planning: 'the cause of, and solution to, all of life's problems'?[1]

The essential 'planning problem' that needs to be addressed in rural areas is the broad fixation with amenity (often rooted in romanticised ideas of the rural) and the lack of emphasis sometimes placed on community needs – apart from the 'need' for high-end housing for wealthier households, used to unlock the surplus value in developable land. The argument here is not that the planning 'belt' should be unconditionally loosened, but rather that local context and situation should play a bigger role in determining the approach taken by planning in different circumstances. Planning should respond to the social reconfiguration of rural areas and the inequalities in housing access. It should support the rural economy by supporting rural workers. And this needs to be achieved while sensible amenity protections are maintained – so that the countryside remains countryside.

Planning has already delivered a degree of flexibility, with the rural exception sites approach examined in Chapter 4 being a clear example of this. But these more flexible interventions exist in the shadow of a one-size-fits-all approach. This is illustrated by key settlement policy, which generally asserts that housing and other forms of development are most appropriate in larger settlements and designated service centres. This would make a lot of sense if planning authorities controlled, or exerted significant influence over, the use of *all* land and existing buildings. They could then ensure that people have access to the housing they need, where they need it, including in smaller villages, by prescribing rules on use and occupancy. But without that control, it is the market that distributes those resources, through private transactions, and it is planning (the grant or denial of development permission) that shapes land values. This happens because the value of a piece of land is almost entirely dependent on what can be built upon it. Where more profitable uses are allowed, landowners 'internalise' benefit in the form of private profit (Ryan-Collins *et al*, 2017: 32–3). By relaxing controls on the conversion from less profitable uses to housing, values may be evened out – and rents lowered. But where more profitable uses are denied, value is corralled and concentrated in developable land. Hence, key settlement policy – or the designation of villages as 'protected' areas – makes those villages expensive. And where settlement protections are overlaid with further restriction – green belt, AONB designations, or both – that expensiveness, and social exclusivity, is further amplified.

Planning drives gentrification in some rural areas, corralling investment into the villages that it has, *de facto*, designated as *exclusive* in its settlement hierarchy. This does not happen everywhere. Accessibility, amenity and the strength of nearby urban economies (supplying rural market entrants) will factor in the production of these problems and mean that in some areas, with much weaker economies, lower accessibility and more limited amenity, the landscape of rural challenges will look very different. Settlement hierarchies are used, implicitly or explicitly, almost everywhere. But where markets are weaker (and there are no second home buyers, lifestyle downshifters or retiring households), property in small villages will not be bought up by market entrants and yet those communities can still be starved of investment – becoming isolated pockets of poverty, inaccessible without a car and bereft of essential services. So, the one size fits all approach may generate problems, albeit different problems, in a variety of rural contexts.

Planning reform in urban areas tends to focus on delivering increased certainty for the development sector (see Breach, 2019; 2020). The *discretionary* nature of planning – with decisions made on a case-by-case basis by local politicians – generates risk for businesses. There has been a call, from some quarters, for greater frontloading of community involvement in planning, essentially confining that involvement to plan-making and then removing it from the consideration of planning applications. In essence, this would push the (English) planning system to a zonal approach, where development progresses 'by right' if it is compliant with rules and codes set out in a Local Plan. There have been recent moves in this direction, through the system of outline planning permission, local development orders (see Chapter 4) and 'permission in principle' experiments (Gallent *et al*, 2019b). Then, in terms of material changes in land-use, permitted development rights (Clifford *et al*, 2019) have removed the requirement for planning scrutiny altogether from some projects. The effects of all of this have been keenly contested, with opposing camps split between those who lament the loss of 'democratic scrutiny' (and effective oversight) and those who have always viewed planning as an impediment to housing delivery and economic growth.

At the time of writing, there is a very significant debate happening over the future shape of the planning system in England. Reports by the Centre for Cities (Breach, 2019; 2020) and by the Policy Exchange (Airey and Doughty, 2020) think tanks appear now to have anticipated and influenced the general thrust of government's thinking. In August 2020, the Ministry of Housing, Communities and Local Government (MHCLG[2]) published a White Paper detailing proposed changes to the planning system in England. 'Planning for the Future' (MHCLG, 2020a) argued that England needs a faster and simpler planning system, one that helps rather than hinders development, and one that gives clarity to the development sector and therefore reduces risk, drives down capital costs and delivers more housing that is more affordable to more people. The formula for achieving this is, as predicted above, is to do away, in most cases, with discretionary case-by-case permissioning of development by planning committees and shift to a by-right system of the type described earlier. The White Paper proposed three situations, or area types, for development control: growth areas, renewal areas and protected areas. The first ones would probably be urban or urban edge locations where significant growth is being promoted or sought. Here, development would be permissioned via a range of consenting mechanisms including local development orders. The second ones might be areas in which a range of development opportunities, at mixed scales, are being planned and pursued. It is conceivable that some larger market towns might be subject to renewal area permissioning rules, perhaps with instruments such as 'permission in principle' (that is, 'in-plan permission' attached to land allocated for development) being used to advance development with minimum, or only technical recourse, to planning committees.

No one really knows where villages sit within this schema, and it now seems likely that the triad of area types will give way to something more nuanced by the time legislation is brought before Parliament.[3] But the general expectation is that lower and lowest tier rural settlements will be in 'protected areas' and subject to a continuation of existing development control practices – so in much the same situation that they find themselves in now.

But the 2020 White Paper, now superseded by the Levelling Up and Regeneration Bill (DLUHC, 2022), was only one part of the planning reform jigsaw. Government had already embarked on a significant programme of deregulation since 2013, removing many conversions to residential use from local planning scrutiny. In September 2020, it moved to reform the Use Classes Order, creating a new Use Class E that brings together a range of commercial high street functions into a single land-use class. This turned out to be a precursor for further deregulation, with government then proposing that anything falling into Use Class E could be converted to residential use without planning permission. Shops, cafés, small offices and a range of other community infrastructure will be allowed to disappear if the owner wishes to convert it into flats or houses. Then, early in 2021, government consulted on a revision of the National Planning Policy Framework, the centre-piece of which was a curtailment of local authorities' use of Article 4 Directives to block permitted development, although its presented goal was to respond to the Building Beautiful, Building Better Commission's (BBBBC, 2020) conclusion that 'ugliness' in development should be rejected in favour of 'beauty' (a point on which few commentators would disagree – see Spiers, 2018: 138). Therefore, MHCLG consulted on a tracked version of the NPPF, newly populated with the word 'beauty' and, at the same time, published a new National Model Design Code (MHCLG, 2021b) intended to provide a blueprint for that 'beauty' in all forms of residential and commercial development.

While the pace and direction of reform is currently unknown – the responsible ministry has been renamed and a new Secretary of State appointed – it seems likely that deregulation of planning controls will continue at pace in much of England, although rural areas will see fewer changes, with government seeking to placate more conservative attitudes towards the direction of future development and the role of communities, and local politicians, in the planning process.

The goal of planning reform in England has generally been to accelerate the pace of housing development in response to an alleged undersupply of new homes. In some rural areas, this is also a primary goal – but one reserved for larger market towns where jobs and growth are concentrated. Villages have a set of different needs. They have been redlined against (or 'protected' from) growth, and for many adventitious buyers they provide refuges from the pace of change being promoted in urban settings. It would not be possible to solve the problems of villages by zoning them for development and by giving landowners and housebuilders a free pass to do as they wished (see also Spiers, 2018: 127, who argues that when the public appears to *lose trust* in planning, the response is often to promote its 'de-politicisation' and argue for greater market responsiveness).

Rather, the solution lies in approaches based on good local understanding and evidence, active enabling of innovation, community-based action and a jettisoning of district-wide prescriptions for rural areas (*building trust* in communities and gaining support – see Spiers, 2018: 127). But something also has to happen nationally: there has to be a plan for rural areas that assigns them a clear role – a role perhaps in post-carbon futures, in new patterns of working, in the promotion of healthier lifestyles and a role also in tackling gross inequalities (in other words, more positive planning for rural areas and places – see Spiers, 2018: 139). For a long time, smaller village locations have been sites of rampant neoliberalism, which has either resulted in social exclusion and gentrification (for those located in prized amenity areas) or neglect (for those in laggard regions). Planning alone cannot deliver a future for rural areas. This will depend also on public investment in services, education and infrastructure – contributions to 'levelling up'. But planning can do the following:

1. Lead on understanding the varied needs of rural places and especially smaller villages, working with communities, key charities and national networks. Leadership involves listening to local evidence and acting upon it. There are numerous examples, some cited earlier in this book, of communities understanding the need for tailored solutions and adaptations that have been ignored by a planning approach fixated with orthodoxy.
2. Invest in rural housing and planning enablers, whose task it is not only to spot opportunities, but to argue for a broader understanding of the

dynamics of rural places and advocate for innovations that advance new roles for rural areas, of the types noted above. Networks of local rural advocates with a broader remit are needed, which are able to think reflexively about rural futures.
3. Promote more community involvement in rural planning and not less. Reject the shift to deregulation and zoning in general terms and allow communities to actively pursue deviations away from 'general planning' approaches, coupling this with land, tax and finance reforms of the types discussed later in this chapter. In essence, deregulations that empower community rather than private interest, are a good thing. It will incubate innovation and fuel community-led housing and other innovations.
4. Remove small village locations from general prescription and top-down solutions: allow them to define their own development trajectories within a broader framework of amenity, landscape, social and economic development goals.

Land

The difficulties and expense of bringing land into public or community ownership is a significant barrier to progressing new models of housing development in rural areas. In the last chapter, examples were presented of communities struggling to solve development dilemmas because of a lack of affordable land. The problem of land monopoly has been a talking point for at least the last 200 years and before that, the feudal system was a source of political and social unrest, which seldom boiled over – as it did in the Peasants' Revolt of 1381 – but remained a visible source of social injustice for centuries. Once freed from English rule, the Republic of Ireland instigated its own reforms that allowed less restricted use of rural land by citizens and communities (Satsangi *et al*, 2010). And once given devolved powers, Scotland has followed a similar path – seeking to bring more land under community ownership and stewardship (see below).

But in England, the land question has perhaps been less prominent, with private ownership and control presented as a natural and unassailable state that provides (the illusion of) social, political and economic stability. For a long time, advocacy of land reform has been a minority sport – derided as a leftist project borne of spitefulness rather than any sense of social justice, which is delivered instead through the advancement of land and property privatisation of the sort that the Conservatives promoted in the 1980s through the right to buy. But there is today a growing awareness of how a range of linked crises – of unaffordable housing, financial instability, inequality and public health – are rooted in the use and abuse of land

(Hetherington, 2015; 2019; 2021; Shrubsole, 2019; Christophers, 2019; 2020). This has prompted renewed interest in the issue and also renewed social and political campaigning (Kenny, 2019: 766). More specifically, and linked to our purpose, the concentrated ownership of land, whose value is contoured by planning, is a major obstacle confronting community-led housing. The occasional scheme gets off the ground because of fortuitous circumstances but many more are thwarted by the land barrier. There is a clear case for land reform that supports those community-led developments and community ownership of land.

The average *price paid* for a hectare of farmland in England at the beginning of 2019 was just under £17,300 (Knight Frank, 2019). In contrast, land with planning permission for residential use ranged in *estimated value*, in the same year, from £370,000 per hectare in Bolsover, assuming a development density of 35 units/ha, to £165,475,000 in Kensington and Chelsea, assuming a density of 400 units/ha (MHCLG, 2020c). The average price of 'housing land' in the North East (well away from the distorting effect of London prices) was just over £660,412 per hectare – 38 times the average price of farmland in England. This underlying value of land is reflected in the cost of housing. Site exceptions reduce the cost of housing by negotiating a price for land that exceeds (current use) *agricultural value* but is lower than (intended use) *housing value*. But more generally, necessary planning restriction corrals value into developable land, with that value ultimately being extracted by private landowners when land is developed or sold on with planning permission. Indeed, the granting of planning permission for change of use – from farming to housing – generates a windfall gain. In some instances, the value of land can rise 100-fold or more, literally overnight. Monbiot *et al* (2019: 11) argue that this uplift in land value, sometimes called a planning gain (but not to be confused with agreed contributions to public infrastructure), has been created by society through public investment, and in fairness should belong to society. That argument has been made before:

> [...] roads are made, streets are made, railway services are improved, electric light turns night into day, electric trams glide swiftly to and fro, water is brought from reservoirs a hundred miles off in the mountains – and all the while the landlord sits still [...] To not one of those improvements does the land monopolist contribute, and yet by every one of them the value of his land is sensibly enhanced. (Churchill, 1909)

But society – comprising citizens, communities and other public interests – must pay extravagant fees to landowners, in the form of house prices and rents that reflect value uplift. This 'transfer of wealth' deprives communities and local authorities of the resources needed to address their own needs, including the broadly shared need for affordable homes (Monbiot *et al*, 2019: 11). It also, according to Monbiot and colleagues, crowds out public amenities and denies fair access. It shuts down opportunities to pursue activities of 'pleasure, fitness and peace of mind'. It is, in essence, a source of public deprivation and private power, which restricts civic and political life (Monbiot *et al*, 2019: 11).

This reality underpins the case for land reform – approaches to purchase and compensation that bring land into either public or community ownership, resulting in a fairer distribution of value, reflecting the state's (and society's) *central role* in creating that value.

Besides direct transfers of ownership, there is a broad spectrum of possible interventions centred on the use of land. Some are concerned with the 'just' operation of real estate markets and aim to reduce the social harm caused by rising economic rents. Planning or tax policies can seek to curb rents in a variety of ways. Interventions may promote health goals, barring particular uses in proximity or increasing access to land for recreation. Interventions that curb rents *and* promote fairer benefit from land development include land value capture tools that try to socialise rents in some way. However, there is inherent contradiction in these goals: lower rents mean less potential to extract public benefit. For that reason, the orthodoxy of land policy in England has been to perpetuate a growth in economic rents through land rationing while trying to siphon off public benefits through value capture (Ryan-Collins *et al*, 2017: 30). But this approach continues to produce significant wealth inequalities given the limited siphoning that is possible, and because of the very tight land rationing and development rules that constrain possible public gains.

Thinking on land reform, in that context, has shifted to direct control of land. How can land be brought into public ownership and made available for community use? Where infrastructure including new housing is needed, compulsory purchase order (CPO) powers exist to bring land into public ownership, but there are problems with the current system (Lyons, 2014). CPO is controversial and seen by some as an affront to 'natural' private property rights. Many local authorities have little experience of their effective use, and they are rooted in outdated legislation from the nineteenth century (Lyons, 2014: 69), when land needed to be compulsorily purchased for the building of railways. But one problem, more than any other, has limited the use of CPO: although the Land Compensation Act 1961 required that the 'hope value attributable to the prospect of development […] be disregarded, allowing for land to be acquired at close to current use value, in many cases agricultural value' (p. 70), subsequent case law and precedent has led to the conclusion that future permission for an alternate use should be factored into CPO valuation. Local authorities obliged to pay intended rather than current use value for land therefore transfer the value created by public investments back to the private owner. This means that the sort of public land assembly that produced New Towns after the Second World War are not possible without changes to compensation rules. Such changes appeared possible in 2019, ahead of the General Election, when the Labour party pledged to '[…] set up a new English Sovereign Land Trust, with powers to buy land more cheaply for low-cost housing' (Labour Party, 2019: 78). For a future Labour government to deliver on this pledge, a new Land Compensation Act would be needed, linking compensation (payable to private landowners) more closely to current use value. Drawing on Wei Yang and Partners and Freeman (2014), the Lyons Housing Review (which was commissioned by the Labour Party) argued that 'CPO powers should be based upon current use value plus a generous premium rather than the future use value once development is complete' (Lyons, 2014: 71). Yang and Freeman proposed 'tapered premiums', with landowners receiving 300 to 400 per cent of current use value: 3 or 4 times the price of farmland (far less than the current price ratios noted above). In instances where local authorities were intending to sell land for private development on larger sites brought into public ownership, this system of value capture would support public investment in enabling infrastructure. For smaller rural sites adjacent to villages and small towns, the result would complement 'exceptions' on agricultural/unallocated land, extending to the acquisition of infill sites currently under other uses. Presumably, an English Sovereign Land Trust would need to demonstrate a need for 'low cost housing' before embarking on such purchases. This would be easy to do in a great many rural amenity areas.

The transfer of land into public ownership could be a precursor to *community control and use*, with land gifted to community trusts or housing associations. It was shown in the last chapter that community land trusts (CLTs) provide a vehicle for delivering affordable housing and thereafter controlling its use. These trusts are often viewed as an outlet for community frustration and ambition – an opportunity to take control of local circumstances and, through co-operation, deliver forms of housing suited to a community's needs (Hudson *et al*, 2019). Community-based action of this type commands support across the political spectrum, aligning with the left's ethic of mutualism and the right's predilection towards self-help. It was noted in Chapter 4 that in the United States, land trusts have a strong association with the civil rights movement (see also Monbiot *et al*, 2019). In the UK, the idea of land being held in trust – for the benefit of 'low income, low wealth' groups – provided part of the template for Ebenezer Howard's Garden Cities. The number of new CLTs in the UK rose from 120 in 2017 to 250 in 2019 (Hilditch, 2019).

But as noted in Chapter 4, the growth of this sector is inhibited by land availability. Philanthropic donations or leases, or public transfers – of land and buildings – have been catalysts for trust activity in many areas, but these do not provide a consistent and regular means of supporting community-led housing. Mechanisms for directly bringing land into community ownership are limited. The Localism Act 2011 introduced a 'Community Right to Bid' for assets of community value, which must nevertheless be purchased at market value (and only at reduced cost where a landowner is motivated to sell to the community, as in the case of the Fox Inn at Loxley, see Chapter 4). Similarly, the Self-build and Custom Housebuilding Act 2015 together with the Housing and Planning Act 2016 place a statutory duty on local authorities to take positive action in support of community and individual self-build. This can mean further releases of public land for such projects or including expressed demand for self-build (reported in 'self-build registers') in calculations of objectively assessed need for housing, resulting in enlarged land allocations. Such measures may impact indirectly on land prices, but they do not involve any private land being *systematically* brought under public or community control.

The same situation initially prevailed in Scotland, where there has been a series of land reform acts over the last 20 years. Following devolution in May 1999, the Scottish Parliament moved to abolish feudal tenure and associated payments – 'feu' duties to superior landlords. It also set up a Scottish Land Fund, in 2001, to assist communities with the purchase of private land. The Land Reform (Scotland) Act 2003 then created a right for rural communities, with a population of fewer than 10,000 inhabitants, to have *first refusal* to purchase private land coming onto the market (similar to the community right to bid moratorium period created in England a few years later). But crofting communities were handed the right to buy land at any time, even if the landowner did not wish to sell. More recently, the Land Reform (Scotland) Act 2016 established a community 'right to buy land to further sustainable development' (Part 5), which like the right handed to crofting communities compels landowners to sell land to a community (or nominated third party) if that sale is judged by the Scottish Land Commission to support sustainable development. The delivery of sustainable forms of development, which support the ambitions (and deliver against the needs of) rural communities, has become the overarching goal of land reform in Scotland (Ross, 2019: 1), which has provided a platform on which to deliver a range of community projects. Supporters of the reforms argue that the Scottish Government is concerned with 'enabling communities' to meet their own needs and that landowners are having to

Figure 5.1 Colonsay Harbour, Scalasaig. © dun_deagh. CC BY-SA 2.0.

Case 5.1: The shifting context for community land purchase and planning in Scotland: Colonsay, Argyll and Bute

The Isle of Colonsay, in Scotland's Inner Hebrides, has an area of roughly 4,000 hectares and a population of just 124. The island's main settlement is Scalasaig, which hosts the majority of Colonsay's facilities – a shop and post office, a parish church, a micro-brewery, a doctor's surgery, a village hall and a hotel and bar (see Figure 5.1). A briefing note from the Communities Housing Trust (CHT) in 2021 noted that Colonsay's population has been aging in recent years and there is a 'worrying lack of young people'. This is partly due to the shortage of affordable housing on the island. About 40 per cent of houses are now second or holiday homes (let seasonally by Colonsay Estate rather than to local residents) and on the rare occasion when homes come onto the market, they are often 'priced above the means of local people'. The challenge – a dearth of jobs and homes in a place rich in amenity and attractive to adventitious purchasers – is common to many rural amenity areas, but arguably more acute in Colonsay given its relative isolation, pristine coastline and spectacular landscape.

It was in this context that the Colonsay Community Development Company (CCDC) was established in 2000. Alarmed by the slow demise of the island community, the Company came together to pursue five goals: to relieve poverty; advance education; assist with the provision of housing; promote trade and industry; and help put the community on a more sustainable footing. Since its inception, the CCDC has sought opportunities to achieve these goals and has tried to work with the *Colonsay Estate* to access the land needed to build homes and develop new employment opportunities.

The Estate has been owned for more than a hundred years by the 'Barons Strathcona and Mount Royal'. The Estate website says that it is now 'working with the community on the development of a complex of affordable housing to enable key workers to move to the island and to provide suitable sheltered housing for elderly residents.' However, relations between the Estate and the local community have not always been positive. A deal to purchase land at Scalasaig for community-led housing collapsed in 2013 when CCDC could not meet the price expectation of Lord Strathcona. Likewise, a community buyout of the island's only hotel failed for the same reason. The owner's asking price, of £535,000, was above the community's valuation. The letting of homes to holidaymakers – a more lucrative proposition than letting to residents, many of whom have ended up living in caravans – has been another source of friction between islanders and their 'laird', although Lord Strathcona counters this by pointing out that no houses have been 'taken out of residential letting to self-catering units' for some 20 years. Other disputes have centred on the removal of gravel from beaches in 2013, with Lord Strathcona wrongly blaming islanders, and the opening of Estate-owned holiday lets to tourists in 2020, against the wishes of many local households given the COVID-19 pandemic.

There are signs, however, that the owner has become more willing to engage with the community on land sales over the last few years. Two schemes are of particular interest, illustrating apparently changing attitudes towards land purchase and the more permissive role of Scottish planning in rural schemes. The first of these involved the Colonsay Estate.

In the first scheme, the community sought a land deal that was very similar to the one that collapsed in 2013 when there was a failure to agree a sale price. In 2020, CCDC purchased two plots of land at Scalasaig from the Colonsay Estate. This time, the sale was negotiated by CHT. These comprised one plot of 1.73 ha, to be used (initially) for six new homes and three self-build plots, and another of 1 ha, for two industrial units. The housing site will eventually have a second phase of up to 24 homes. A variety of housing (including self-build) and tenure types (for rent or purchase) will be provided, matching the mix of needs that Scottish communities encounter and all protected by the 'rural housing burden' (occupancy restricted). The purchase was facilitated by a Scottish Land Fund grant of £375,000 as well as awards from Highlands and Islands Enterprise (HEI) and the support of an industrial partner, MOWI, which operates a salmon farm off the coast. CCDC is still seeking further support for project delivery (some of which has been raised via crowdfunding) and the scheme has been slowed by the 2020–2 COVID-19 pandemic. Further contributions to meeting the land purchase cost have been made by Argyll and Bute Council's Business Continuity Committee, and CCDC expects the bulk of build costs to be met from the Rural and Island Housing Fund. The agreement with MOWI is that three of the homes will be leased from the community for their workers, reverting to community ownership, when and if they are no longer needed. The Oban Times reported that the scheme will help 11 families on the island currently in temporary accommodation (the caravans noted above) as well as support MOWI's activities and attract new workers to the island.

The second scheme is a project by West Highland Housing Association to deliver five affordable homes at Lower Kilchattan. Because the Argyll and Bute Development Plan offers 'broad encouragement to small scale (not exceeding 5 dwelling units) housing development on appropriate sites', and because the proposal comprised affordable homes (which was said to 'strengthen the merits of the proposal') on an opportunity site, the scheme was green-lighted without the need for a public hearing (following discussions on application report 17/00041/PP, dated 15 March 2017). One objector pointed to the 'open, rural setting' as being an impediment to the scheme. The planning authority's view was that 'development can be successfully absorbed into the landscape'. A more significant threat to the development was the following objection: '[…] the permission applied for indicates that widening of the existing access road and bell-mouth and the construction of a passing place are to be located on my ground and the applicants have no agreement with me to that effect'. The Officer responded that 'whilst land ownership is not a material planning consideration […] the land required for the passing places has not been included within the application site but a suspensive planning condition will ensure that the work must be carried out prior to any other development commencing'. CCDC noted in November 2018 that 'resolution of the access difficulties with the permitted scheme for 5 houses at Lower Kilchattan are being pursued'. Because this access barrier – known locally as the 'case of the seven gates' – could not be overcome, another Council meeting held on 29 November 2019 looked at the 'option of using a Compulsory Purchase Order (CPO) to obtain a piece of land in order to allow the development of 5 new build affordable houses on Colonsay'. Neither the report nor the minutes of the meeting could be published as this would have revealed the 'financial or business affairs of a particular individual'. However, it was noted that '[…] the Council agreed to the recommendations as outlined in the submitted report' (which remained confidential) and now have the option to compulsory purchase the land. But like other Scottish authorities, Argyll and Bute is reticent about using its CPO powers. West Highland Housing Association listed the scheme as being 'in the pipeline' in December 2020. Like the Scalasaig sites, further progress was now being impeded by the pandemic and the inability of construction workers to get on site.

In terms of *land purchases*, clear breakthroughs have been achieved in the last five years. A once reticent landowner has worked with CCDC on land sales. These sales were preceded by the Land Reform (Scotland) Act 2016, which signalled the Scottish Government's clear resolve to tackle the sorts of community sustainability challenges confronted by Colonsay and other island communities. Part 5 of the 2016 Act came into force on 26 April 2020, following the publication of a Business and Regulatory Impact Assessment (BRIA) on 7 February. CHT, negotiating the sale of the Scalasaig sites on behalf of the community, reminded the Estate that Part 5 would soon come into force and that CCDC would have a strong case for compulsory purchase. It was in that context that the community achieved this significant success. In terms of *planning*, this rural authority works within a more permissive context, where design strictures and discourses of openness do not necessarily stand in the way of essential development, and which supports the broader sustainability of rural places. To that end, there is a willingness to use available powers to unlock sites for new housing.

Sources: Communities Housing Trust: https://www.chtrust.co.uk/case-studies1.html#colonsay
CCDC: https://colonsay.org.uk/our-community/community-development-company
Oban Times: https://www.obantimes.co.uk/2020/05/16/land-sale-builds-better-future-on-colonsay/
Argyll and Bute Council I: https://www.argyll-bute.gov.uk/moderngov/documents/s117149/1700041%20colonsay.pdf
Argyll and Bute Council II: https://www.argyll-bute.gov.uk/moderngov/ieIssueDetails.aspx?IId=93026&Opt=3

adapt to a changing context, with many finding that opportunities are created for those ready to engage positively with communities.[4]

The radical feature of Scottish Land Reform is the rebalancing of power between rural communities and private landowners. The compulsion on landowners to sell to communities will impact negatively on land prices, but communities still pay 'market value' for the land's intended use (suppressed where a planning authority will only grant permission for housing targeted at local need). As in England, the Scottish Parliament continues to grapple with the question of how 'to give planning authorities the ability to acquire development land at values closer to its existing use' (Scottish Land Commission, 2018; see also Adams, 2015 for a broader discussion of challenges). It seems inevitable that a much higher proportion of the value in developable private land, created largely through public investment, will only be captured for community use through radically different compensation arrangements.

An alternative approach to land taxation that discourages owners from hanging onto land allocated for development in local plans (Ryan-Collins *et al*, 2017), through a recurrent land tax, might also incentivise sale or gifting to communities for local housing projects – but only if community owners (CLTs) were exempt from the liability. Otherwise, the new owner would need to transfer the tax burden to housing occupants when market conditions allow (Wyatt, 2019: 8), reducing the affordability of homes. Recurrent land taxes discourage owners from delaying the development of *permissioned sites* and are therefore a mechanism to accelerate housing delivery in growth areas, with knock-on effects for the supply of affordable homes. The speed at which market sites are developed in villages, which are often too small to support on-site affordable housing, is not a critical concern. Bringing *unallocated land* into community ownership, and thereafter granting an exception for housing use, appears to be a more appropriate way forward for villages.

Tax

Tax rules can be adjusted to aid certain types of housing project, including self-build or community-led development, by removing VAT liability affecting build costs (see also Spiers, 2018: 138). But more generally, the 'tax treatment of housing' may be considered a driver of consumption and therefore a determinant of price. How housing consumption is taxed will have general cost implications for buyers. So there is a shift of focus here: from thinking about how to support non-market housing options, through transfers of land to community control, to thinking about the general cost impediment that affects a wider spectrum of households from accessing homes at a more reasonable 'market price'. In essence, the cost impediment that confronts village housing solutions is, in part, rooted in the tax treatment of land and housing. The way they are taxed, relative to other objects of taxation (from payroll earnings to other asset classes), encourages investment, hoarding, and corrals value into real property. That value becomes an impediment to community, private and public answers to housing inequalities in rural areas. Therefore, we conceive tax to be part of a broader fiscal-finance barrier to village housing solutions. Tax shapes consumption, and it is the private consumption of assets that contours value, in preferred assets (housing) and preferred locations (villages).

The consumption of private housing in the UK is shaped by the tax treatment of this *asset*. It was noted in Chapter 2 that housing is a complex commodity, consumed for both the services it delivers (its utility) and for the investment it represents (its exchange value), realised through imputed rent and capitalisation of an appreciated rental value on sale. Both homebuyers and governments globally have come to view housing as an asset: one that delivers personal financial security over time, as residential mortgages are paid off (and net imputed rent grows, leaving households with greater disposable income for consumption and eventually for retirement) and also public spending advantages, as asset-based welfare replaces state welfare (Rossi, 2017).

Since the Second World War, and even during council housing's 'golden age' (see Chapter 3), successive governments have been committed to increasing the level of home ownership and reducing fiscal support for public housing (see Stirling, 2019). There is a general misconception, promoted by those on the political right, that private housing consumption comes at no cost to government (and society more generally) and that public housing is, in contrast, a significant drain on public resources.

But in order to support private housing consumption, governments enacted the series of steps recounted in Chapter 2. Home purchasers were given significant tax breaks: income tax linked to property holding was scrapped in the 1960s and home purchasers benefited from tax relief on mortgage interest in the 1980s. Also in the 1980s, a Financial Services Act opened up the UK banking sector to global investors (Wainwright, 2009: 377). The combination of tax relief and increased credit supply, from international money markets, supercharged both the demand for, and lending on, housing (Ryan-Collins, 2021) and caused the rapid escalation of prices witnessed in recent decades. Tax reliefs have gone, but UK residential property remains undertaxed relative to work and other assets. There is no capital gains tax (CGT) on primary residences (the un-earnt increment arising from price inflation is entirely tax free); capital gains on secondary residences are charged at 27 per cent (or 19 per cent for a home owned by a limited company for the purpose of private letting) rather than the owner's higher PAYE (pay as you earn) rate (for example 40 per cent or 45 per cent); there are a range of tax reliefs on income derived from the letting of 'investment properties'; and Council Tax liability is misaligned with property values, including in many rural areas where prices have risen sharply since the last assessment of 'rateable values' in 1991. Council Tax is a hypothecated *property tax* used exclusively to fund local services, but it is payable by the tenant rather than the *property owner* where a home is let.

Private housing has become a tax efficient asset for *owner occupiers* (encouraged to trade up to bigger homes in order to enlarge the capacity of their 'savings pot'. However, Stamp Duty Land Tax (SDLT) acts as a brake on this – see below), for *landlords* (with CGT on investment property set lower than their PAYE rate and the annual tax liability paid by their tenants), and for *banks*, which originate loans against this 'high quality collateral' (Aalbers, 2017), repackage these as debt securities and then sell them on to investors.

Housing consumption has become a focus for the UK economy, with governments viewing house-price inflation as good inflation – a measure of economic success. For that reason, all political parties have tended to steer clear of interfering with the housing market at this macro level, avoiding measures that could impact on house prices and related financial services. It is the centrality of housing to the national economy, partly rooted in the relative tax treatment of UK homes, which drives price and suppresses affordability. This effect is amplified by the long term decline in real interest rates, which have encouraged homebuyers to take on bigger mortgages at higher loan to value ratios (in an attempt to keep up with escalating prices). The increased volume of mortgage debt makes the economy extremely sensitive to base rate changes, with even modest increases denting consumer confidence (and spending) by raising borrowing and therefore living costs. Across different countries, high levels of domestic mortgage debt encourage central banks to keep a tight rein on interest rates, triggering more borrowing and further asset price inflation.

Kate Barker (2019: 70), a former member of the Bank of England's Monetary Policy Committee, has argued that, in this environment, *new housing supply boosts* – concentrated in urban rather than rural areas – may not be effective in reversing or calming the escalation of house prices, meaning that new market entrants (first-time buyers) will continue to struggle to save deposits for home purchase, irrespective of planning reforms or other interventions on the supply side.

Borrowing rates and housing consumption taxes are critical to the trajectory of house prices – but the gross inter-generational wealth inequalities that rising prices have produced (Resolution Foundation, 2018), especially falling rates of home ownership amongst younger people, have triggered some adjustments. Government has added a transaction tax (SDLT) surcharge on the purchase of second homes and reined-in some of the reliefs, including on CGT, for private landlords. Such moves may affect investment practices in the housing sector, shorten the queue of buyers in some areas (where returns were more marginal), and reduce the bidding up of prices (Barker, 2019: 61–2). Along with Brexit uncertainty, these adjustments caused housing prices to flatten in many parts of the UK during 2019.

Without the COVID-19 pandemic, government may have continued to make adjustments to its tax supports for the housing market, prioritising first-time owner-occupiers over investment buyers. But the closure of the economy in 2020 looked set to slow the housing market, further reducing economic confidence at a time of rising unemployment and falling consumer spending. Government reacted by removing stamp duty on purchases below £500,000, initially until the end of May 2021 before extending this until the end of June and then adding a transition period until September. House prices soared and were pushed into double digits in many areas (Gallent and Madeddu, 2021). It is difficult to untangle the effect of lower transaction taxes from the general flight to housing, traditionally considered a safe investment, during a time of economic volatility. However, a great many purchases were made by existing owners, encouraged to trade up to bigger homes or buy investment properties. Tax has a huge impact on housing consumption and especially on patterns of investment buying. And during 2020 and 2021, investment appears to have been concentrated in rural areas as many London buyers sought homes, with gardens and adaptable space, in green belt villages (Gallent and Madeddu, 2021). Supports for the housing market during COVID-19, ensuring rising prices, confirm the importance attached to housing by the UK Treasury: government's commitment to house-price inflation is undiminished and its enthusiasm for scaffolding prices has never been greater.

But while that commitment, through the tax system, causes acute affordability stresses in rural amenity areas, which are affected by a combination of capital mobility and supply constraints, the reality of housing occupying centre stage in the economic life of the country makes politicians understandably wary of radical shifts in the tax treatment of housing. Despite committing to ending the 'unfairness that sees income from wealth taxed at lower rates than income from work' (Labour Party, 2019: 30), the Labour Party's 2019 General Election manifesto primarily targeted income tax (on workplace earnings) rather than property tax (on un-earnt wealth) as a source of additional public revenue. The commitment to end 'unfairness' (Labour Party, 2019: 30) in fact referred to the application of personal tax rates to CGT liability on second homes and investment property rather than a resurrection of 'Schedule A' income tax (that would see owner-occupiers face a tax on rising asset value, attributed to improvements in local services, including schools, scarcity of new housing supply, and credit supply).

The *object* of taxation – wealth and assets versus earnings through payroll – is a recurrent theme in tax literature, with those authors prioritising 'redistributive justice' over productive efficiency (that is, limiting fiscal drag on the productive economy) always keen to see assets and asset accumulation (and transfer) taxed at an equivalent rate to workplace earnings (Diamond and Mirrlees, 1971). The *Mirrlees Review* for the Institute for Fiscal Studies looked at exactly this issue, recommending the equalisation of personal tax rates on income from all sources (including capital gains) and the implementation of a 'lifetime wealth transfer tax' in place of an 'ineffective inheritance tax' that captures only 'some assets transferred at or near death' (Mirrlees *et al*, 2011: 479).

If at some point in the future a UK government decides to implement structural responses to the inequality and access concerns witnessed in many rural areas, it could do the following: charge CGT on primary residences (see Barker, 2014; 2019), causing a slowing of house-price rises and managed deflation; increase capital gains on second homes to match an owner's PAYE rate (Mirrlees *et al*, 2011; Monbiot *et al*, 2019 – and committed to in the Labour Party's 2019 manifesto); and reform Council Tax, increasing liability for higher value property (Dorling, 2014) and transferring liability onto owners (Monbiot *et al*, 2019). Another possibility would be to abolish residential SDLT and make it part of the CGT liability. This could aid market entry and market mobility for lower income groups who are not first-time buyers and do not enjoy SDLT exemption. Merging SDLT with CGT would transfer the liability from buyers to vendors who, for example, could pay SDLT on a percentage of the price they paid for a property and the CGT as a percentage of the uplift, less retained reliefs. The objective of these changes would be to firstly make housing more affordable overall, and secondly promote the needs of those requiring a home to live in over those wanting to invest. The theory is that the 'market' could be made to cater for a wider spectrum of needs if utility purchases were given priority over investment, though such a big upstream shift would generate a range of economic knock-on effects.

All of these adjustments would impact on the consumption of housing, particularly the consumption of housing for investment, and therefore shorten the queue of buyers looking for rural property. The new tax liabilities would act as a disincentive, eating into revenues (from renting) or capital appreciation. The impact on demand for housing would, in turn, impact on demand for (and therefore the price of) land on which to supply that housing. But the degree of impact would be macro and geographically variable. We might expect to detect shifts in consumption nationally, but the effect on villages could be much smaller given that scarcity probably impacts on value (of housing and land) to a far greater extent than tax liability. That said, it is likely to have *some* effect and, combined with the sorts of land reforms discussed above and new sources of finance, could help support new community-led solutions to housing needs.

Finance

The question of how to pay for non-market housing projects in villages was raised in the last chapter. It could, in part, be paid for through the transfer of land into community ownership, including via a revamped compulsory purchase mechanism. But that would still leave build costs to be met. Relying on local fundraising generates spatial inequalities in the capacity of communities to take forward projects. And often having at least some funding in hand is a prerequisite for accessing support from charitable foundations. This points to inconsistencies in 'finance' for community-led projects. In this section, we will look at both support to communities (where does money come from, and where might it come from in the future?) and sources of funding for public housebuilding, which has diversified in recent years.

Community-led housing

For community projects, finance can come directly – in cash, land or assets – from (a) local fundraising or share issuing; (b) charities and foundations; (c) crowdfunding; (d) central government (currently, or until recently, from the *Community Housing Fund*, and in the future from the *Community Ownership Fund*) or (e) from private gifting or donation.

Indirectly, it can come through partnering arrangements with a registered provider of social housing, in the form of (f) capital funding/grant or (g) land subsidy generated either through the permissioning process or through a site exception where land is made available at closer to agricultural than intended use value (reviewed in Chapter 4). Community-led housing can also receive miscellaneous (h) support from a local authority, in the form of land, loans and grants.

(a) Local fundraising and share issuing usually happens after a community has established an entity that can legally fundraise and issue shares. In the case of the purchase of the Fox Inn at Loxley (detailed in Chapter 4), members of the community set up the 'Loxley Community Benefit Society' with the objective of buying and saving an important community asset. A 'share offer' was then launched, operated and eventually extended until the target amount, of £250,000, was achieved.

(b) Funding from charities and foundations can take the form of grants or loans. Once the Loxley group had hit their target, a request for a further £100,000 was approved from the Plunkett Foundation – half grant and half loan. There are a large number of charities in the UK, funding various kinds of projects. *Locality* (a charity supporting community organisations) estimates that there are more than 4,000 funders of community projects. These tend to offer short-term funding, often seed-corn. They are highly specialist, supporting very particular types of project. They are over-subscribed, with many communities bidding for relatively small pots of money. Application processes can require considerable investment of time. And these funders do not cover 'full economic costs' so need to be supplementary to other sources of finance. Funding for 'land and buildings' is just a part of the charitable funding landscape and includes specialist sources (such as Plunkett, see above) that are concerned with certain types of asset. Other pots in that area target, for example, the preservation of heritage buildings. Some pots might extend to the support of community housing, including the Community Investment Fund or *Power to Change* from the UK National Lottery. Most are concerned with social enterprise, but a few will provide funds to achieve housing outcomes, often in tandem with wider projects.

(c) Crowdfunding could be a potential source of funding for community housing but it has been used mainly for projects focused on general community benefits and cohesion – so, for example, to seed-corn the development of a community garden on derelict land or a community market in a disused building, sometimes just temporarily. *Spacehive*[5] lists a number of projects that have been supported through crowdfunding, most of which are based in and around London. This 'civic crowdfunding

platform' partners with community networks and councils. It aims to provide supplementary funding for projects and works best where there is an abundance of potential contributors who have a direct connection with a project. This sort of crowdfunding tends not to generate the funds needed to buy land and buildings, but it provides communities with the money needed to repurpose buildings where they have already been bought or leased by, or gifted to, a community. It could, for example, help with building conversion costs. Crowdfunding is an updated version of the 'whip rounds' noted in Chapter 4, but helps communities reach a wider audience of private and institutional contributors. *Spacehive* provides a platform where communities can present their project to that audience in the hope of attracting donors. But there is a greater likelihood of effective fundraising in areas of concentrated population and for projects that have many direct participants and beneficiaries.

The major source of funding for community-led housing comes from *(d) central government* or, more specifically, from its 'communities' department (the Department of Levelling Up, Housing and Communities, or DLUHC, after October 2021). Some pots are administered directly and others in partnership with the community groups and networks. A partnership of organisations – the Confederation of Co-operative Housing, Locality, the National Community Land Trust Network and UK Cohousing – operate *Community-Led Homes*, which co-ordinates funding in the (i) group (set up), (ii) site and plan and (iii) build stages. Small grants (typically up to £10,000) are available for group set up, from either DLUHC or the National Lottery (Power to Change). That money can also be crowdsourced, and Community-Led Homes offers guidance and support for that. For the site and plan stage, the main source of support is the Community Housing Fund (more below) from DLUHC. But flexible loan support is available from the Charities Aid Foundation (CAF) which offers a range of repayable loans including loans to cover land purchase of up to £400,000 (and small amounts to cover upfront expenses and fees). Community-Led Homes also offers legal guidance on share issuing, of the type undertaken in Loxley. It can also offer guidance and support for those communities wishing to establish their own registered providers (of social housing) in order to access funding available to that sector. For the build stage, communities can go back to CAF and access another £400,000 to cover development costs. They can also bid for phase 2 Community Housing Fund support, to cover the construction or refurbishment of homes. Overall, Community-Led Homes provides a portal for groups wishing to take forward community housing, directing them to grant and loan finance, the former mainly coming, at the time of writing, from DLUHC and the latter available from CAF on terms that are generally suited to the community-led housing model.

The *Community Housing Fund* in England is administered by Homes England and was established in July 2018. Some £163m of funding was committed to phase 1, to cover *revenue funding*: community-group capacity funding, upfront fees, planning applications and staffing costs. *Capital funding* was available to local authorities wanting to install infrastructure to support community-led housing – roads, site remediation and so on. Phase 1 funding ran until March 2020. Another £163m was committed to phase 2, to cover 'the construction of new homes and conversion/refurbishment of existing properties; including acquisition and/or remediation of land for development' or the 'the acquisition of existing properties for conversion or refurbishment'. This mix of revenue and capital funding was designed to support genuinely community-led housing, rather than housing that could otherwise have been funded through Section 106 contributions. The housing needed to be 'affordable in perpetuity' so could take the form of discounted market (with a resale price covenant), shared ownership, social rent, affordable rent or rent to buy. The future of the Community Housing Fund is currently unknown, with decisions on its future having been suspended during the COVID-19 pandemic. In March 2021, government announced the creation of a £150 million *Community Ownership Fund*, which will provide groups with match-funding of up to £250,000 for the purchase of community assets, or more for sports related assets (MHCLG, 2021a). Broader in intent than the Community Housing Fund, the creation of the Ownership Fund comes on the back of disappointment with the outcomes of *community right to bid* initiatives (see previous chapter – and MHCLG, 2021a) which have seldom ended with the transfer of assets into community ownership. Although not focused on housing, this fund could be accessed to purchase assets needed to support the delivery of community-led homes, including sites earmarked for mixed use, or land needed for the transfer of community uses away from a site, already in public ownership, needed for housing (see the Ferring example, Chapter 4).

Some Community Land Trusts have been seeded through (e) *private gifting or donation*. There are numerous examples of very particular sets of local circumstances leading to community-led housing by CLTs. Some examples were given in the last chapter. Others include the Beer Community Land Trust in East Devon, which was originally established with a mix of loans and grants from the District Council and the Homes and Communities Agency (which had its functions split between Homes England and the Regulator of Social Housing in 2018) but has since commenced development on land vacated by the Beer Social Club. Land for the club was donated privately, but the club itself became non-viable. Members of the club therefore agreed to donate their shares, and in effect the land, to Beer Community Land Trust, which started redeveloping the site for affordable housing – four two-bed houses and two two-bed flats – at the end of 2020 (https://www.beerclt.org/project2). Many landowners choose to donate land (or grant long leases on peppercorn rents) directly to parish councils, and this sometimes happens ahead of the granting of site exceptions. Some of English Rural Housing Association's recent developments have occurred on gifted land. In 2016, for example, the association completed a development of six affordable homes at Vyvyan Cottages, Iden Green in Kent. That development complemented another scheme, also of six homes, completed in the same village in 1995. 'The land for the current site was made available by the Parish Council, having been gifted to them by the current Viscount Rothermere [as part of the Harmsworth Memorial Trust] at the same time he made land available for the initial six homes' (Collett, 2016).

In the Iden Green case, the push for additional housing came from the Parish Council (Benenden Parish) and could therefore be considered 'community-led'. It is often the case that community-led housing is delivered *in partnership with a registered provider*, using a combination of (f) *capital funding and* (g) *land subsidy*. The involvement of a registered provider would probably prevent the community from accessing resources from the Community Housing Fund, and this would certainly be the case if any housing built made use of Section 106 contributions. However, registered providers are still eligible for loans from CAF. An alternative for some communities might be to establish their own registered provider of social housing (registering with Homes England). A number of rural housing associations began life in this way, registering with the Housing Corporation after 1964 and then accessing housing association grants after 1974. This remains a possibility today. But again, that would shift them onto a different footing – into the charities sector and away from the purely community-led model, strictly defined. The most important sources of finance for community-led housing remain: local fundraising, grants/loans from charities, government support (which often means central government, but can also mean land, loans and grants from local government – see below), or gifting and donations.

Finally, and sitting between private gifting and new models of council housing, introduced below, are the *supports provided by local authorities* to community land trusts operating in their jurisdictions. There are a number of ways that authorities can support community-led housing, including through the gifting of land (often to parish councils, which then establish a CLT in order to progress the development of that land – unless they wish to work with an existing registered provider), through grant support using cash contributions from Section 106 agreements (cash in lieu of on-site contributions), or through the issuing of loans to a trust, with money sourced from regular revenues or from the Public Works Loan Board lending facility – see below. The Beer Community Land Trust, referred to above, received a £1 million loan from East Devon Borough Council to support the delivery of affordable homes. A significant challenge, in the absence of public land to build on, is the cost of acquiring land in the private market.

Indeed, what is lacking in England is a mechanism to seed CLTs through private land acquisition (including in instances when an owner may not wish to sell), of the type that is possible in Scotland. It is much more usual to work in partnership with landowners, hoping for donations or at least a willingness to sell land to a community at a reasonable cost, close to current use value. But because not all communities have the patronage of a benevolent aristocrat, who can write the gift off against tax liability, there is a case for a more muscular approach to bringing land under community ownership, as discussed above.

Council housing

Our concern for council housing at this juncture is in fact a concern with new finance opportunities, ahead of exploring the future of council-led provision in villages in Chapter 6. 2019 marked the hundredth anniversary of the Addison Act: 100 years since the legislation that brought about exchequer subsidy for council housing and ushered in the era of direct state involvement in building homes for mass consumption – for general need. Besides community-led housing, the state might yet have an important role to play (again) in rural areas, mainly because its own finance options have significantly broadened during the last 20 years. It may also find new ways to provide consistent support to community-led housing, including through those finance options.

The sale of council homes to sitting tenants combined with restrictions on building programmes put an end to mass public housing after 1980. Margaret Thatcher, writing in her 1993 memoirs reflected: 'The state, in the form of local authorities, has frequently proved an insensitive, incompetent and corrupt landlord [therefore…] as regards the traditional post-war role of government in housing – that is, building, ownership, management and regulation – the state should be withdrawn from these areas just as far as possible' (Thatcher, 1993: 599). During the Labour years (1997 to 2010), the seeds were sown of a new, arms-length approach, to council building. The Local Government Act 2003 allowed authorities to set up trading companies. And although the Conservative-led Coalition government (from 2010) placed further restrictions on council borrowing for the purpose of house-building (fixing a cap on Housing Revenue Account (HRA) spending in 2012, which was eventually lifted in 2018), it also extended legislation allowing the setting up of trading companies through the Localism Act 2011. Austerity meant that councils were not allowed to grow the public debt (Ryan-Collins *et al*, 2017: 220), but deregulation and pursuit of market solutions meant that they were allowed to become market actors.

During the 2000s, many councils began to think again about restarting their building programmes. Anything funded from the HRA (in other words 'traditional' council housing) would be subject to the right to buy – what was the point, therefore, of building affordable homes that would quickly be lost to private sale? But it was also recognised that overall housing supply had fallen significantly below need since the 1970s, clearly because council programmes had been curtailed. Therefore, many local authorities saw the trading companies as a means of contributing to local housing supply, by using the new legislation to set up local housing companies, which were also allowed to be joint ventures with private partners.

This model had one clear advantage: local authorities can borrow, at close to sovereign rates, from the Public Works Loan Board. 'The PWLB lending facility is operated by the UK Debt Management Office (DMO) on behalf of HM Treasury and provides loans to local authorities, and other specified bodies, from the National Loans Fund, operating within a policy framework set by HM Treasury. This borrowing is mainly for capital projects' (DMO, 2020). So unlike other developers reliant on conventional commercial finance (which is often short term with rates in excess of five per cent), local authorities – and their trading companies – have preferential access to relatively cheap credit (loans repayable over one to 50 years, typically at a rate of less than two per cent for standard new loans or less than one per cent for premature repayment, with fixed rates based on gilt yields[6]). Some local authorities also have land banks. Put these two things together and the case for *local authority-led* building becomes clear. And because there is no draw-down from the HRA, any affordable housing built through this model, subsidised by the sale of market housing, will not be subject to the right to buy.

This means that local authority-led housing can be undertaken by a local housing company, using cheap public credit, by a joint-venture (with a private partner – including a landowner) or through an existing ALMO-based entity. The significant point here is that local authorities identifying a need can begin to build again – and be part of a diversified approach to supplying housing in rural areas (Spiers, 2018: 138). A route has therefore opened up for a new type of council housing, including in smaller village locations. Examples of authority-led housing are provided in the next chapter, revealing what can be achieved in villages and in larger rural settlements.

Conclusions

A linked array of impediments confronts village housing projects, including that of land availability and cost. Private ownership of land ensures that private interest benefits disproportionately from the 'rezoning' of land for development – that is, the allocation of land for housing use in local plans – and its subsequent build-out and sale. There is a long-standing debate in this area, stretching back hundreds of years. The general thrust of that debate is that society, and public investment, seeds the value that is harvested by landowners. Churchill (1909) captured the essence of the argument in his famous 'mother of all monopolies' speech, cited above. But it is not only investments in infrastructure that create or drive up land costs: tax policy also plays a part in amplifying inessential demand for housing, and the planning system's prioritisation of rural amenity means that any land available for development will command a significant premium, over agricultural value, where market fundamentals are strong. The combination of factors driving value creation/price inflation then create a critical funding challenge for the providers of non-market housing in rural areas. In short, it is expensive to develop village housing even though farmland is relatively cheap and plentiful. This is the reality exploited by site exceptions, which permit the building of affordable housing on farmland outside a village's development envelope, or on other sites not allocated for housing use.

The examples given of exception site developments in Chapter 4 were all positive. Landowners were willing to engage with land trusts and registered providers in those cases. But exceptions policy has not always proven popular with rural landowners, who have not been satisfied with the return on the sale of land. Recognising that issue, government mooted the idea of 'entry-level exceptions' in 2018 (see Chapter 4) which was reworked into its 'First Homes' framework. As originally envisaged, this new approach to building on relatively small plots of farmland (and other plots not allocated for housing use) would have allowed landowners to mix sale and affordable housing and not required them to work with local communities. Despite rowing back on these ideas in the 2019 revision of NPPF (MHCLG, 2019), they ultimately found their way into the 'First Homes' re-revision. The move to entry-level, and then 'First Homes', exceptions demonstrates an obvious truth: development needs to serve the aspirations of 'willing' private landowners. Allowing them to build exactly what they like on their land was a step too far in 2018, but it has been the direction of travel under Conservative governments. Deregulation – through local development orders, permission in principle and First Homes exceptions – that empowers the development sector at the expense of communities and public interest has been a clear narrative during the last decade of planning in England.

But this formula has fuelled the gentrification of many villages and the decline of others. There is a case for greater control over rural land, realised through land reform. The object of that reform will be to grow and empower community actors including land trusts. At the same time, there is a case for an approach to planning that consistently prioritises community interest and potentially supports the new interest in local authority-led housebuilding in rural towns and villages. A broad programme of reform could look like this:

1. An approach to *rural planning* led by rural housing/planning enablers, which puts community interest on an equal footing with amenity and which rejects top down formulations of rural interest but is rather evidence-led and flexible enough to support community-led projects.
2. An approach to *rural land use*, which is again guided by community interest and includes a facility to bring land under community control for the purpose of delivering against housing or other community needs. This is likely to require compulsory purchase powers and (landowner) compensation arrangements similar to those in place in Scotland, but with an extension to limit compensation to current use value plus an incentive premium.
3. Reform of housing taxes that aims to curb inessential consumption: a return to the taxation of estimated imputed rent from ownership could help rebalance the accrued benefits from work and asset-holding, making housing generally more affordable. This is a complex thing to do, with likely profound consequences. So in terms of tax liabilities

in rural areas, there is a case for pursuing greater fairness in the first instance: extended council tax bands, better reflecting the value of high-end property in villages; an impact levy on second homes and holiday lets; a rate of CGT on second homes that is equal to the vendor's PAYE rate, or 40 per cent, whichever is higher; and discourage the registration of second homes for non-domestic business rates (as holiday lets) by extending the minimum let period and lowering the small business rates relief threshold on homes previously registered for council tax (that is, homes that have been flipped rather than being genuine self-catering lets).
4. An extension of *public finance* for community-led projects that includes a bigger pot of money for acquiring land at closer to agricultural value (realised through new compulsory purchase powers) for all sorts of community-led projects. The same facility for local authorities acquiring land through LHCs for 100 per cent affordable housing (or perhaps also affordable private renting for local need – see Lafford Homes example in next chapter). A broadening of flexible finance for community projects (including through CAF – and underwritten by government) would aim to accelerate community land acquisitions and projects, challenging the monopoly of private land ownership in rural areas.

These sorts of reform would greatly assist current community-led projects. More obvious sources of funding and finance would likely encourage new groups to form. And a streamlined means of bringing affordable land under community control, without protracted processes in which landowners are the 'kingmakers', would have a similar effect. These reforms would also enable other approaches to housing delivery in villages to gain traction, including self and community build and also low impact developments outside village envelopes. These extended forms of community-led housing are reviewed in the next chapter. Beyond support for community-led housing, general tax reforms would assist with the 'de-assetisation' of housing, discussed in this current chapter and introduced in Chapter 2. Because homeownership brings a range of tangible and intangible benefits, from security and peace of mind to reduced pressure on household finances, especially in later life, a complete de-assetisation of rural housing is neither possible nor desirable. But tax changes could make that asset, and linked benefits, more accessible to a broader spectrum of socio-economic groups in rural areas and elsewhere. Therefore, our recipe for reform is two-fold: to lend greater support to community-led housing through land stewardship; and to support the ambition of homeownership across the wider market.

Notes

1. From *The Simpsons*, of course. Original reference 'to alcohol'.
2. MHCLG has now become DLUHC, the Department for Levelling Up, Housing and Communities.
3. The 2022 Levelling Up and Regeneration Bill (LURB) has ended the focus on automatic, or 'in principle' (in plan) permissioning for development. Government suffered a series of political setbacks, some of which were attributed to its proposed planning reforms and how they might 'disempower' communities within the planning process.
4. Personal correspondence with the Communities Housing Trust, 19 May 2021, who cited the case of a landowner who agreed to release six plots of land near Aviemore to the community for zero cost. CHT worked to service the plots, returning two to the landowner, who then sold these for self-build at a price that exceeded the value of releasing four plots to the community for half market price (for affordable housing).
5. www.spacehive.com
6. www.dmo.gov.uk/responsibilities/local-authority-lending/current-interest-rates/ (accessed 6 January 2022)

6
Self-build and custom housebuilding, off-grid and council-led development: the future

Extending discussions started in Chapters 4 and 5, our examination of rural housing futures now turns to three promising pathways: getting more homes 'self-built'; opening up opportunities for low-impact and off-grid development, which challenge the entrenched orthodoxies of rural planning; and increasing the presence of council-led housing. These are not the limit of housing futures in rural areas. Our major prescription is for extended community stewardship and control over land. We have also offered views on tax that aim to support wider access to homeownership across the general housing market. But our focus now is on emergent opportunities within both the 'community-led' domain and in the area of council-led provision, which will continue to play important roles in assisting lower-income households in villages that would otherwise continue to gentrify, losing their economic and social vitality.

Introduction

Chapter 4 looked mainly at community-led projects, sometimes framed by broader community or neighbourhood planning activities. It also considered rural housing projects that rely on flexible planning, notably the site exceptions approach. That chapter ended by examining some of the barriers that stand in the way of current projects, preparing for a broader discussion of key frameworks – planning, land, tax and finance – in Chapter 5. Reform of those frameworks could bring significant change to patterns of housing production and consumption. Community-led housing (and other community projects) could benefit significantly. But other models might also gain greater traction. Self-build – either individual or by community groups – for example, is hampered by a combination of land and finance constraints. In pressured housing markets, it may work well for self-builders with deep pockets, but *affordable schemes* can struggle to get off the ground in villages. The purpose of this chapter is to look at emergent village housing models. Besides self-build, we focus on low-impact off-grid ('one planet' housing) and also on the type of local authority-led development that might be suited to, and advanced, in villages.

The mix of housing delivery models in this chapter is likely to fit different circumstances. In areas with more active communities, and a surfeit of know-how, community-led schemes – including self-build – may be more important. Elsewhere, perhaps in our 'depleting' villages (see Chapter 1), there may be a need for local councils to lead on affordable housing projects that form part of a wider economic vitalisation. Geography and established culture will also determine what is appropriate. Low impact developments, often associated with alternative lifestyles, have a tendency to locate in areas of more limited development pressure. They are products of an experimental mind-set and examples developed to date are more commonly found well away from areas of concentrated population, or in national parks that have been keen to incubate housing forms that have a lighter footprint and diverge from the look and feel of 'traditional' development. Land is the critical ingredient for all of these models: land for self or group builders that is affordable, land for public projects where land banks have been exhausted, and land beyond village envelopes that can support what are essentially low-impact new settlements in the countryside.

Self-build and custom housebuilding

UK housebuilding is dominated by industrial production – a small number of large companies build most new homes. In 2019, just over 80 per cent of housing completions were attributed to the private sector (HM Government, Live Table 213) and in 2018, 58 per cent of total housing output came from just 10 companies. Four of those companies – Barratt, Persimmon, Taylor Wimpey and Bellway – build a third (33 per cent) of England's housing.

It has been suggested that this profile and power asymmetry in UK housebuilding generates two problems. First, big companies control the land market and labour supply, squeezing out smaller providers.

And second, the lack of smaller companies limits interest in smaller sites, reducing competition and driving up cost. It also leads to housing quality issues: standardised, 'routine' build aims to control cost and limit risk (of cost overrun and failure to successfully navigate planning). This means that big companies build the same housing, with the same design and materials, resulting in residential monotony that invites rejection by communities who fear increasing 'placeless-ness' if new housing is permitted. The few big companies also enjoy significant corporate influence, through lobbying by the Home Builders Federation (HBF), over planning policy. Planning rules are designed to support their business models – with an emphasis on big sites and deregulation through local development orders and so on (see Gallent *et al*, 2021). There has been less attention paid to small sites (until recently). Control of the land market, noted above, is exercised through option agreements – treaties between landowners and developers, with the developers buying 'the option' to complete the purchase at a later date. Big companies, with significant spending power, control the lion's share of immediately developable land (allocated in local plans) and also accumulate strategic land banks (comprising land not yet allocated for development or in areas where there is no current local plan). Their aim is to be in the driving seat if and when that land is allocated and becomes developable. There is a perennial debate on land banking and its function within the development process: the Royal Town Planning Institute (RTPI, 2007) has accused developers of seeking to influence house prices through land hoarding, by slowing the pace of development (trickling homes onto local markets at a rate below the (market) 'absorption rate', thereby generating pent up demand and more intense competition between buyers). But neither the Office of Fair Trading (2008) nor Lichfields (2017) have found any substantive evidence of this.

The jury is out on much of the above, but the skewed profile of private provision is thought to limit the capacity of private enterprise to give attention to smaller sites. It has been argued recently, by the Home Builders Federation (HBF), that 'plurality' in the sector needs to be rebuilt (Home Builders Federation, 2017: 25) so more small sites, of limited interest to the top 10 companies, get built out. Plurality – having more SMEs and specialist providers – is viewed as a way of upping overall housing supply. But it is also a way to re-energise many different types of housing provision in rural areas: new private partners for community-led and 'self-build' projects, or even specialist rural providers for local authority-led joint ventures – companies that are trusted partners in village development and can actively contribute to place-making and continuity in rural design and housing delivery.

Countries with a broader mix of small, medium-sized and large housebuilders tend to have larger self-build sectors. This is also true of some post-socialist economies (Stephens et al, 2015). This is perhaps because the absence of big companies, funded by share issuing and flotation on stock markets, leaves space for different models and alternative ways in which individuals and communities can meet their own needs. The spatial distribution of self-build housing varies significantly across the United Kingdom, contoured by instrumental drivers such as land availability and cost, as well as by broader factors including demography (for instance ageing populations in some locations) and cultural attachment to established production norms. Although the self-build and custom housebuilding sector produces an estimated 10 per cent of new housing each year across the United Kingdom, there are very significant regional variations, with output at its lowest in the south-east of England and significantly higher in Wales, Scotland and Northern Ireland as well as in a selection of remoter rural regions within England. The popular perception of self-build in the UK is of one-off bespoke projects for high-end clients – which is something that is regularly seen in the south-east of England and in other pressured markets, often key amenity ('exchanging') areas where land is expensive (see previous chapters), build costs are high (because there may be too few small companies competing for this work) and finance is difficult to access (as banks have not been providing accessible finance for self-builders). However, in reality, there is a diverse range of models, from 'do-it-yourself' self-constructed 'tiny homes' through to technically elaborate architectural commissions likely to win planning approval on the grounds that they are 'truly outstanding, reflecting the highest standards in architecture, and would help to raise standards of design more generally in rural areas' (MHCLG, 2021c: Para, 80). Therefore, although the median cost of an individual self-build home (including land purchase) was reported to be £460,000 in 2020 (Self Building and Renovating, 2020), costs can vary enormously in relation to land, specification and development model, as well as scale and regional differences in building costs. Field (2020: 22) lists 10 distinct community-led and self-organised development models, with those touched upon here, and also in Chapter 4, listed in Table 6.1. It is in recognition of this diversity of development pathways and outcomes that policy labelling in the UK changed from 'self-build' to 'self-build and custom housebuilding' in 2015, with self-build used to denote housing that has been designed and built specifically for a client, and custom-build to cover individual 'off-the-shelf' packages.

A growing body of research has focused on the potential of self-build to add to the available mix of housing in England; how this model

Table 6.1 Selected models of community-led and self-organised housing (Field, 2020, *abridged*)

Type	Characteristics/Case studies
Self-build housing	Tailor-made or designed properties, arranged by individuals or groups for their own use, including homes built by the residents themselves (Cases 6.1 and 6.2)
Custom-build housing	Where households have made use of a specialist provider/developer to finalise the 'customising' of homes to their own choosing
Self-help housing	Bringing empty or derelict properties back into use through renovation works undertaken by community projects (Case 4.3)
Community land trusts/ development trusts	Housing and other assets being owned or managed for community benefit, and at permanently affordable costs (Cases 4.3, 4.4 and 4.5)
Cohousing	Creating mutually supportive neighbourhoods that combine self-contained dwellings with other shared spaces, buildings and facilities (Case 6.2)
Low-impact housing	The design and development of dwellings to maximise the protection of the local and natural environment (Cases 6.3 and 6.4)

might be facilitated by planning and finance; and the impact it might have on both overall supply and individual housing circumstances in different areas. Hamiduddin (2017) notes that England and the rest of the UK is an outlier internationally, both in terms of the weight placed on housing delivery by a few companies and the under-development of a self-build sector.

Proponents of self-build highlight the many advantages of directly involving consumers and communities in the production of housing. Benson and Hamiduddin (2017: 4) cite three main pluses: general contribution to housing supply; contribution to affordability (as self-builders are no longer funding developers' profits); and ensuring that different kinds of sites are matched to different kinds of builder. Furthermore, and besides this *systemic resilience in diversity* argument – connecting a diversity of providers to a diversity of development opportunities and needs – 'user involvement' in the building of homes can bring positive social benefit, developing homes and communities in tandem (Hamiduddin and Gallent, 2016). It therefore ensures that people have a direct stake in the places – and not only the homes – they build.

There is of course additional complexity in self or custom built housing, with participants getting more involved in issues of finance, planning and design and also dealing with legal advisors and subcontractors (Lloyd et al, 2015: 29). It is also the case that the barriers affecting other models, including community land trust developments, also confront self-builders: these relate to planning, land and finance and also to technical support, for people or groups who may not have considered self-build before and may therefore have little knowledge of this route. Proponents accept that land availability plays a critical role in holding back this form of development. It is the *sine qua non* for self-build, meaning that if this issue can be resolved then the potential of this sort of housing, which many more people might embrace, could be unleashed (Obremski and Carter, 2019: 188).

The Self-Build and Custom Housebuilding Act 2015 and Housing and Planning Act 2016 have established a 'right to build', requiring local authorities to maintain a register of people or groups seeking land on which to build their own homes. Thereafter, authorities must have regard to the level of local interest in self-build when drawing up development plans and formulating policies on housing, land disposal and regeneration. The ambition behind this legislation is that the contribution of individually commissioned or self-built homes to total housing output could double in the next decade – rising to 20 per cent by 2030.

Different forms of self and custom building present different opportunities and possibilities in villages. Individual self-build has the potential to meet a range of needs in rural areas, from the high-end projects undertaken by wealthier families – some of which have been featured on Channel 4's *Grand Designs* since 1999 – to the low-cost builds suited to those on more limited budgets. These individual self-builds are private projects, constrained by planning rules and by the availability of suitable building plots. The average price of a building plot in England is £200,000 but there is significant locational variation behind this figure. Typical build costs range from £300 to £3,000 per square metre[1], with land cost being by far the most important variable. In some instances, existing homeowners may engage in self-build projects, demolishing a current home and building a new one. They might also partition the plot on which their current home is sitting, creating an opportunity for themselves, a relative or a stranger to build an additional dwelling.

The Right to Build legislation has provided the impetus, backed by a statutory requirement, to progress policies and approaches that respond to the demand for self and custom homes within local authority areas. The maintenance of self-build registers is one measure of how quickly local authorities are moving. It has been reported in *Planning Resource* (Marrs, 2020) that a fifth of authorities had failed to establish a register by the end of the statutory (three-year) implementation period and others have been charging substantial registration fees or requiring interested households to demonstrate local connection (NaCSBA, 2021). But while some areas are arguably dragging their feet and showing little interest in self-build, others are enthusiastically embracing its potential. Teignmouth District Council and Swindon Borough Council have been requiring developers to incorporate self-build plots into larger development schemes. South Shropshire District Council's Build Your Own Affordable Home scheme specifically targets the problem of rural housing affordability by using the site exception approach (see Chapter 4) to support the construction of self-builds (with ground floorplates of up to 100 square metres) with the resale value of homes capped by a covenant, thereby ensuring that they remain affordable to local households in perpetuity. Perhaps the most ambitious rural self-build project currently being taken forward, however, is Cherwell District Council's attempt to create a new village, of up to 1,900 units, largely comprising self-build and custom-build homes. That project is detailed below (Case 6.1).

Figure 6.1 Graven Hill self-build village, Bicester, South Oxfordshire. © Iqbal Hamiduddin.

Case 6.1: Graven Hill self-build village, South Oxfordshire

The idea of creating a complete new settlement through self-build might appear radical in the context of the developer-led industrial housing delivery processes that now prevail in the UK. But self-build of this kind was the dominant mode of settlement production in England until the late-nineteenth century. When fully realised, Graven Hill (see Figure 6.1) will be, by far, the UK's largest contemporary self-build development – an entirely new village of approximately 1,900 homes (on a 188 ha site) to the south of Bicester, South Oxfordshire – and represent a scale of rural 'self-provided housing' not seen in the country since the 'plotland' schemes of the early twentieth century (Hall and Ward, 1998).

Graven Hill is a product of both local circumstances and the impetus provided by central government's localism agenda. This part of Oxfordshire has endured acute housing pressures in recent years, which have resulted from the usual development constraints and the demand pressures associated with the county's accessibility to London. Its smaller settlements have struggled to deliver the sorts of housing opportunities required by local households and the county's growing population. Against this backdrop, the closure of the Graven Hill military depot site, and plans for its subsequent disposal by the Ministry of Defence (MOD), provided the local authority, Cherwell District Council, with a significant opportunity to bring forward a model of housing delivery that was acknowledged to be potentially much more affordable than standard developer-led housing (given developers' pursuit of significant returns). Crucially, the local authority and its leader, Barry Wood, had the foresight and ambition to seize the opportunity presented by the site while also enjoying high-level political support from David Cameron's Coalition government (2010 to 2015), which saw this kind of self-build development as being entirely consistent with the 'mutualism' that it sought to promote through its localism agenda. Graven Hill offered the government an opportunity to demonstrate what might be achieved through the 'empowerment' of local communities.

Self-build at the scale proposed at Graven Hill requires innovation across the land–planning–finance nexus. Inspiration for the scheme was drawn from the Dutch new town of Almere, where a streamlined planning and development process was applied in the

Homeruskwartier self-build district. This involved the provision of ready-to-develop serviced plots framed by a simplified permissioning process. In relation to *land*, Cherwell District Council acquired the Graven Hill site in 2011 for the sum of £38 million (suggesting a per hectare land cost substantially below the estimated post-permission cost of development land in Cherwell[2], DCLG, 2015b) and established its own council-owned delivery vehicle, Graven Hill Village Development Company (GHVDC), to perform the roles of estate developer and manager. The development company drew up a masterplan, divided the site into individual plots and provided the services – including water, sewage connection and power – needed by prospective self-builders. With regards to *planning*, the District Council granted outline planning permission for development: individual plots come with a 'plot passport' detailing the basic development requirements and constraints for each self-build home. As long as the final design of a home meets the specifications set out in the passport, detailed planning permission is guaranteed within 28 days. The successful applicant then has a two-year window in which to complete the build, during which time they are not allowed to live on-site in temporary accommodation. This is a common practice, with self-builders living in adjacent caravans, during more normal one-off self-build projects. The bar on caravans (Homebuilding and Renovating, 2021) is intended to induce speedier completions and reduce potentially negative neighbour effects. In terms of public *finance*, the local authority's financial commitment was limited to purchasing and preparing the site, with these costs (including domestic service costs) being recovered from onward sales to self-builders, registered providers and other developer groups. Finance for the purchase was raised from plot and onward land sales. Wider infrastructure contributions (for a mix of community assets and landscaping) were financed through a combination of plot sales and planning agreements reached on more conventional development elements, including Graven Hill Apartments. Overall, the up-front financial commitment by the local authority was less than that incurred by other councils taking forward more conventional schemes, involving the direct construction of homes. At Graven Hill, those costs were borne by self-builders, via private borrowing.

Individual self-builders often encounter difficulties raising mortgage finance for one-off schemes. In the case of Graven Hill, the development company created a 'one stop shop' to enable prospective builders to access land, finance and an off-the-shelf custom-build design for those wishing to bypass the design process.

The first wave of plots was released to the market in July 2016, with construction starting in early 2017. Roughly 500 units had been completed by the beginning of 2020, representing a build-out rate comparable to a housebuilder on a larger development site (Lichfields, 2016). Graven Hill has shown how local authorities can take control of development opportunities, if they commit to establishing bespoke development vehicles and tailored planning approaches. However, while homes are more affordable to first occupants than off-the-shelf housing purchased from regular housebuilders, rising resale values in an otherwise constrained market will of course prevent that dividend being passed on to future buyers (there have been few resales of self-build homes at Graven Hill since 2017, but asking prices appear broadly similar to those for similarly-sized homes in Bicester). It has been reported that besides the individuality of housing design, the potential for greater value uplift from self-build (given savings relative to purchasing from a volume builder) is a major incentive to prospective self-builders (Tanner, 2019). As with any housing, they want affordability for themselves but they also want to profit significantly from future sale. For that reason, the Graven Hill model would need to be mixed with South Shropshire-style resale capping if its affordability benefits were to be retained in perpetuity. Such restrictions could of course be applied selectively, on plots where self-builders meeting particular access criteria were granted price-concessions to aid affordability, with the cost of those concessions met through unrestricted sales. As it stands, Graven Hill's self- and custom-build homes are offered to the open market and subject to no resale restrictions. A separate element of affordable housing has been provided by Bromford Housing Association, comprising an initial wave of 32 two-, three- and four-bedroom shared ownership homes. The scale of the Graven Hill project means that it can support a range of housing types for builders on a range of budgets: cost savings are achievable through design and material choices. Smaller projects in villages, however, perhaps taken forward by CLTs, may need to think about how cost and social benefits are sustained for successive occupiers.

Sources: Homebuilding and Renovating: https://www.homebuilding.co.uk/advice/graven-hill

Graven Hill Village Development Company: https://www.gravenhill.co.uk/resources/planning-permission/
Lichfields (2016): https://lichfields.uk/media/1728/start-to-finish.pdf
iNews (Tanner): https://inews.co.uk/inews-lifestyle/money/self-build-house-profit-graven-hill-oxfordshire-247794
Conservative Home: https://www.conservativehome.com/localgovernment/2018/11/barry-wood-in-britain-the-number-opting-to-build-a-home-is-way-behind-other-countries-but-not-in-cherwell.html

Although the *right to build* legislation noted above has the potential to accelerate *individual* self and custom build where authorities establish the frameworks needed to facilitate easier access to land and finance, *community build projects* have been a more common means of delivering lower cost homes. This form of collective action benefits from a pooling of resources and skills, which plays a critical part in reducing build costs. It also delivers something distinctly different from individual self-build: the opportunity to consolidate community ties, rooted in both a shared need and a shared approach to addressing that need.

Community build projects

Self-build has clear potential in small village locations. Individually designed and constructed homes can more easily 'fit in' with the existing pattern of development, which itself has been shaped by small-scale incremental additions over a number of decades or even centuries. This sort of development, often carried out by people who have the means to purchase and develop sites in the open market, can contribute positively to existing character and may be preferred over the 'standard' products bolted onto villages by regular builders. However, self-build at this scale can be expensive and only accessible to wealthier individuals. There is also no guarantee that it will be in keeping with the village. Much depends on the taste of the self-builder and on the strength of local planning controls. Individual self-build, unless orchestrated at greater scale, is a socially exclusive housing pathway in more expensive villages. The more affordable option is often *community build*, facilitated by the release of land at a discounted price, via a planning exception that supports the development of affordable homes, and taken forward by an entity that is able to act on behalf of a group and access the finance or grant support needed to bring down development costs. Different delivery models are available to community-build projects, ranging from cohousing to collaborative ventures that deliver individual homes (see Field, 2020). Such delivery models can be led by community land trusts, which then employ a resident-managed leasehold model to ensure that homes remain affordable over the longer term.

Self-build or self-commissioning is clearly complementary to the community ethos of the models examined in Chapter 4. Besides positive 'place making' effects (Hamiduddin, 2017), getting together and building bespoke homes with friends and neighbours is likely to foster a sense of rootedness and co-operative sociability that no other form of housing production can offer (Field, 2020). There is considerable interest, worldwide, in the different models of collaborative or community-led housing that range from the creation of 'intentional community' through cohousing (Field *et al*, 2021), to looser 'deliberative' models such as Germany's collective-build or *Baugruppen*, where groups of people come together to build homes on land allocated for that purpose, pooling skills, time and resources. *Baugruppen*, or 'building groups', are not community land trusts. Once the homes are completed, land title for separate units passes to individual owners. Assuming land was purchased freehold, by the group, some form of share of freehold will become the basis of ownership. Homes are not 'affordable' in the sense used in the UK (that is land- or grant-subsidy-dependent), although this route to ownership, like other models of self- or custom-build may have been more affordable to the participants than regular off-the-shelf purchase, given the labour input they themselves have provided and the avoidance of the developers' premium.

But unless there is a mechanism for suppressing and retaining future resale value – of the type employed in South Shropshire, where a title clause requires that homes are offered to the market at no more than 60 per cent of market value for six months – any affordability will be lost once a home is resold. Restrictive covenants are one means of protecting the affordability of units where first occupiers benefited from some form of land or build subsidy. Perhaps a more comprehensive approach is for a land trust to co-ordinate the group build and, once homes are completed, for that trust to retain an ownership share that allows it to control onward sale. Some analyses of the German model caution that 'community build' can be a source of conflict as much as harmony (Obremski and Carter, 2019: 189–90), with close and prolonged co-working becoming a cause of personal antagonism, sometimes resulting in the collapse of groups and people walking away from schemes.

The co-ordination provided by a community land trust, and the arms-length involvement of co-ordinating trustees, may resolve this issue. It is often the case that CLT-based schemes, including some of those detailed in Chapter 4, already include an element of self-build. Trusts either commission sub-contractors to undertake construction or renovation (of buildings being converted or returned to residential use), or ask future residents to do some of the work themselves (usually just

Figure 6.2 Forgebank Cohousing, Halton, Lancashire. © Luke Mills.

the labouring, leaving highly skilled work to specialists). The 'intended occupier builds or commissions' principle is implicit in all genuine self-build, but in the case of community schemes led by CLTs, there may also be an element of training provided – including for National Vocational Qualifications (NVQ) – that targets the upskilling of participants with a view to enhancing their future employability. CLTs can access grant funding to reduce build costs, but if they do not wish to partner a registered provider (see Chapter 4), then self-build offers another means of achieving greater affordability, at least for first occupants. Many of these features, and considerations, are illustrated in the case of Forgebank Cohousing (Case 6.2).

Case 6.2: The cohousing model: Forgebank Cohousing, Halton, Lancashire

The impetus for cohousing schemes differs from other self- and custom-build models because they are more explicitly concerned with creating an enduring community that shares common resources. These 'intentional communities' aim to balance a desire for privacy and independence with the communality, and social interaction, that comes from sharing certain spaces and facilities. In a rural context, cohousing schemes can appear to mimic the sociability and mutualism attributed by some to 'traditional' village life. Shared spaces substitute (or complement) the pubs or village halls that provide venues for regular community events. But like traditional housing, homes within a cohousing scheme tend to be fully independent, with their own kitchens, living rooms and outdoor spaces. The shared spaces that mark them out as cohousing schemes will include communal gardens, workshops, and even bookable guest bedrooms. Cohousing schemes are typically home to between 20 to 40 households – small enough for residents to get to know each other, and even share group meals, but large enough to maintain support for a regular schedule of activities (Field *et al*, 2021). Larger cohousing schemes, such as those found in Denmark – where the modern cohousing model originated – are often divided into sub-units, each with its own common house and attendant facilities. In keeping with the communal ethos, individual homes are usually leasehold, with the freehold maintained by a cohousing group (set up as a community interest company or similar) or sometimes by a separate land trust.

Forgebank Cohousing – located in the village of Halton, three miles to the east of Lancaster (see Figure 6.2) – is an example of a larger cohousing scheme, comprising 41 homes of mixed size and tenure, and housing a community of 61 adults and 17 children (Lancaster Cohousing, 2021a). Halton is the larger of two settlements within the parish of Halton-with-Aughton. It had a resident population of 2,227 at the 2011 Census. The project's founding group aimed to create a fully sustainable community rooted in the cohousing model. Thirty-five of the homes are leased on 999-year terms, with the freehold retained by Lancaster Cohousing Ltd, a resident-owned not-for-profit company, while the remaining six were offered to the market freehold – as a source of cross-subsidy for the project (see below).

The scheme is sometimes referred to as 'Lancaster Cohousing', a name that hints at its origin. The founding resident group came together in 2006 with the aim of developing homes in the city of Lancaster. The group sought to purchase land from British Waterways for its development, but the sale stalled and collapsed after the vendor switched from a private sale to an open tendering process. After that, the group struggled for a number of years to secure an alternative site within the city. Such struggles are a common experience of collaborative build and community housing groups, particularly in the UK, where there is limited familiarity with these models and few support structures (Hamiduddin, 2017). The earliest groups often tried to bid for land as loose collectives of private buyers, but many soon realised that they needed to form community interest or benefit companies in order to be taken seriously when bidding for development land. After several rounds of land search, Lancaster Cohousing Ltd identified a site adjacent to the River Lune at Forge Bank Mill, or Halton Mills as it was then known. The site lacked current planning permission for residential use, but a condition on future re-use stipulated that the existing mill would need to be used commercially (which was a clear deterrent against regular commercial redevelopment of the site, thereby suppressing the value of the land). Lancaster Cohousing carefully considered the implications of this and worked on developing a viable business plan for the mill. Taking account of these hurdles, the group agreed to purchase the site (split across three separate land titles) in 2011 from its private owner for £600,000, plus VAT.

Much of the cash needed for land acquisition and legal fees was provided by group members (13 households bank-transferred the cash to Lancaster Cohousing in the days before the purchase), but development finance was sought from specialist lenders including the Co-operative and Triodos banks, which required the group to meet stringent housing pre-sale terms and conditions. The outright freehold sale of six homes, noted above, provided the group with roughly £1 million of the necessary £8 million of development finance. The group was also successful in obtaining grants to support the redevelopment of the old mill building into a community hub and to establish a renewable energy scheme on the site, comprising a mix of solar, biomass and hydroelectricity. Group members worked directly on the scheme's communal projects, contributing 'sweat equity' as a means of reducing the overall development cost. Discounts on homes, reflecting early risk-taking (in the form of contributions to the land purchase prior to planning permission being granted) and sweat equity contributions, were agreed with group members. The latter were costed at £15 per hour for management contributions and statutory minimum wage for labouring, paid in the form of deductions against members' cash contributions.

A key challenge for Lancaster Cohousing Ltd was the lack of familiarity within the local planning authority of these sorts of cohousing schemes. For that reason, the group sought to engage early and maintain a dialogue with the local planning team, with a view to raising mutual understanding of the development model, on the part of the planners, and also the detail of planning obligations, placed on the cohousing group. Planning approval was secured in 2011 and work began soon thereafter, with the main phase of development completed in 2013. This included not only the first residential units but also the renovation and reuse of the old mill building as a 'common house' (for regular communal meals and gatherings) along with a shared laundry, food larder and bike store. High ecological standards were a key part of the development vision, with all new buildings achieving the Passivhaus standard and meeting the Code for Sustainable Homes Level 6. The Forgebank Cohousing scheme is described as an 'intergenerational cohousing community, that encourages social interaction and is built on ecological values': it aspires to be an exemplar in sustainable design, with 'close links to Halton and the wider community'.

Today, the scheme is often labelled an 'eco-housing community' that has sought to offer an alternative housing model, demonstrating the potential of collective action. Some of the homes built at the early stages of the project are now being sold to new leaseholders. These are no longer 'affordable homes': indeed, Lancaster Cohousing notes that the houses at Forgebank 'normally sell for more than equivalent, more conventional, homes because of the added value of the facilities that come with them'. The average sale price of homes in Halton in the year to November 2021 was just under £270,000. Two-bedroom freehold terraced homes can be purchased for around £150,000. The average sale price is inflated by a high proportion of larger detached properties. In comparison, two Forgebank homes were being offered to the market in late 2021 for £285,000 and £349,000 (both three bedrooms, with the latter occupying three floors). The eco-homes are significantly more expensive than similarly sized 'conventional' homes in Halton, and there is a recognition that they were far more affordable for first occupiers, many of whom 'had contributed very significantly to the creation of LCH [and therefore] paid a reduced price to take account of the 'sweat equity' value they had put in' (at the rates noted above) while others 'had taken significant financial risk over the life of the project [and] received a discount' (Lancaster Cohousing, 2021b). First occupiers choosing to sell up and relocate are able to capitalise on their sweat equity and risk taking, making self-build a 'good investment'. While this means that affordability is not retained in perpetuity, it also points to the social and economic benefits (of initial affordability and later profitability) of participation in self-build community housing projects. Even ones where affordability is not protected over the long term have a part to play in helping group builders access homeownership at a lower cost.

Sources: Lancaster Cohousing (2021a): https://lancastercohousing.org.uk/About
Lancaster Cohousing (2021b): https://lancastercohousing.org.uk/join/HomesForSaleOrRent
NaCSBA (2021): https://selfbuildportal.org.uk/case-studies/lancaster-co-housing-project/
Detailed Project Timeline: https://miro.com/app/board/o9J_lfolEog=/

Low-impact 'one planet' development

Low-impact development (LID), in its current forms, gained popularity in the 1980s. Early examples met with opposition from local councils, which regularly took enforcement action against low-impact homes built by lifestyle downshifters without the requisite planning permission or because of their failure to meet standard building regulations. Fairlie (1996) has tracked the evolution of the modern LID movement across the UK, defining it as 'development that through its low impact either enhances or does not significantly diminish environmental quality' (Fairlie, 1996; xiv). LID is offered as an alternative to conventional development, being more affordable to construct and aiming, through the use of local materials and traditional building techniques, to blend in with rural landscapes. It is not a solution to housing need in all situations and, unlike other 'models' examined in this book, is as much a *way of life* as a development approach or model. However, it is often suited to highly sensitive landscapes and illustrates how community access to land and flexible planning can combine to deliver unexpected housing opportunities.

Maxey (2009: 8) attributes the following characteristics to LID: locally adaptive, diverse and unique; made from natural, local materials; of an appropriate scale; visually unobtrusive; enhancing bio-diversity; based on renewable resources; autonomous in terms of energy, water and waste; increasing public access to open space; generating little traffic; linked to sustainable livelihoods; and co-ordinated by a management plan.

There are numerous examples of LID across the UK, which range from the more peculiar builds to ones that appear more outwardly conventional – albeit with very clear 'eco' credentials – and perhaps with potential to be mainstreamed. A few are single buildings – including 'That Roundhouse' at Brithdir Mawr in Pembrokeshire, whose infamy (owing to protracted planning disputes) turned it from *'The'* to *'That' Roundhouse*. Others comprise entire model developments including

Figure 6.3 Community hub at Tir-y-Gafel, Pembrokeshire. © Tao Paul Wimbush.

Hockerton Housing Project in Nottinghamshire, *Findhorn Ecovillage* in Moray, Scotland, and *Lammas Ecovillage*, again in Pembrokeshire (see case 6.3 below). Planning policy has taken considerable time to catch up with the demand for LID, often in more isolated rural areas that have been attractive to lifestyle downshifters for several decades. The National Planning Policy Framework for England (MHCLG, 2021c) makes no mention of low impact development and dedicates only a few lines to rural housing: planning needs to be 'responsive to local circumstances', and this might of course open the door to innovation or alternative development models, but there is no clear presumption in favour of doing things differently. In relation to broader economic development, the following line offers some hope to advocates of new ways of serving communities: 'sites to meet local business and community needs in rural areas may have to be found adjacent to or beyond existing settlements, and in locations that are not well served by public transport. In these circumstances it will be important to ensure that development is sensitive to its surroundings, does not have an unacceptable impact on local roads and exploits any opportunities to make a location more sustainable (for example by improving the scope for access on foot, by cycling or by public transport)' (MHCLG, 2021c: Para. 85). Evidence suggests that the demand for alternative ways of living in rural areas has focused outside of England, especially in Wales.

Case 6.3: Low-impact development in Wales: Tir-y-Gafel, Pembrokeshire

Lammas eco-hamlet in Pembrokeshire, or *Tir-y-Gafel* in Welsh, has achieved considerable fame as a trailblazing low-impact development whose struggle to gain planning consent contributed to the development of the Welsh national 'One Planet Development' policy, later integrated into the Welsh Government's Technical Advice Note (TAN) 6. The overall vision of the scheme was to support a 'return to the land' for nine households who would be able to derive three-quarters of their income from small scale agricultural activities on their own smallholdings on the site, and enable the households to live off-grid in self-built low impact dwellings constructed from local, sustainable materials and using traditional construction methods. Although small, and relatively isolated, the scheme is in keeping with the prevailing settlement pattern of farming-based hamlets and small villages in this part of west Wales.

The scheme was taken forward by Lammas Low-Impact Initiatives Ltd, an organisation that grew from the environmental concerns of its members and which was formally instituted as a co-operative in 2007, enabling its growing body of members to invest and become shareholders in a range of socially and environmentally focused initiatives. The Lammas proposal for Tir-y-Gafel sought to capitalise on local planning policy support, set out in Policy 52 of Pembrokeshire's Joint Unitary Development Plan, adopted in 2006, for low-impact development. The policy established the principle of permitting low-impact development that was able to pass eight key tests relating to its environmental, social and economic contribution alongside public benefit; the low use of resources; the re-use of existing buildings where feasible; integration into the landscape and no adverse visual effects; engage with agriculture, forestry and/or horticulture in a countryside location; provide a sufficient livelihood for residents on site; involve a number of adults sufficient to run the enterprise; and be operated by a trust, co-operative or similar structure where more than one family is on site. The Lammas group was able to pass these tests, although Policy 52 was intended to support more traditional agricultural practice rather than the permaculture proposed at *Tir-y-Gafel*. A planning application for the site (2007) alongside a management plan (2008) detailed how the project would make a positive and sustainable contribution to the local area (Lammas, 2021a, b). The application ran to 800 pages but was refused on technical grounds that were disputed by the group, prompting two further applications before the project received approval in August 2009 following a Welsh Government public hearing. Despite the council's support for low impact development in the county, the form of proposed development at *Tir-y-Gafel* – self-built homes using an array of locally sourced materials and not conforming to any contemporary vernacular – was disliked by many critics. The leader of Pembrokeshire County Council, John Davis, condemned the decision to approve the scheme as 'setting a dangerous precedent' (Wimbush, 2009).

Lammas's purchase of the 31-hectare *Tir-y-Gafel* site, for which it had agreed a sale option from Gafel Farm on condition of planning approval, was financed through the upfront sale of the nine 999-year smallholding leases on the site. Because the land was not permissioned for a conventional build, the purchase cost did not exceed agricultural value and the smallholders were left to finance their own builds. However, further fundraising was needed to cover the cost of building a community hub as the heart of the scheme (see Figure 6.3), a hydro-power generator and infrastructure that included access roads and a children's playground. The group also needed to purchase a minibus. These costs were mostly met through the support of shareholders and money raised from 'friends' of the co-operative. Additional income was raised from television companies, which were keen to feature the eco-community in their programming.

Despite the early difficulties in obtaining planning permission, Lammas has been able to largely fulfil its vision of a low impact, off-grid and production-based 'eco-hamlet'. The significance of the scheme lies in its demonstration of an alternative way of living in rural areas, linking the building of admittedly unconventional homes with sustainable, land-based livelihoods. *Tir-y-Gafel* helped transform planning policy in Wales. It was an important step on the road to TAN 6's support for low-impact development and provided a model for other off-grid eco-villages (Forde, 2017). While neither the homes built nor the lifestyles lived may be to everyone's taste, the lesson here is that planning can adapt to a broader set of aspirations and lend support to less intensive patterns of settlement.

Sources: Lammas (2021a): https://lammas.org.uk/en/welcome-to-lammas/
Lammas (2021b): https://lammas.org.uk/en/research/ (Tolle, J. (2011) Towards sustainable development in the countryside? A case study of the first eco-hamlet under Pembrokeshire Planning Policy 52, Unpublished Dissertation, Swansea University)
Wimbush (2009): The Process: Lammas's experience of the planning system December 2006 – August 2009. Lammas Low Impact Initiatives Ltd.

Popular presentations of sustainable development and sustainable living frequently cite evidence that the human footprint, the consumption of land and resources, is larger than the entire planet. The lack of a 'planet B' is a rallying call for many environmental campaigns. These debates have prompted the idea of 'one planet' development or living. Numerous groups are now pushing this agenda: these include Bioregional's 'one planet living vision', the global 'one planet network', technology-based solutions from 'oneplanet.com', the 'one planet summit' in Paris in 2019, and Wales's 'one planet council' – supporting one planet developments of various kinds. The label has become ubiquitous. It references a mode of living that acknowledges the need to live within the Earth's resource capacity by reining back prevailing patterns and levels of consumption. The various groups listed above have advanced proposals as to how we can all live within resource limits, by adopting green technologies and promoting low-impact development (Obremski and Carter, 2019: 11).

It was noted above that the movement has gained particular traction in Wales, building on a long tradition of embracing alternative technologies and lifestyles. Harris (2019: 32) notes that, since devolution, the Welsh Government has looked to deviate from English planning practice, supporting models of development that are more embedded in Welsh contexts and connect with particular opportunities for living differently in Wales. Many of its one planet developments, supported through the granting of 'exceptions' to standard planning practice, seek different human–nature relationships that protect biodiversity and promote landscape restoration. In the few schemes that have progressed, there has been a focus on new forms of self-built housing development in the open countryside. Indeed, after years of local wrangling, the Welsh Government published a 'One Planet Development' practice guidance note in 2012, which drew inspiration from policy development and local projects in Pembrokeshire (see Case 6.3). General Policy on rural planning is contained in TAN6 – on planning for sustainable rural communities. That policy, alongside the broader Planning Policy Wales, serves up the usual edict that 'development in the countryside should be located within and adjoining settlements and that new building in the open countryside away from existing settlements should be strictly controlled'. But the One Planet Development guidance, which is a companion to TAN6, deviates from that general approach and is focused on 'One Planet Development in rural locations outside existing settlements' (Welsh Government, 2012: Para. 1.2).

Along with TAN6, it defines 'one planet development' as being both a physical imprint and lifestyle that ensures a much lighter ecological footprint and does not diminish environmental quality. These developments are light touch, are land-based and provide for the complete needs of residents within five years, have a low and prescribed ecological footprint, have very low carbon buildings, are defined and controlled by a binding management plan and must be the sole residence of proposed occupants. These one planet developments look very much like the LID described by Fairlie and later writers, including Maxey.

Although LID is clearly an outlier in this book, the philosophy it embodies and the corresponding flexibility required whenever off-grid development proposals meet standardised planning processes, offers lessons for a broader array of development types. When the usual planning straitjacket is loosened, rural areas are able to embrace land-use and development models that can contribute positively to wider societal goals. Where projects lessen the carbon footprint, there is a strong case for flexible planning to support a combination of social objectives and environmental priorities: affordable homes on farmland released either at close to agricultural value (because of the retained restriction on any regular build) or at a significantly discounted price relative to full development value (because of rules on occupation, and land-based production, that can be expected to severely limit the market for the offered lifestyle). It is the *niche nature* of these types of affordable homes and lifestyles, and related public benefit from carbon reduction, which makes it *reasonable*, relative to the desire to preserve the openness and character of rural areas, to offer these flexibilities in response to the regular nexus of land–planning–finance constraints and the legitimate desire to live differently in the countryside. LID requires a radical rethinking of planning constraint.

As with the 'standard' site exceptions approach, land that would not otherwise be available for housing needs to be made available – and the cost of that land must be kept low, enabling wide project participation. Community ownership of land, through a trust or co-operative structure, provides the means of long-term stewardship, although in the case of LID it is the management plan and required participation in land-based production or site maintenance, rather than any restrictive covenant on forward sale, which ensures the long-term affordability of homes. It does so by tightly limiting the appeal/possibility of living in an eco-community for the many people whose livelihoods are tied to the conventional economy. This is true in the case of *Tir-y-Gafel* above and also, to some extent, in the more conventional build represented here by Hockerton Housing Project (Case 6.4).

Figure 6.4 Low impact housing at Hockerton, Nottinghamshire.
© Rob Annable. CC BY-NC-SA 2.0.

Case 6.4: Low-impact housing at Hockerton, Nottinghamshire

Hockerton Housing Project is a small scheme of five highly sustainable homes set in a 10-hectare site (comprising a lake and small reservoir, cultivated areas, an orchard and areas hosting wind turbines), on the edge of the village of Hockerton in Nottinghamshire (see Figure 6.4). Like the later Lammas project at *Tir-y-Gafel* (see case 6.3), the Hockerton scheme is an exemplar of 'holistically sustainable' rural LID. The founding group set out to create '[…] a community that was sustainable in all senses of the word: environmentally and without sacrifice to Western standards of living. Common to most 'eco' buildings is the idea that we need to use as little energy as possible; and the energy we do use needs to be sustainable' (EBuilding, 2017). The scheme was initiated by Nick Martin, an experienced builder of low-energy buildings, who purchased the site in the early 1990s with the intention of developing a demonstration project. A core group of prospective residents, initially comprising friends and relatives, was expanded to include those responding to a call for participants. Early ideas for the scheme were sketched out in 1993. Nick Martin had previously collaborated with Brenda and Robert Vale, 'green architects' and authors of 'The Autonomous House' (Vale and Vale, 1975), which provides a guide to constructing energy-self-sufficient homes with a conventional appearance. The Vales were commissioned to provide the design for Hockerton, proposing earth-sheltered homes that benefit from high thermal mass and reduced visual and ecological impact.

Securing planning consent proved to be a significant challenge, despite the enthusiastic support of the local authority's chief architect (NaCSBA, 2021). Few authorities at that time had experience with low-impact development and even the underpinning principles of sustainable development and build were in their infancy. Discussions with the local planning authority – Newark and Sherwood District Council – were therefore protracted, which triggered a loss and turnover of group members. Local authority planners expressed concerns over the 'loss' of productive agricultural land and doubts over the technical feasibility of the scheme. However, in August 1996, the advice offered to the planning committee was that the project at Hockerton would make a positive contribution to sustainable development, taking into account the social and environmental activities being proposed, and the emphasis being placed on limiting ecological impact. Indeed, the land management plan that formed part of the planning application included a provision to limit car ownership and require each household to contribute 300 hours of volunteer time to maintain the site each year. The obligations to be placed on residents were broadly set out in a Section 106 agreement, with requirements detailed in accompanying documents and in the management plan. These were then incorporated into the leasehold agreement for each individual home. The freehold for the site is retained by Hockerton Housing Project Ltd.

The project was developed as a group self-build, project-managed by Nick Martin and the architects. The group set up a temporary legal entity to oversee the build, *Hockerton Housing*, comprising one member from each prospective household. Approximately half of the construction work was undertaken directly by group members, and the other half by contractors under the project manager's supervision. This arrangement kept the cost of the build relatively low: £65,000 for all five homes at 1998 prices. Each household financed the building of their own home. At a project level, the infrastructure comprising the main access road, reservoir and lake, and the visitor centre completed in 2004, were originally paid for by a loan from the Co-operative Bank, later refinanced with mortgages from the Ecology Building Society. The specialist nature of the design and build, and associated risks, meant that standard high street borrowing was not an option for Hockerton Housing Project.

Overall, although energy use has been higher than originally forecast – in part because of the teenagers living on the site and the greater level of working from home than anticipated – homes at Hockerton Housing Project use only 10 per cent of the energy of typical UK housing. The project has also successfully maintained its community ethos and is widely regarded as a vanguard project that has helped raise the profile of low impact development across the UK. An important epilogue, however, relates to the loss of affordability incurred at resale. At the time of writing (November 2021), one of the homes was on sale for close to £400,000. This is about 10 per cent higher than the per-foot cost of a conventional home in Hockerton, and many multiples of the build cost in 1998. One explanation for this loss of affordability is that although quite 'onerous' conditions are placed on leaseholders, the queue of buyers for this type of property and lifestyle in England has been substantially lengthened by growing environmental awareness and by the rarity of this sort of opportunity. If such schemes become more commonplace then the cost of participation can be expected to fall substantially.

Sources: Diggers and Dreamers (2021): https://diggersanddreamers.org.uk/community/hockerton-housing-project/
EBuilding Blog (2017): https://ebuilding.blog/hockerton-housing-project
Hockerton Housing Project (2021): https://www.hockertonhousingproject.org.uk/about-us/faq/
NaCSBA (2021): https://selfbuildportal.org.uk/case-studies/case-studies-hockerton/

Local authority-led village housing

New models of local authority-led housing were introduced and briefly discussed in the last chapter and also touched upon in Case 6.1, involving Cherwell District Council's creation of a council-owned development company to deliver the Graven Hill self-build scheme. Local authorities were once important contributors to affordable housing supply in rural locations, proving critical support to rural economies (see Chapter 3). Through the Local Housing Company (LHC) model, they may come to play an important role again. Morphet and Clifford (2017: 62) observe that 'those authorities engaging in housing provision tend to have larger populations, with more staff, and higher housing need. However, it is important to note that housing delivery and housing companies are not just the province of large local authorities. *Many smaller, rural councils are successfully building housing each year, and many of these wish to increase their output of properties'*. Local authorities are building across all tenures (Morphet and Clifford, 2017: 48), but it is not absolutely clear where that building is happening from available evidence: whether concentrated in larger towns or dispersed to smaller sites. North Kesteven District Council, in Lincolnshire, is a largely rural authority that is blighted by relatively high levels of reported homelessness. During the period of the HRA debt cap (between 2012 and 2018) it became frustrated by its inability to directly build new council homes (Morphet and Clifford, 2017: 24). In response, it set up its own housing company – Lafford Homes – to provide private rented accommodation. It struggled to secure land for development but eventually reached an agreement with a local owner and built 27 homes for rent. Through its company, the council planned to secure more sites for housing and also purchase existing homes for private letting to local people. But the focus of its efforts is in Lincoln or nearby towns including North Hykeham (population around 14,000).

Brown and Bright (2018) have noted at least a partial village focus for some housing companies, claiming that council housebuilding and companies can overcome a private sector 'reluctance to consider the provision of affordable rented homes in specific locations such as villages' (p. 34). For that reason, companies in rural areas have been directed to search for sites, often very small sites, which 'could potentially enable better matching of [new housing] to geographical housing need' (p. 30). These authors cite several examples of council-led village housing delivery. In the East Riding of Yorkshire, for instance, the local authority is drawing from its HRA (there is no company) to purchase land for construction and to buy Section 106 properties from developers. Brown and Bright note that 'if need is identified in a small village, the council can consider buying a single property for refurbishment and letting' (p. 53). It works with a rural housing enabler to facilitate these actions (p. 54). Northumberland is another example of an authority with a village focus, promoting 'sustainable economies and communities' and emphasising the needs of older residents. In the seven years to 2015, the council built 288 homes, but noted 'high land values in rural and coastal areas' as a particular impediment to providing affordable homes (p. 57). Although much of its programme was funded from the HRA (and again, not via a company), it also worked with local communities (and Community Action Northumberland) to secure additional funding from the

Community Housing Fund (see Chapter 5), delivering homes that could not otherwise have been delivered, including via Section 106 contributions. Another rural example was Stroud, a rural amenity area stretching into the Cotswolds AONB with significant affordability challenges. As well as restricting the resale of properties sold under the right to buy (under Section 157 of the Housing Act 1985), Stroud District Council has been using Homes England grants and RTB receipts for new council-led building. Spending rules allow it to re-use those receipts, totalling almost £2.5 million in 2019/20, within a three-year window. A maximum of 30 per cent of the funding for new affordable rented homes can be sourced from those receipts, with the remaining 70 per cent having to come from other sources including rental income or borrowing. Stroud's strategy for new council homes is mainly focused on strategic sites and larger towns. Its approach in rural areas has been to work in partnership with communities and registered providers: '[…] the Council has recently become a member of the Gloucestershire Rural Housing Partnership for the delivery of schemes on rural exception sites and will work with the rural housing enabler to identify suitable sites to meet local need. Through that partnership it will be decided which provider is best suited to deliver schemes in each Parish' (Stroud District Council, 2020: 14). Land availability is a major constraint to local-authority led housing. The council notes that:

> The land owned by the Council which is suitable for development is a limited and finite resource and the Council also needs to identify land for purchase on the open market or by negotiation. This will need officers to be able to compete with developers for these sites and to act quickly with offers. (Stroud District Council, 2020: 8)

Public land is a focus for many councils getting back into direct build, and many projects comprise demolition and replacement of existing council homes. But once land already owned by councils is exhausted, they must join the queue of private buyers looking to acquire land for development. Stiff competition for that land causes a bidding up of prices – and high land costs means less resource available, either from council revenues or borrowing, for the actual building of affordable homes. Indeed, what emerges from recent work on council-led building is that challenges persist – around land availability, land prices and funding. Housing companies are a powerful tool for local authorities, but not an absolute panacea in rural areas. Some have prioritised land search and acquisition, seeing this as the biggest challenge. Others have focused on acquiring

Figure 6.5 CGI of new council-led development at Park Lanneves, Bodmin, Cornwall. © Treveth Holdings LLP.

existing stock, where this is not beyond their financial reach. The rural focus has been on the use of traditional mechanisms, including site exceptions, which involve multiple partners. Authorities are certainly working with community land trusts and have in some instances used their resource – including recycled funds from right to buy sales and monies borrowed from the PWLB – to fund the building of homes on land that has been brought under community ownership (Beswick *et al*, 2019: 8). Many rural schemes are hybrid, using a mix of funding pots including those for community-led projects. But authorities and housing companies can give considerable impetus to village housing projects. They are potentially powerful leaders and partners, redirecting effort and investment to rural locations, as illustrated in Case 6.5.

Case 6.5: Council-led housing delivery at Park Lanneves, Bodmin, Cornwall

It was noted in Chapter 4 that the south-west of England, and especially the county of Cornwall, has seen an acceleration of house prices in recent years, made worse by a decentralisation of housing consumption choices linked to the COVID-19 pandemic (Gallent and Madeddu, 2021), which has driven down affordability for the region's existing residents. Mulholland (2021) notes that Cornish workers typically earn 70 per cent of the average UK wage but face above-average housing costs: the in-area earnings to house price ratio is 1:14, making Cornwall one of the least affordable counties in England. Although pressures extend across the market, with recent price hikes making already expensive housing more expensive, the real pinch point for local households is felt in the private-rented sector. This is due to a long-term undersupply of rental housing and the recent transfer of many properties to short-term holiday letting, in response to burgeoning 'staycation' demand (Mullholland, 2021). It was against the backdrop of longer-term trends that Cornwall County Council took the decision to establish its own arms-length development company. Treveth Holdings LLP – *Treveth* meaning 'homestead' in Cornish – will deliver 1,000 mainly affordable homes for sale or rent by 2024, creating a new revenue stream that the council hopes will offset central government funding cuts (Cornwall County Council, 2020). The county council has a controlling share in Treveth while its partner shareholder is *Corserv*, a council-owned group of public interest businesses. Profits and income streams generated by Treveth are returned to the council: these derive from the development of open market homes, for sale and rent, and are recycled into the development of affordable housing. The first wave of homes is planned for larger villages and towns including Liskeard, Redruth, Camborne and Bodmin, where a profitable scale and mix of housing can be delivered on sites owned by the council.

The Park Lanneves scheme on the outskirts of Bodmin (see Figure 6.5) is one of Treveth's first wave local authority-led housing developments. It reuses public land – the site of the former St Lawrence Hospital – and uses market development to finance affordable homes. The 100 homes being developed at Park Lanneves comprise 60 for private letting and 10 for private sale. The remaining 30 are made up of 21 social lets and nine homes being offered for shared ownership. The objectives of the scheme are to address the shortage of private rental sector (PRS) opportunities in this part of Cornwall while adding to the county's depleted stock of council homes, available to families drawn from its local waiting list. All prospective residents, whether for the private or affordable homes, will need to demonstrate that they currently live or work in the county. Construction of the homes is being undertaken by the Midas Group: they will be compliant with forthcoming (2025) energy efficiency regulations and feature solar panels and air source heat pumps (UK Construction Online, 2021). Seasonal precarity (and price volatility) is a significant problem in Cornwall's private rental sector, with tenants sometimes offered the shortest possible assured shorthold tenancies so that landlords can switch into short lettings during the holiday seasons. Treveth's rented homes are offered on three-year renewable lets, providing a new gold standard in security of tenure (in the absence of secure tenancies) (Treveth Homes, 2021).

The comprehensive planning of new development on public land has a long history and was foundational to the delivery of new towns after the Second World War. However, as the memory of this close tie-in between land, planning and finance has faded, some critics have objected to local authorities 'marking their own homework' and even pitched the charge of 'cronyism' because of the special relationship between planning and council-owned development companies (Petherick and Sumner, 2019). Such criticism evidences how far planning has moved away from the 'spirit of 1947' when one of its main functions was to facilitate local authority development in the form of council homes and associated infrastructure. The expectation today is that it will confine itself to the fast and efficient licensing of private land development. But if there is to be a beneficial return to mixed-mode housing delivery, and greater opportunities for households to enter the non-market sector, local authorities will need to mark more of their own homework in the years ahead. Planning permission for Park Lanneves was approved with little comment or dissent, perhaps showing that council housing is back. However, reliance on *existing* public landholdings limits the reach of local authority-led housebuilding. It is confined to larger sites such as St Lawrence's Hospital or old Highways Depots. Only through exceptions mechanisms can land be brought forward for council build at a village scale. These are an inconsistent source of land in some areas, with the affordability of homes now threatened by 'first homes' policies (Chapter 4). Prioritising local authority-led build on exception sites, or bringing village land into public ownership, could extend the reach of council housing into smaller villages.

Sources: Cornwall County Council (2020): https://www.cornwall.gov.uk/media/l3cbakvb/cornwall-council-statement-of-accounts-2019-20.pdf
Treveth Homes (2021): https://www.treveth.co.uk/latest-news/treveth-starts-work-on-100-new-homes-for-bodmin/
UK Construction Online (2021): https://www.ukconstructionmedia.co.uk/market_leads/work-underway-on-100-home-bodmin-development/

But the critical constraint in all local-authority led projects is land availability and cost. Unless a site exception is agreed, rural development will in many instances be prohibitively expensive, making it difficult if not impossible to deliver affordable homes. The capital gains tax rate on land sales in the UK is lower than tax on other property sales, and less than the higher and lower income tax bands. Purchase of land on the open market will always mean that a significant share of land rent, capitalised on sale, remains in private hands. The benefit to communities – through the socialisation of that rent – is always limited where local authorities, as prospective developers, are obliged to pay intended rather than existing use value. It was noted in Case 6.5 that criticism has been levelled at local authorities for permissioning development on their own landholdings – for 'marking their own homework'. That criticism would be greatly amplified if they were able to bring farmland into public ownership and then permission it for housing use. However, this sort of 'socialisation' of rent was the cornerstone of public housing delivery for decades. The shift away from this practice marks a critical change in political priority: from public to private interest planning. That is not to say that willing landowners cannot be important partners in public projects, but where there is resistance to development that promotes social sustainability, the sorts of land reforms outlined in Chapter 5 remain an obvious means of supercharging the capacity of local authorities to enable and support affordable housing projects in villages, ensuring that a larger share of the value locked up in land can be extracted for community benefit.

Reflections

All of the activities tracked in this chapter – self-build and custom housebuilding, low impact development and local authority-led development – are already happening and each has a long and unique history. Self and custom build has recently been presented as a route to promoting an essential 'right to the city', or indeed a 'right to the rural' (see Salet *et al*, 2020). Supporting individuals and communities to meet their own needs is an important priority in rural areas and especially in villages. Land trust arrangements and the practice of self-build are closely intertwined and so there has been substantial overlap between the coverage provided in this chapter and the broader discussion of land trusts offered in Chapter 4. Community-led housing schemes that include an element of self-build capture the dual benefits of reduced development cost and potentially increased sociability, although a significant challenge, evidenced in both the conventional builds and LID, is the loss of that affordability through onward sale. Affordability is not always secured through sale restrictions or rules, although this can happen where a scheme benefited from a land subsidy or charitable grant, with the managing trust or co-operative then protecting that affordability through a planning agreement.

Because this book is not centrally concerned with the 'ecology' of rural dwelling, the examination of LID in this chapter is an outlier relative to the conventional models and concerns – of planning, land and finance – dealt with in other chapters. However, important lessons can be taken from these innovative models, some of which are transferrable to other housing projects. The first lesson is that unconventional builds offer cost benefits, especially when delivered through an element of self-build. Those cost benefits are reaped during the build itself and when a home is in occupation. Housing affordability, seen in the round, is about both capital and running costs – this is why registered providers have been installing a range of energy-saving features in their homes in recent years, although none brings the costs down to the level of the Hockerton Housing Project. The second lesson is that by making space for alternative forms of development, planning can assist those households seeking to lighten their carbon footprint to access affordable homes in rural areas. The planning framework developed by the Welsh Government has created this space. It is not without its critics, but it demonstrates that not all environmental objectives are predicated on 'strong' and inflexible planning or rooted in rural protection. Rather, flexibility offers an alternative pathway to sustainable development outcomes with potentially broader societal benefit.

Finally, local authorities have a clear leadership and enabling role to play in meeting rural housing needs. That is not to downplay the importance of community-led projects, but innovative authorities – ready to pick up the toolkit of housing options now available to them – are a crucial ally to communities. Local authority-led housing is already beginning to gain momentum. In villages, that momentum is constrained by the regular nexus of barriers noted earlier in this book. But through reform, of the types noted in Chapter 5, there will be every chance for these models to become more important in the years ahead. Council-led housebuilding programmes depend on the availability of public land and on mechanisms to bring land into public ownership. Those mechanisms have been greatly weakened over the last 60 years. Shifting the balance between public and private interest in the land market is an important political issue. The direction of travel in Wales and Scotland, exemplified by support for 'one planet' exceptions and by broader land reforms, has been markedly different from the neo-liberal market priorities that prevail in England. It is those priorities, the protection of landowner interest and inflation of private profit, which stand in the way of progressive answers to the village housing dilemma.

Notes

1. See https://householdquotes.co.uk/cost-to-build-a-house/
2. The post-permission land value estimate, per hectare, for Cherwell in 2015 (the oldest figures available) was almost £2.6 million (DCLG, 2015b), assuming 100% private housing and nil affordable housing or CIL contributions. Government land value estimates outside London assume a density of 35 units per ha.

7
A future for villages

What are the drivers for positive change and what are the barriers? Rural areas have seen incremental change in the approach to affordable housing delivery for more than a hundred years. Arguably the only radical episode in those hundred years was the advent of interwar council housing. But the overall narrative has been towards increased private consumption – given impetus by bank lending and tax policy – and often a rapid social reconfiguration of villages in amenity areas. Housing has become a financial asset, with patterns of access and cost producing deepening inequalities. The potential change driver for many countries has been the realisation that those inequalities threaten social cohesion, undermine inter-generational fairness and perpetuate unsustainable consumption. There has been a growing chorus of discontent with recent housing outcomes. The aim of this final chapter is to connect the case for change to villages. It also addresses the 'reward myth': the idea that the countryside is essentially a retirement retreat or playground for the wealthy. This myth weakens the link between community and economy, limiting the role that rural areas might play in decarbonised economic futures. Support for rural economies, and for a post-carbon transition, now provides a core rationale for ensuring wide access to affordable housing in the countryside.

Introduction

In this book we have tracked the narrative of village housing over the last hundred years through three important episodes. First, the interwar reliance on landowners to provide tied housing and post-war diversification of responses to rising housing access difficulties, including from the public and third sectors; second, recent responses that are community-led or rely on new flexibilities in planning intervention; and third, actions that disrupt established production processes: self-build, low impact development and a re-emergence of council provision. These episodes were set against a broader backdrop of structural constraint – our planning–land–tax/finance nexus – and opportunities, through reform, to reduce that constraint. The purpose of this concluding chapter is to think again about the need to intervene in village housing situations and reappraise some of the actions and opportunities highlighted in earlier chapters. We ask: why not simply leave things as they are ('let the market decide')? If changes are made, what will be their broader purpose beyond distributional justice (for rural places and economies)? What are the main prescriptions offered, and are there any alternatives? And what are the prospects for change in the years ahead?

Let the market decide

For a variety of reasons, markets have been left to distribute housing in villages. Villages are not sites of planned growth and for a long time they were not seen as contributors to wider economic well-being. Some villages are islands of neo-liberalism, bordered by hinterlands of acute development constraint. This is particularly true of villages in core amenity areas. The constraint comes from rural planning edicts that are still present in policy frameworks across much of the United Kingdom (despite Wales's support for LID in open countryside and the more permissive attitude displayed by many local authorities in Scotland) and arguably dominant in England. In that context, the market 'decides' the distribution of a constrained housing resource, supported by supercharged bank lending, historically low interest rates, and housing's preferential tax treatment relative to other assets. A range of property and rural life publications feed prospective homebuyers and investors with an irresistibly romantic view of rural property and the wider countryside. Together with other investor and home-maker targeted media, they present high-end housing investment, middle-class art and culture, elite private education, and preservation of rural life as a complete package. Refurbished farmhouses, now with tennis courts, or former farm workers' cottages knocked through to provide 300 square metres plus of living space are the quintessence of rural living. There is a complete rural economy geared to cater for this type and level of investment and consumption. Newby (1980) drew attention to its emergence in his book *Green and Pleasant Land*, pointing to the rising division between remnant agricultural communities and middle-class newcomers, who have since replaced hops and barley with grape vines and general village stores with miniature art galleries and bespoke bakeries: £7.50 for the finest European long-fermentation sourdough. The market did this, aided by planning restriction and an emphasis on preservation of amenity and the 'monumental' countryside (Abercrombie, 1926). In regions with strong economies, or those accessible to feeder regions, distributional justice is metered out by the market, bringing gentrification – of housing, lifestyles, services and educational choice. It all works very well, for those in a position to benefit, who capture equity growth in property and lifestyle advantages. This complete economy also (probably) delivers trickle-down: jobs in the bakeries, in the private schools and in the maintenance of someone else's property. This is perhaps an extreme picture of rural social change, but it is one that is certainly commonplace in lowland 'exchanging' amenity areas: in the Surrey Hills, the Chilterns, in the Cotswolds (see Figure 7.1) and in Cornwall.

Elsewhere, the same market forces produce different outcomes: either a watered-down version of the above or a lack of investment in rural amenities in left-behind rural places, where schools and services have been centralised and no decent quality housing is available. Public intervention – *deciding to not let the market decide* – will look very different in different places. In amenity areas, land prices are set by a strong market. Any attempt to build housing without some circumvention of normal land market 'rules' will be confronted by the near-insurmountable hurdle of cost, meaning that either no affordable homes can be built or the number delivered is far less than the number needed. In other areas, low in perceived amenity and with little to attract market entrants, local authorities will ponder the logic of investments that aim to anchor communities rather than consolidate people and services in larger towns.

The distributional justice argument – intervene to prevent people and places from being left behind – is a strong one, but also needs scaffolding with an underlying community and economic logic. The distribution of a resource so vital to the well-being of people in rural areas can surely not be left to the market: but what is the wider benefit – *the case* – for doing things differently?

A post-carbon rural

Two years ago, the global economy was on the cusp of change: the pace of that change has arguably been accelerated by the COVID-19 crisis. It

Figure 7.1 Cottages in Wroxton, Oxfordshire. © Elena Gallent Madeddu.

has brought the realisation that things really can go wrong. It has provided a glimpse of what real crisis looks like and the implications it has on everyday life. The coronavirus pandemic has been followed by economic recession, but also by an opportunity to move more rapidly towards a greening of the global economy, thereby forestalling the more catastrophic crisis of climate change. Not all countries will grasp that opportunity. The failure of leadership will remain a defining image of 2020.

A former US president quipped, in May 2020, that the crisis had 'torn back the curtain' on poor leadership, with a lot of leaders not 'even pretending to be in charge' (Burch and Eligson, 2020). This is likely to mean that vested economic interests will continue to steer economic policy and direction in some countries, but many democracies do appear ready to embrace change: signs of a post-carbon future are now visible. How can rural areas make a full contribution to that future?

Rural areas need economic futures, not only for their own residents, but as a means of greening national economies. This point has been made by Phillips and Dickie (2019): *post-carbon ruralities,* with rural areas contributing very significantly towards climate goals, are possible but also contested. Present patterns of high-end consumption are a direct challenge to that contribution, squeezing out alternative ways of living, promoting car dependency (which is high among affluent residents and weekenders), increasing rural living costs in general and housing costs more specifically, reducing labour supply (for new industries) and resulting in competing narratives of rurality and rural futures.

Those competing narratives are of the rural as a *playground* – 'a place of consumption for new second homeowners, tourists, food consumers' – or as a *post-carbon landscape* and 'site for the (often contested) deployment of renewable energy – wind farms, solar farms, biomass' (Gallent and Scott, 2017). Linked to the latter, the rural is portrayed as a *supplier of eco-system services,* providing functions and services essential to human well-being, from recreation to flood alleviation or carbon storage (Gallent and Scott, 2017).

There are a mix of imageries here: the playground narrative brings together high-end consumption with nostalgia for an imagined rural past (of the type found in property and rural life media), where 'authenticity' depends on limiting development and change, preserving ('in aspic') the heritage of the landscape and promoting versions of middle-class lifestyle imported from suburbia. The post-carbon narrative has two components: the first is concerned with ecological footprint, how people live, produce and consume. That part of the story is faithfully captured in Wales's promotion of 'one planet development', with communities shunning modern consumption habits and finding ways to become increasingly self-sufficient. The second component advances the narrative of a working countryside, but with agriculture paired with green industries and managed ecosystem services. That narrative needs a workforce and the workforce needs access to housing and essential services. High-end consumption and the preservation emphasis of rural planning is not compatible with either part of a post-carbon green future. So here is the economic logic, or scaffolding, for distributional justice in the housing market. Sometimes that justice is already very close to being achieved or is not the major concern of planning. Elsewhere, injustice is very keenly felt. But everywhere, competing narratives of the rural are present. Lobby groups tend to generalise the diversity of spatial realities, arguing broadly for emphasis on protection or on the pursuit of new economic opportunity. Planning policy – or the policy that frames local discretion in the United Kingdom – tends to be vague on how to balance these perspectives, asking local authorities to look case-by-case at local situations. Where consumption interests are dominant, consumption – or *playground* agendas – take root; elsewhere, the desire to promote economic opportunity tends to be stronger.

The obvious repost to this is that some rural areas are suited to new development trajectories, including green industries, and others are not. Areas of landscape amenity, peppered with heritage villages, need protection from obtrusive development. But the combination of that protection, including constraints on housing supply, and rampant market demand for housing and amenity generates an exclusive form of rurality – and the overriding dominance of a singular narrative. Our argument is that there needs to be room for different, overlapping and co-existing narratives: which support social inclusion and a right to share in rural resources, including the housing resource.

Tackling inequalities

What prescriptive conclusions are we offering? Inequalities in housing access are a barrier to realising the post-carbon future envisaged above. In its place, we will have a future of high-end inessential consumption that limits the future potential and contribution of rural areas to the greening of national economies. The obvious general prescription is for governments to change the narrative, placing new emphasis on climate goals and the sorts of rural development that contribute to achieving those goals: there is certainly scope in England for government to be less ambiguous on this front, including in its drafting of planning reforms. But our concern has been with direct actions, which create new opportunities for households to access affordable homes while, simultaneously, calming those patterns of consumption that cause a bidding up of rural land and house prices. We have considered action on four fronts:

First, *planning* that leads on understanding the varied needs of rural places and especially villages; that invests in rural housing and planning enablers; that promotes more community involvement in rural planning – rejecting deregulation but allowing communities to actively pursue deviations from generalised planning approaches ('community exceptions'); and that frees small village locations from general prescription and top down solution, allowing them to define their own development trajectories.

Second, a reorientation of *land* rights towards public and community actors by reforming current compulsory purchase and compensation arrangements. Essentially, allow communities to acquire land at closer to current use or agricultural value for community projects or 100 per cent affordable housing (rebadged *community housing* and genuinely affordable to those who need it).

Third, change the incentives for housing consumption and especially inessential consumption. Through a palette of *tax reforms*, it is possible to restructure the housing market and prioritise the needs of full-time residents. The greatest positive effect on rural markets might be achieved through an equalisation of personal tax liability on assets and payroll income: so un-earnt capital gains charged at the personal tax rate. Similarly, an extension of council tax bands to better reflect the value of high-end property, and also impact levies on second homes, are likely to shrink the queue of market entrants looking for rural property, and therefore act on the price of both housing and land (sweetening the pill of land reform for landowners). There is a more general argument that imputed rent, capitalised on sale, should be taxed – through capital gains on first homes. The logic here is that 'income' is not derived from workplace earnings alone but from a mix of asset-based earnings and payroll. Income and wealth inequalities could be closed through taxes on housing. But this argument is more complex and opens up a wider debate on the structure of the economy and the role of housing therein. Even taxes on second homes are controversial, as we note below.

And fourth, *community action* has a key role to play in opening up housing opportunities in small village locations. It needs consistent funding. There is a strong case for the extension and expansion of the Community Housing Fund (or future equivalent) and also government support for flexible lending arrangements to Community Land Trusts and similar entities. Land reform and impact levies on second homes could also provide local authorities with opportunities to grow housing delivery and acquisition in villages, forming part of a broader finance package to support local authority-led housing.

Through this programme, or something similar, rural housing markets can be opened up. Village housing for working households, for full time residents, will be instrumental in supporting a wider spectrum of rural narratives.

An obtainable future?

Is any of this achievable? Village housing in amenity areas has considerable investment value. Owners regularly demonstrate their readiness to defend the status quo (Coelho *et al*, 2017). On the other hand, many rural residents and communities are working to secure more sustainable futures, in which workers on lower and average wages are helped to secure good quality affordable housing through community-led projects and acceptance of innovative planning interventions. And yet, limited interventions are not a threat to asset values. Some of the most prized and expensive homes are in amenity villages. While some non-market housing is provided in villages, most is directed to market towns and other service centres. There has been a significant social reconfiguration of rural places during the last 50 years. Small local projects do not change the overall direction of travel towards significant rural gentrification, with a large part of the rural housing stock becoming increasingly expensive and exclusive. The village housing challenge tracks the general housing crisis, sharing both its supply and consumption components. Achieving a level of supply in villages that would significantly and meaningfully deflate house prices is not going to happen. It would undermine amenity and risk the heritage those villages embody. This means that the 'housing crisis' in villages is weighted towards the demand side (homes removed from local and full-time use) and that is arguably where resolution must be sought.

The COVID-19 pandemic of 2020–2 illustrated the appetite of many people, around the world, to consume rural housing. Insane images of rural flight – hundreds of thousands of people leaving cities and decamping to second homes and holiday lets in nearby countryside – evidenced the scale of amenity-driven consumption of rural housing. The immediate concern, in March and April 2020, was the potential for this exodus to spread infection and overload rural healthcare services (see Gallent, 2020; Gallent and Hamiduddin, 2021). But the lasting concern is for the way in which rural housing markets are structured by the 'symbolic violence' of market choice, and the exercise of class-based market power, which excludes and drives gross inequality (Gallent and Madeddu, 2021; Goode, 2021). Rural society has been in a state of flux for at least the last 50 years. There is no simple binary between local and non-local households and trying to confer housing rights based on length of residence or family connection is, quite understandably, a contentious and difficult undertaking (see Rogers, 1985). However, the distinction between essential and inessential consumption is much easier to make. There are also agreed criteria for determining who is a 'key worker' or contributing to the foundational economy. The COVID-19 pandemic has shone a brighter light on this issue, showing how dependent societies are on their essential service, retail and farm workers – amongst many others. Measures to limit housing consumption to essential need, partly or completely, might win support if the nature of essential need were clarified. Likewise, communities already agree on specialist support packages for key workers. Essential need is the desire to put down roots and live in a place. It is measured only by full-time residence. Inessential need, on the other hand, includes the seasonal consumption of amenity. There are arguments *for* second homes in rural areas, ranging from increased service use, tax contribution and market support. The market liberal view sees benefit for second homeowners, linked to recreational opportunity and the formation of identity, and also benefit for host communities and their housing markets. Hilber and Schöni (2018) have argued that second homes support an ecosystem of local spending and also secure macro wealth equalities. If the second homeowners were gone then rural house prices would be lower. Wealth would be ring-fenced into urban markets: therefore, these market entrants are the distributors of wealth by virtue of their investment choices. That wealth, as Shucksmith (1990b) observed in the Lake District more than thirty years ago, concentrates in the hands of local homeowners – but also acts as a barrier to wider housing access.

Like Shucksmith, our prescription for this malaise is positive rather than restrictive, promoting greater fairness in access to homeownership rather than trying to curb locational and tenure choice. Private housing is a source of private wealth and supports public spending, leading to a circulation of capital and economic growth. Rural housing markets are part of that circulation of capital and they share in private wealth generation, but there are two challenges. First, if general restrictions are applied to rural housing markets (restrictions on occupancy or even, potentially, on private sale transactions – see Brooks, 2021) then rural areas do not share in growth and spending. Such interventions risk a levelling down relative to unrestricted areas. Rural households would become poorer if market supports, such as second homes, were entirely removed. Equity in housing would shrink relative to outstanding loans, with a growing sense of impoverishment reflected in reduced consumer spending and less money circulating in local economies. Every housing market has investment buying and it drives house prices, wealth and spending, but here comes the second problem. Less affluent groups are locked out by the rise in house prices caused by investment and supply pressures. Existing homeowners benefit and contribute via spending to economic growth. But there is an ever-present risk of rising inequality. It seems sensible to address that through non-restrictive interventions that do not threaten personal economic well-being and public spending. That is where the combination of planning, land and tax/finance reform detailed in Chapter 5 is important: *use CPO powers to purchase farmland at close to agricultural land; pay tapered compensation and transfer land to community stewardship, enabling CLTs to build for shared ownership but retain onward sale control of housing*. This seems to us to be a route to shared rather than stunted prosperity – levelling up rather than levelling down. That strategy aims to ensure that more people in villages are in a position to benefit from the prosperity and security arising from home ownership.

The assetisation of housing detailed in Chapter 2 is only a 'bad thing' if it is allowed to become a barrier to market entry. Fair assetisation means allowing as many families as possible to share in the personal and financial benefits of home ownership, including through shared ownership. What we have seen in recent years is a surge, a tidal wave, of unfair assetisation. The volume of 'adventitious' purchasing in the market is far greater today than it was in the 1980s. A rentier class – engaged in residential capitalism, including via Airbnb in many villages – has been driving growth in the housing market for at least the last decade. The view that the housing market can only 'work properly' if there is a big enough queue of first-time buyers able to get onto the housing ladder has been supplanted by the belief that the market can work perfectly well if enough wealthy people are prepared to splash cash in the housing market or re-mortgage in order to buy additional homes. The broader social benefits of homeownership have been sacrificed for the benefit of housing investors.

This means that answers to the land question – mechanisms for bringing land under the stewardship of communities – and new supports for the provision of affordable homes, for rent or ownership depending on the detail of local need, need to work in tandem with continuing investments in housing that provide necessary market supports. The 'market support' argument is important for all housing and all areas. UK wealth is concentrated in housing, with homes providing the collateral for household borrowing and also occupying centre-stage in an economy dependent on financial services (and other services) linked to housing consumption and debt creation. For that reason, governments have been wary of disrupting the current pattern of consumption. At the same time, the freedom to consume property, for whatever essential or inessential purpose, is often presented as an inalienable right. But today these arguments contend with the spectacle of villages bereft of full-time residents, second homeowners (some of them UK lawmakers) breaking lockdowns to visit their weekend retreats, and rural services and economies struggling to provide for rural residents. Inessential housing consumption contributes to the experience of rural poverty: setting limits, through planning restriction (barring, for example, the use of homes as holiday lets), and introducing meaningful disincentives (impact levies on second homes) now seems sensible. These would preclude no one from living in villages but would – as we have suggested above – open up a wider range of more inclusive futures for the countryside. In 1999, a Cabinet Office report into the future of rural economies argued that '[…] without adequate provision of […] affordable housing, large parts of rural England risk becoming the near-exclusive preserve of the more affluent sections of society. This risk poses an important challenge to the goal of achieving balanced communities'.

Times have changed. The UK government that came to power in 1997 seemed to believe that the housing market should not be allowed to create 'no-go' areas. Distributional justice was embedded in the goal of achieving 'balanced communities'. But to what extent does this remain a priority of government today? The Conservative-led Coalition that came to power in 2010 set a housing benefit cap on households having to pay exorbitant rents in the private market. This effectively forced many lower income households out of central London: the market had decided and government acted. A lack of investment in public housing over the last forty years has created no-go areas. Private renting, paid for with housing benefit, was touted as a substitute for public housebuilding: but when the costs of that approach spiralled, government was quick to lay the blame at the door of landlords (playing by government's game-rules) and tenants (accused of living at the taxpayers' expense) rather than their own policy failings. The current government is more pro-market and pro-deregulation than any other in the last 50 years. On the one hand, this does not bode well for rural communities. But on the other, the combination of Brexit fallout and the COVID-19 crisis provides a unique opportunity to hold government to its word, and pursue a radical levelling up agenda for village housing.

References

Aalbers, M. B. (2017) 'The variegated financialization of housing', *International Journal of Urban and Regional Research*, 41(4), 542–54.
Aalbers, M. B. and Christophers, B. (2014) 'Centring housing in political economy', *Housing, Theory and Society*, 31(4), 373–94.
Abercrombie, P. (1926) 'The preservation of rural England', *Town Planning Review*, 12(1), 5–56.
Adams, D. (2015) 'Explaining public interest-led development', *Urban Land Reform Briefing Paper No. 4*, Glasgow: University of Glasgow.
Airey, J. and Doughty, C. (2020) *Rethinking the Planning System for the 21st Century*. London: Policy Exchange.
Ambrose, P. (1974) *The Quiet Revolution: Social change in a Sussex village, 1871–1971*. Falmer: Sussex University Press.
Armstrong, W. A. (1993) 'The countryside'. In *The Cambridge Social History of Britain, 1750–1950, Volume 1: Regions and Communities*, edited by F. M. L. Thompson, 87–154. Cambridge: Cambridge University Press.
Atkinson, R. and Jacobs, K. (2020) *What Do We Know and What Should We Do About Housing?* Los Angeles: Sage Publications.
Barker, K. (2014) *Housing: Where's the plan?* London: London Publishing Partnership.
Barker, K. (2019) 'Redesigning housing policy', *National Institute Economic Review*, 250(1), R69–R74.
Barlow, J. and Chambers, D. (1992) *Planning Agreements and Affordable Housing Provision*. Falmer: University of Sussex Centre for Urban Regional Research.
Baxter, D. and Murphy, L. (2018) 'A new rural settlement: fixing the affordable housing crisis in rural England'. Accessed 25 August 2021. https://www.ippr.org/files/2018-06/1530194000_a-new-rural-settlement-june18.pdf.
BBBBC (Building Better, Building Beautiful Commission) (2020) *Living with Beauty: Promoting health, wellbeing and sustainable growth*. London: BBBBC.
BCLT (Bradwell Community Land Trust) (2020) *The Principal Project that Led to the Founding of Bradwell CLT*. Bradwell: BCLT.
Beard, M. (1989) *English Landed Society in the Twentieth Century*. London: Routledge.
Beauregard, R. A. (1994) 'Capital switching and the built environment: United States, 1970–89', *Environment and Planning A*, 26(5), 715–32.
Benson, M. and Hamiduddin, I. (2017) 'Self-build homes: social values and the lived experience of housing in practice'. In *Self-build Homes: Social discourse, experiences and direction*, edited by M. Benson and I. Hamiduddin, 1–15. London: UCL Press.
Beswick, J., McCann, D. and Wheatley, H. (2019) *Building the Social Homes We Need*. London: New Economics Foundation.
Boughton, J. (2019) *Municipal Dreams: The rise and fall of council housing*. London: Verso Books.
Bourdieu, P. (1986) 'The forms of capital'. In *Handbook of Theory and Research for the Sociology of Education*, edited by J. Richardson, 241–58. Westport, CT: Greenwood.
Bowie, D. (2017) *Radical Solutions to the Housing Supply Crisis*. Bristol: Policy Press.
Bradley, Q. (2021) 'The financialisation of housing land supply in England', *Urban Studies*, 58(2), 389–404.
Bramley, G. and Watkins, D. (2009) 'Affordability and supply: the rural dimension', *Planning Practice and Research*, 24(2), 185–210.

Breach, A. (2019) *Capital Cities: How the planning system creates housing shortages and drives wealth inequality*. London: Centre for Cities.

Breach, A. (2020) *Planning for the Future: How flexible zoning will end the housing crisis*. London: Centre for Cities.

Brooks, S. (2021) *Second Homes: Developing new policies in Wales*. Cardiff: Welsh Government.

Brown, T. and Bright, J. (2018) *Innovation in Council Housebuilding*. London: Local Government Association.

Buller, H. and Gilg, A. W. (2012) *Rural Housing, Exurbanization, and Amenity-Driven Development: Contrasting the 'haves' and the 'have nots'*. Aldershot: Ashgate.

Buller, H. and Hoggart, K. (1994) *International Counterurbanisation: British migrants in rural France*. Aldershot: Avebury.

Buller, H., Morris, C. and Wright, E. (2003) *The Demography of Rural Areas: A literature review*. London: DEFRA.

Burch, A. D. S. and Eligson, J. (2020) 'Obama says US lacks leadership on virus in commencement speeches', *New York Times*, 16 May. Accessed 6 January 2022. http://www.nytimes.com/2020/05/16/us/barack-obama-2020-commencement-graduation-speech.html.

Castles, F. G. (1998) 'The really big trade-off: home ownership and the welfare state in the new world and the old', *Acta Politica*, 33(1), 5–19.

Chaney, P. and Sherwood, K. (2000) 'The resale of right to buy dwellings: a case study of migration and social change in rural England', *Journal of Rural Studies*, 16(1), 79–94.

Cherry, G. E. (1979) 'The town planning movement and the late Victorian city', *Transactions of the Institute of British Geographers*, 4(2), 306–19.

Christaller, W. (1933) *Die zentralen Orte in Süddeutschland*. Jena: Gustav Fischer.

Christophers, B. (2019) 'Putting financialisation in its financial context: transformations in local government-led urban development in post-financial crisis England', *Transactions of the Institute of British Geographers*, 44(3), 571–86.

Christophers, B. (2020) *Rentier Capitalism: Who owns the economy, and who pays for it?* London: Verso.

Churchill, W. (1909) 'The mother of all monopolies', from a speech delivered at the King's Theatre, Edinburgh, 17 July 1909.

Claxton, P. (2020) 'Cottingham's council housing, Part II from 1930: new forms of housing provision', *Municipal Dreams* blog, 20 October. Accessed 24 May 2022. https://municipaldreams.wordpress.com/2020/10/20/cottinghams-council-housing-part-ii-from-1930/.

Clifford, B., Ferm, J., Livingstone, N. and Canelas, P. (2019) *Understanding the Impacts of Deregulation in Planning: Turning offices into homes?* London: Palgrave Pivot.

Cloke, P. (1977) 'An index of rurality for England and Wales', *Regional Studies*, 11(1), 31–46.

Cloke, P. (1979) *Key Settlements in Rural Areas*. London: Routledge.

Cloke, P. (2006) 'Conceptualizing rurality'. In *Handbook of Rural Studies*, edited by P. Cloke, T. Marsden and P. Mooney, 18–28. London: Sage Publications.

Cloke, P. and Edwards, G. (1986) 'Rurality in England and Wales 1981: a replication of the 1971 index', *Regional Studies*, 20(4), 289–306.

Coelho, M., Dellepiane-Avellaneda, S. and Ratnoo, V. (2017) 'The political economy of housing in England', *New Political Economy*, 22(1), 31–60.

Collett, M. (2016) 'Royal opening for Kent affordable rural homes', *English Rural*, 2 March. Accessed 14 March 2022. https://englishrural.org.uk/royal-opening-for-kent-affordable-rural-homes/.

Cope, H. (1999) *Housing Associations: The policy and practice of registered social landlords*. London: Springer.

Cornwall Council (2015) *Second and Holiday Homes*. Truro: Cornwall Council.

Countryside Agency (2004) *What Makes a Good Parish Plan?* Cheltenham: Countryside Agency.

Cox, J. (1998) 'Poverty in rural areas is more hidden but no less real than in urban areas', *British Medical Journal*, 316(7), 722–30.

Crook, T., Henneberry, J. and Whitehead, C. (2015) *Planning Gain: Providing infrastructure and affordable housing*. London: John Wiley.

Danbom, D. B. (2017) *Born in the Country: A history of rural America*. Baltimore: Johns Hopkins University Press.

Dartmoor National Park Authority (2019) *Settlement Profile: South Tawton*. Newton Abbot: DNPA.

DBIS (Department for Business Innovation and Skills) (2010) *Local Growth: Realising every place's potential*. London: DBIS.

DCLG (Department for Communities and Local Government) (2015a) *Government Response to the Communities and Local Government Select Committee Inquiry into the Community Rights*, Cm 9052. London: DCLG.

DCLG (Department for Communities and Local Government) (2015b) *Land Value Estimates for Policy Appraisal*. London: DCLG. Accessed 4 January 2022. http://assets.publishing.service.gov.uk/government/uploads/system/uploads/attachment_data/file/407155/February_2015_Land_value_publication_FINAL.pdf.

DEFRA (Department for Environment, Food and Rural Affairs) (2021) *Statistical Digest of Rural Areas, August 2021 Edition*. London: DEFRA.

DEFRA (Department for Environment, Food and Rural Affairs) (2022) *Statistical Digest of Rural England, May 2022 Edition*. London: DEFRA.

DETR and MAFF (Department of the Environment, Transport and the Regions and the Ministry of Agriculture, Fisheries and Food) (2000) *Our Countryside – The Future: A fair deal for rural England*. London: DETR and MAFF.

Diamond, P. and Mirrlees, J. (1971) 'Optimal taxation and public production II: tax rules', *American Economic Review*, 61(3), 261–78.

DLUHC (2022) *Levelling Up and Regeneration Bill*. London: Department for Levelling Up, Housing and Communities.

DMO (UK Debt Management Office) (2020) *PWLB Lending Facility*. Accessed 6 January 2022. http://www.dmo.gov.uk/responsibilities/local-authority-lending/.

DoE (Department of the Environment) (1981) *Proposed Modifications to the Cumbria and Lake District Joint Structure Plan*. London: DoE.

DoE (Department of the Environment) (1991) *Circular 7/91 Planning and Affordable Housing*. London: DoE.

Dorling, D. (2014) *All That is Solid: How the great housing disaster defines our times, and what we can do about it*. London: Penguin.

DTLR (Department for Transport, Local Government and the Regions) (1998) *Modern Local Government: In touch with the people*. London: DTLR.

Dunn, M., Rawson, M. and Rogers, A. (1981) *Rural Housing: Competition and choice*. London: Allen and Unwin.

Engels, F. (1962) *The Housing Question*. Moscow: Progress Publishers (originally published 1872).

Fairlie, S. (1996) *Low Impact Development*. Charlbury, Oxfordshire: Jon Carpenter.

Farthing, S. and Ashley, K. (2002) 'Negotiations and the delivery of affordable housing through the English planning system', *Planning Practice and Research*, 17(1), 45–58.

Fera, G. and Ginatempo, N. (1985) *L'Autocostruzione spontanea nel mezzogiorno*. Milan: Franco Angeli.

Field, M. (2020) *Creating Community-led and Self-build Homes: A guide to collaborative practice in the UK*. Bristol: Policy Press.

Field, M., Coates, C., Colenutt, B., Fitzpatrick, D., Hamiduddin, I., How, J., Hudson, J., Laganakou, G., McCourt, T. and Seaborn, D. (2021) *Practical Guide to Cohousing: For developing cohousing communities, community led homes, hubs and stakeholder organisations*. London: UK Cohousing Network.

Field, M. and Layard, A. (2017) 'Locating community-led housing within neighbourhood plans as a response to England's housing needs', *Public Money and Management*, 37(2), 105–12.

Fielding, A. J. (1982) 'Counter-urbanisation in Western Europe', *Progress in Planning*, 17(1), 1–52.

Fine, B. (2001) *Social Capital versus Social Theory: Political economy and social science at the turn of the millennium*. London: Psychology Press.

Forde, E. (2017) 'From cultures of resistance to the new social movements: DIY self-build in West Wales'. In *Self-build Homes*, edited by M. Benson and I. Hamiduddin, 81–95. London: UCL Press.

Forrest, R. and Murie, A. (1983) 'Residualization and council housing: aspects of the changing social relations of housing tenure', *Journal of Social Policy*, 12(4), 453–68.

Friedmann, J. (1973) *Retracking America: A theory of transactive planning*. New York: Anchor Press.

Gallent, N. (1995) 'Policy, partnership and people: provision and perceptions of social housing in rural Wales in the 1990s', doctoral dissertation, Aberystwyth: University of Wales.

Gallent, N. (1997) 'Improvement grants, second homes and planning control in England and Wales: a policy review', *Planning Practice and Research*, 12(4), 301–10.

Gallent, N. (1998) 'Local housing agencies in rural Wales', *Housing Studies*, 13(1), 59–81.

Gallent, N. (2013) 'Re-connecting "people and planning": parish plans and the English localism agenda', *Town Planning Review*, 84(3), 371–97.

Gallent, N. (2019) *Whose Housing Crisis? Assets and homes in a changing economy*. Bristol: Policy Press.

Gallent, N. (2020) 'COVID-19 and the flight to second homes', *Town and Country Planning*, 89(4/5), 141–4.

Gallent, N. and Bell, P. (2000) 'Planning exceptions in rural England: past, present and future', *Planning Practice and Research*, 15(4), 375–84.

Gallent, N. and Ciaffi, D. (eds) (2014) *Community Action and Planning*. Bristol: Policy Press.

Gallent, N., De Magalhaes, C. and Freire Trigo, S. (2021) 'Is zoning the solution to the UK housing crisis?', *Planning Practice and Research*, 36(1), 1–19.

Gallent, N., De Magalhaes, C., Freire Trigo, S., Scanlon, K. and Whitehead, C. (2019b) 'Can "permission in principle" for new housing in England increase certainty, reduce "planning risk", and accelerate housing supply?', *Planning Theory and Practice*, 20(5), 673–88.

Gallent, N. and Hamiduddin, I. (2021) 'COVID-19, second homes and the challenge for rural amenity areas', *Town Planning Review*, 92(3), 395–402.

Gallent, N., Hamiduddin, I., Juntti, M., Kidd, S. and Shaw, D. (2015) *Introduction to Rural Planning: Economies, communities and landscapes*. London: Routledge.

Gallent, N., Hamiduddin, I., Kelsey, J. and Stirling, P. (2020) 'Housing access and affordability in rural England: tackling inequalities through downstream intervention or upstream reform', *Planning Theory and Practice*, 21(4), 531–51.

Gallent, N., Hamiduddin, I., Stirling, P. and Kelsey, J. (2019a) 'Prioritising local housing needs through land-use planning in rural areas: political theatre or amenity protection?', *Journal of Rural Studies*, 66, 11–20.

Gallent, N., Mace, A. and Tewdwr-Jones, M. (2002) 'Delivering affordable housing through planning: explaining variable policy usage across rural England and Wales', *Planning Practice and Research*, 17(4), 465–83.

Gallent, N., Mace, A. and Tewdwr-Jones, M. (2005) *Second Homes: European perspectives and UK policies*. Aldershot: Ashgate.

Gallent, N. and Madeddu, M. (2021) 'COVID-19 and England's decentralising housing market: what are the planning implications?', *Planning Practice and Research*, 36(5), 567–77.

Gallent, N. and Robinson, S. (2011) 'Local perspectives on rural housing affordability and implications for the localism agenda in England', *Journal of Rural Studies*, 27(3), 297–307.

Gallent, N. and Robinson, S. (2012) *Neighbourhood Planning: Communities, networks and governance*. Bristol: Policy Press.

Gallent, N. and Scott, M. (2017) 'Introduction'. In *Rural Development and Planning, Volume I*, edited by N. Gallent and M. Scott, 1–30. London: Routledge.

Gallent, N. and Tewdwr-Jones, M. (2000) *Rural Second Homes in Europe*. Aldershot: Ashgate.

Gallent, N. and Tewdwr-Jones, M. (2007) *Decent Homes for All: Planning's evolving role in housing provision*. London: Routledge.

George, H. (1905) *Progress and Poverty: An inquiry into the cause of industrial depressions and of increase of want with increase of wealth – the remedy*. New York: Pantianos Classics (originally published 1879).

Gibb, K. (2009) 'Housing studies and the role of economic theory: an (applied) disciplinary perspective', *Housing, Theory and Society*, 26(1), 26–40.

Gilg, A. W. and Kelly, M. (1997) 'Rural planning in practice: the case of agricultural dwellings', *Progress in Planning*, 47(2), 75–157.

Gkartzios, M., Gallent, N. and Scott, M. (2022) *Rural Places and Planning: Stories from the global countryside*. Bristol: Policy Press.

Gkartzios, M. and Lowe, P. (2019) 'Revisiting neo-endogenous rural development'. In *The Routledge Companion to Rural Planning*, edited by M. Scott, N. Gallent and M. Gkartzios, 159–69. London: Routledge.

Gkartzios, M. and Shucksmith, M. (2015) '"Spatial anarchy" versus "spatial apartheid": rural housing ironies in Ireland and England', *Town Planning Review*, 86(1), 53–72.

Goode, C. (2021) '"Escape to the country": the implications of coronavirus upon the English housing crisis'. In *Living with Pandemics: Places, people and policy*, edited by J. R. Bryson, L. Andres, A. Ersoy and L. Reardon, 173–83. Cheltenham: Edward Elgar.

Gray, K. A. (2008) 'Community land trusts in the United States', *Journal of Community Practice*, 16(1), 65–78.

Halfacree, K. (1993) 'Locality and social representation: space, discourse and alternative definitions of the rural', *Journal of Rural Studies*, 9(1), 23–37.

Hall, C. M. and Müller, D. K. (eds) (2018) *The Routledge Handbook of Second Home Tourism and Mobilities*. London: Routledge.

Hall, P. (2014) *Cities of Tomorrow: An intellectual history of urban planning and design since 1880*. Chichester: John Wiley.

Hall, P. and Ward, C. (1998) *Sociable Cities: The legacy of Ebenezer Howard*. Chichester: John Wiley.

Hamiduddin, I. (2017) 'Community building, self-build and the neighbourhood commons'. In *Self-build Homes: Social discourse, experiences and direction*, edited by M. Benson and I. Hamiduddin, 17–37. London: UCL Press.

Hamiduddin, I. and Gallent, N. (2016) 'Self-build communities: the rationale and experiences of group-build (Baugruppen) housing development in Germany', *Housing Studies*, 31(4), 365–83.

Harris, N. (2019) 'Exceptional spaces for sustainable living: the regulation of one planet developments in the open countryside', *Planning Theory and Practice*, 20(1), 11–36.

Harrison, E. (2019) '"They are treating us with contempt": the complexities of opposition in an English village', *Journal of Rural Studies*, 68, 54–62.

Harvey, D. (1974) 'Class-monopoly rent, finance capital and the urban revolution', *Regional Studies*, 8(3–4), 239–55.

Harvey, D. (1978) 'The urban process under capitalism: a framework for analysis', *International Journal of Urban and Regional Research*, 2(1–3),101–31.

Harvey, D. (1981) 'The spatial fix: Hegel, von Thünen, and Marx', *Antipode*, 13(3), 1–12.

Harvey, D. (1982) *The Limits to Capital*. Oxford: Basil Blackwell.

Haynes, R. and Gale, S. (2000) 'Deprivation and poor health in rural areas: inequalities hidden by averages', *Health and Place*, 6(4), 275–85.

Hetherington, P. (2015) *Whose Land is Our Land? The use and abuse of Britain's forgotten acres*. Bristol: Policy Press.

Hetherington, P. (2019) 'Land, property and reform'. In *The Routledge Companion to Rural Planning*, edited by M. Scott, N. Gallent and M. Ghartzios, 79–88. London: Routledge.

Hetherington, P. (2021) *Land Renewed: Reworking the countryside*. Bristol: Policy Press.

Hilber, C. A. and Schöni, O. (2020) 'On the economic impacts of constraining second home investments', *Journal of Urban Economics*, 118, 1–16.

Hilber, C. A. and Vermeulen, W. (2016) 'The impact of supply constraints on house prices in England', *Economic Journal*, 126(591), 358–405.

Hilditch, M. (2019) 'The local heroes: what is the future for community land trusts?'. *Inside Housing*. Accessed 6 January 2022. https://www.insidehousing.co.uk/insight/insight/the-local-heroes-what-is-the-future-for-community-land-trusts-60307.

HM Government (1945) *White Paper on Housing, Cmd. 6609*. London: HMSO.

HM Government (1987) *Housing: The government's proposals – White Paper, Cmd. 214*. London: HMSO.

Hodge, I. and Monk, S. (2004) 'The economic diversity of rural England: stylised fallacies and uncertain evidence', *Journal of Rural Studies*, 20(3), 263–72.

Hoggart, K. (1988) 'Not a definition of rural', *Area*, 20(1), 35–40.

Hoggart, K., Buller, H. and Black, R. (1995) *Rural Europe: Identity and change*. London: Routledge.

Hoggart, K. and Henderson, S. (2005) 'Excluding exceptions: housing non-affordability and the oppression of environmental sustainability?', *Journal of Rural Studies*, 21(2), 181–96.

Home Builders Federation (2017) *Reversing the Decline of Small Housebuilders: Reinvigorating entrepreneurialism and building more homes*. London: HBF. Accessed 8 June 2018. https://www.hbf.co.uk/documents/6879/HBF_SME_Report_2017_Web.pdf.

Hudson, J., Scanlon, K., Fernandez-Arrigoitia, M. and Saeed, S. (2019) *The Wider Benefits of Cohousing: The case of Bridport*. London: London School of Economics.

Hulme, T. J. (2010) 'Urban governance and civic responsibility: interwar council housing in Buxton', *Midland History*, 35(2), 237–55.

International Independence Institute (1972) *The Community Land Trust: A guide to a new model for land tenure in America*. Cambridge, MA: Center for Community Economic Development.

Keen, S. (2018) 'The housing crisis: there's nothing we can do … or is there?', *Eco-cognito* blog, 27 March. Accessed 19 March 2021. https://www.ecocognito.com/twitawoo/post/housing-crisis-explained-nothing-we-can-do/.

Kemeny, J. (1980) 'Home ownership and privatisation', *International Journal of Urban and Regional Research*, 4(3), 372–88.

Kemeny, J. (1981) *The Myth of Home Ownership: Public versus private choices in housing tenure*. London: Routledge.

Kemeny, J. (2005) '"The really big trade-off" between home ownership and welfare: Castles' evaluation of the 1980 thesis, and a reformulation 25 years on', *Housing, Theory and Society*, 22(2), 59–75.

Kenny, T. (2019) 'Land for the many and a new politics of land', *Planning Theory and Practice*, 20(5), 763–8.

Kime, Elliott (2019) 'Has St Ives' second home ban backfired?', *Financial Times*, 13 September. Accessed 4 August 2022. https://www.ft.com/content/6abb85e8-c349-11e9-ae6e-a26d1d0455f4.

Knight Frank (2019) *Farmland Index Q1 2019*. London: Knight Frank.

Krippner, G. (2005) 'The financialization of the American economy', *Socio-economic Review*, 3(2), 173–208.

Labour Party (2019) *It's Time for Real Change: The Labour Party manifesto 2019*. London: The Labour Party.

Lake District Special Planning Board (1977) *Draft National Park Plan*. Kendal: LDSPB.

Lake District Special Planning Board and Cumbria County Council (1980) *Cumbria and Lake District Joint Structure Plan – Written statement*. Kendal: LDSPB and CCC.

Law, C. M. (1967) 'The growth of urban population in England and Wales, 1801–1911', *Transactions of the Institute of British Geographers*, 41 (June), 125–43.

Lichfields (2017) *Stock and Flow: Planning permissions and housing output*. London: Lichfields.

Lichfields (2018) *Local Choices? Housing delivery through neighbourhood plans*. London: Lichfields.

Liu, N. and Roberts, D. (2013) 'Counter-urbanisation, planning and house prices: an analysis of the Aberdeen housing market area, 1984–2010', *Town Planning Review*, 84(1), 81–105.

Lloyd, M. G., Peel, D. and Janssen-Jansen, L. B. (2015) 'Self-build in the UK and Netherlands: mainstreaming self-development to address housing shortages?', *Urban, Planning and Transport Research*, 3(1), 19–31.

Locke, J. (2002) *The Second Treatise of Government*. New York: Dover Publications (originally published 1689).

Lowe, S. (2011) *The Housing Debate*. Bristol: Policy Press.

Lyons, M. (2014) 'The Lyons housing review: mobilising across the nation to build the homes our children need'. Accessed 20 November 2019. https://www.policyforum.labour.org.uk/uploads/editor/files/The_Lyons_Housing_Review_2.pdf.

Maclennan, D. (1979) 'Housing economics: a review and introduction', *Scottish Journal of Political Economy*, 26(3), 325–9.

Marrs, C. (2020) 'Councils using "dirty tricks" to block people joining self-build registers"', *Planning Resource*, 22 January. Accessed 7 January 2022. https://www.planningresource.co.uk/article/1671554/councils-using-dirty-tricks-block-people-joining-self-build-registers.

Marsden, T., Murdoch, J., Lowe, P., Munton, R. and Flynn, J. (1993) *Constructing the Countryside*. London: UCL Press.

Martin, E. W. (1962) *The Book of the Village*. London: Phoenix House.

Matheson, A. (2010) 'Localism focus is an opportunity for stronger leadership in communitues', *Planning Resource*, 13 August. Accessed 5 May 2021. https://www.planningresource.co.uk/article/1021621/localism-focus-opportunity-stronger-leadership-communities.

Maxey, L. (2009) 'What is low impact development?'. In *Low-impact Development: The future in our hands*, edited by J. Pickerill and L. Maxey. Accessed 26 March 2021. http://lowimpactdevelopment.wordpress.com.

MHCLG (Ministry of Housing, Communities and Local Government) (2019) *National Planning Policy Framework*. London: MHCLG.

MHCLG (Ministry of Housing, Communities and Local Government) (2020a) *Planning for the Future – White Paper*. London: MHCLG.

MHCLG (Ministry of Housing, Communities and Local Government) (2020b) *Affordable Housing Supply: April 2019 to March 2020, England*. London: MHCLG.

MHCLG (Ministry of Housing, Communities and Local Government) (2020c) 'Land value estimates for policy appraisal 2019'. Accessed 5 January 2022. https://www.gov.uk/government/publications/land-value-estimates-for-policy-appraisal-2019.

MHCLG (Ministry of Housing, Communities and Local Government) (2021a) *Community Ownership Fund: Policy paper*. London: MHCLG.

MHCLG (Ministry of Housing, Communities and Local Government) (2021b) *National Model Design Code*. London: MHCLG.

MHCLG (Ministry of Housing, Communities and Local Government) (2021c) *National Planning Policy Framework*. London: MHCLG.

Milbourne, P. (1997) 'Housing conflict and domestic property classes in rural Wales', *Environment and Planning A*, 29(1), 43–62.

Milbourne, P. (2006) 'Rural housing and homelessness'. In *Handbook of Rural Studies*, edited by P. Cloke, T. Marsden and P. Mooney, 427–44. London: Sage Publications.

Miller, M. (2010) *English Garden Cities: An introduction*. Swindon: English Heritage.

Ministry of Housing and Local Government (1958) *House Purchase: Proposed government scheme, Cmd. 571*. London: House of Commons Parliamentary Papers Online.

Mirrlees, J., Adam, S., Besley, T., Blundell, R., Bond, S., Chote, R., Gammie, M., Johnson, P., Myles, G. and Poterba, J. (2011) *Tax by Design: The final report of the Mirrlees Review*. London: Institute for Fiscal Studies.

Monbiot, G., Grey, R., Kenny, T., Macfarlane, L., Powell-Smith, A., Shrubsole, G. and Stratford, B. (2019) *Land for the Many: Changing the way our fundamental asset is used, owned and governed*. London: The Labour Party.

Moore, T. (2021) 'Planning for place: place attachment and the founding of rural community land trusts', *Journal of Rural Studies*, 83 (April), 21–9.

Moore, T. and McKee, K. (2012) 'Empowering local communities? An international review of community land trusts', *Housing Studies*, 27(2), 280–90.

Morphet, J. and Clifford, B. (2017) *Local Authority Direct Provision of Housing*. London: National Planning Forum and RTPI.

Mulholland, T. (2021) 'Tackling Cornwall's housing crisis', *Western Morning Press*, 31 August. Accessed 6 January 2022. https://www.treveth.co.uk/latest-news/tackling-cornwalls-housing-crisis/.

NaCSBA (National Custom and Self-Build Association) (2021) 'Numbers wanting to self build grows despite "dirty tricks" from a growing minority of local authorities'. Accessed 7 January 2022. https://nacsba.org.uk/news/self-build-registers/.

National Community Land Trust Network (2020) 'What is a community land trust?'. Accessed 6 January 2022. https://www.communitylandtrusts.org.uk/about-clts/what-is-a-community-land-trust-clt/.

Nelson, P. B. (2001) 'Rural restructuring in the American West: land use, family and class discourses', *Journal of Rural Studies*, 17(4), 395–407.

Newby, H. (1977) 'Tied cottage reform', *British Journal of Law and Society*, 4(1), 94–103.

Newby, H. (1980) *Green and Pleasant Land? Social change in rural England*. Harmondsworth: Penguin Books.

Obremski, H. and Carter, C. (2019) 'Can self-build housing improve social sustainability within low-income groups?', *Town Planning Review*, 90(2), 167–93.

Office of Fair Trading (2008) *Homebuilding in the UK: A market study*. London: OFT.

O'Sullivan, A. (2012) *Urban Economics*. New York: McGraw-Hill.

Owen, S. (2002) 'From village design statements to parish plans: some pointers towards community decision making in the planning system in England', *Planning Practice and Research*, 17(1), 81–9.

Owen, S. and Moseley, M. (2003) 'Putting parish plans in their place: relationships between community-based initiatives and development planning in English villages', *Town Planning Review*, 74(4), 445–71.

Pahl, R. E. (1965) *Urbs in rure,* Geographical Papers No. 2. London: London School of Economics and Political Science.

Pahl, R. E. (1966) 'The rural–urban continuum', *Sociologia Ruralis*, 6(3), 299–329.

Pahl, R. E. (1975) *Whose City? And further essays on urban society*. Harmondsworth: Penguin.

Paris, C. (2019) 'Second homes, housing consumption and planning responses'. In *The Routledge Companion to Rural Planning*, edited by M. Scott, N. Gallent and M. Gkartzios, 273–86. London: Routledge.

Parker, G. (2014) 'Engaging neighbourhoods: experiences of transactive planning with communities in England'. In *Community Action and Planning: Contexts, drivers and outcomes*, edited by N. Gallent and D. Ciaffi, 177–200. Bristol: Policy Press.

Parker, G. and Salter, K. (2016) 'Five years of neighbourhood planning: a review of take-up and distribution', *Town and Country Planning*, 85(5), 181–8.

Parker, G. and Salter, K. (2017) 'Taking stock of neighbourhood planning in England 2011–2016', *Planning Practice and Research*, 32(4), 478–90.

Parker, G., Wargent, M., Salter, K., Dobson, M., Lynn, T., Yuille, A. and Navigus Planning (2020) *Impacts of Neighbourhood Planning in England*. Reading: University of Reading.

Pendall, R. (1999) 'Opposition to housing: NIMBY and beyond', *Urban Affairs Review*, 35(1), 112–36.

Petherick, S. and Sumner, S. (2019) 'Councillor lands £10,000 role on Bath and north east Somerset council housing company', *Bath Chronicle*, 12 April. Accessed 4 August 2022. https://www.somersetlive.co.uk/news/somerset-news/councillor-lands-10000-role-bath-2747882.

Phillips, M. and Dickie, J. (2019) 'Post-carbon ruralities'. In *The Routledge Companion to Rural Planning*, edited by M. Scott, N. Gallent and M. Gkartzios, 521–47. London: Routledge.

Pidd, Helen (2014) 'How Lake District holiday homeowners are pushing out local residents', *The Guardian*, 9 July. Accessed 4 August 2022. https://www.theguardian.com/uk-news/2014/jul/09/lake-district-homeowners-local-residents.

Piketty, T. (2014) *Capital in the Twenty-First Century*. Cambridge, MA: Harvard University Press.

Quigley, J. M. (ed.) (1997) *The Economics of Housing*. Cheltenham: Edward Elgar.

Quilgars, D. and Jones, A. (2010) 'Housing wealth: a safety net of last resort? Findings from a European Study'. In *The Blackwell Companion to the Economics of Housing: The housing wealth of nations*, edited by S. J. Smith and B. A. Searle, 295–315. Chichester: Wiley-Blackwell.

Regulator of Social Housing (2015) *A Guide to Regulation of Social Housing*. London: HM Government.

Resolution Foundation (2018) *A New Generational Contract: The final report of the Intergenerational Commission*. London: Resolution Foundation.

Robinson, R. (1979) *Housing Economics and Public Policy*. Basingstoke: Macmillan.

Rogers, A. W. (1985) 'Local claims on rural housing: a review', *Town Planning Review*, 56(3), 367–80.

Rolnik, R. (2013) 'Late neoliberalism: the financialization of homeownership and housing rights', *International Journal of Urban and Regional Research*, 37(3), 1058–66.

Ross, A. (2019) 'The evolution of sustainable development in Scotland: a case study of Community Right-to-buy law and policy 2003–2018', *Sustainability*, 11(130), 1–18.

Rossall Valentine, D. (2015) *Solving the UK Housing Crisis*. London: Bow Group.

Rossi, U. (2017) *Cities in Global Capitalism*. London: John Wiley.

Rowley, T. (2006) *The English Landscape in the Twentieth Century*. London: Hambledon Continuum.

RTPI (Royal Town Planning Institute) (2017) *Opening up the Debate: Exploring housing land supply myths*. London: RTPI.

Rural Coalition (2017) *Rural Coalition Statement 2017: Good practice – case studies*. Rural Coalition. Accessed 27 May 2022. https://rsnonline.org.uk/images/stories/publications/rural-coalition/Rural%20Coalition%20Statement%202017.pdf.

Ryan-Collins, J. (2021) 'Breaking the housing–finance cycle: macroeconomic policy reforms for more affordable homes', *Environment and Planning A: Economy and Space*, 53(3), 480–502.

Ryan-Collins, J., Lloyd, T. and Macfarlane, L. (2017) *Rethinking the Economics of Land and Housing*. London: Zed Books.

Salet, W., D'Ottaviano, C., Majoor, S. and Bossuyt, D. (2020) *The Self-Build Experience: Institutionalisation, place making and city building*. Bristol: Policy Press.

Sandford, M. (2021) *Assets of Community Value: Briefing Paper 06366*. London: House of Commons Library.

Satsangi, M., Gallent, N. and Bevan, M. (2010) *The Rural Housing Question*. Bristol: Policy Press.

Saunders, P. (1978) 'Domestic property and social class', *International Journal of Urban and Regional Research*, 2(1–3), 233–51.

Saunders, P. (1984) 'Beyond housing classes: the sociological significance of private property rights in means of consumption', *International Journal of Urban and Regional Research*, 8(2), 202–27.

Savage, M., Warde, A. and Ward, K. (2003) *Urban Sociology, Capitalism and Modernity*, 2nd Edition. Basingstoke: Palgrave Macmillan.

Savage, W. G. (1919) *Rural Housing*. London: TF Unwin.

Sayer, A. (2016) *Why We Can't Afford the Rich*. Bristol: Policy Press.

Scottish Land Commission (2018) 'Land value capture to have a proactive role in place making'. Accessed 22 November 2019. https://landcommission.gov.scot/tag/land-value/.

Sendra, P. and Fitzpatrick, D. (2020) *Community-Led Regeneration: A toolkit for residents and planners*. London: UCL Press.

SHBC (Surrey Heath Borough Council) (2022) 'Neighbourhood Development Orders'. Accessed 6 January 2022. http://www.surreyheath.gov.uk/residents/planning/planning-policy/neighbourhood-planning/neighbourhood-development-orders.

Short, J. R. (1982) *Housing in Britain: The post-war experience*. London: Taylor and Francis.

Shrubsole, G. (2019) *Who Owns England? How we lost our green and pleasant land, and how to take it back*. London: HarperCollins.

Shucksmith, M. (1981) *No Homes for Locals?* Farnborough: Gower.
Shucksmith, M. (1990a) 'A theoretical perspective on rural housing: Housing classes in rural Britain', *Sociologia Ruralis*, 30(2), 210–29.
Shucksmith, M. (1990b) *Housebuilding in Britain's Countryside*. London: Routledge.
Shucksmith, M. (2018) 'Re-imagining the rural: from rural idyll to good countryside', *Journal of Rural Studies*, 59, 163–72.
Sillince, J. A. A. (1986) 'Why did Warwickshire key settlement policy change in 1982? An assessment of the political implications of cuts in rural services', *Geographical Journal*, 152(2), 176–92.
Sindt, R. P. and Guy, D. C. (1985) 'Economics of rural housing: challenges and changes', *Housing and Society*, 12(3), 147–60.
Smith, S. J. and Searle, B. A. (2010) 'Housing wealth as insurance: insights from the UK'. In *The Blackwell Companion to the Economics of Housing: The housing wealth of nations*, edited by S. J. Smith and B. A. Searle, 339–60. Chichester: Wiley-Blackwell.
Spiekermann, K. and Aalbu, H. (2004) *Nordic Peripherality in Europe*. Stockholm: Nordregio.
Spiers, S. (2018) *How to Build Houses and Save the Countryside*. Bristol: Policy Press.
St Ives Town Council (2016) *St Ives Area Neighbourhood Development Plan 2015–2030*. St Ives: St Ives Town Council.
Stephens, M., Lux, M. and Sunega, P. (2015) 'Post-socialist housing systems in Europe: housing welfare regimes by default?', *Housing Studies*, 30(8), 1210–34.
Stirling, P. (2019) 'Constructing London's housing market: national housing strategy and market mediation', unpublished PhD thesis, London: University College London.
Stirling, P., Gallent, N. and Purves, A. (2022). 'The assetisation of housing: A macroeconomic resource'. *European Urban and Regional Studies*, March. Accessed 5 August 2022. https://doi.org/10.1177/09697764221082621.
Stroud District Council (2020) *Strategy for New Council Homes 2020–2024*. Stroud: SDC.
Sturzaker, J. (2010) 'The exercise of power to limit the development of new housing in the English countryside', *Environment and Planning A*, 42(4), 1001–16.
Sturzaker, J. (2011) 'Can community empowerment reduce opposition to housing? Evidence from rural England', *Planning Practice and Research*, 26(5), 555–70.
Sturzaker, J. (2019) 'Settlement, strategy and planning'. In *The Routledge Companion to Rural Planning*, edited by M. Scott, N. Gallent and M. Gkartzios, 369–77. London: Routledge.
Sturzaker, J. and Shaw, D. (2015) 'Localism in practice: lessons from a pioneer neighbourhood plan in England', *Town Planning Review*, 86(5), 587–609.
Taylor, M. (2008) *Living Working Countryside: The Taylor review of rural economy and affordable housing*. London: DCLG.
Thatcher, M. (1993) *The Downing Street Years*. London: HarperCollins.
Townley, C. (2021) 'Four council cottages at Mickleton: Rural council housing in Gloucestershire before the First World War'. Accessed 6 January 2022. http://municipaldreams.wordpress.com/2021/01/26/four-council-cottages-at-mickleton/.
Tunstall, B. (2015) 'Relative housing space inequality in England and Wales, and its recent rapid resurgence', *International Journal of Housing Policy*, 15(2), 105–26.
Vale, B. and Vale, R. (1975) *The Autonomous House*. New York: Universe Books.
Wainwright, T. (2009) 'Laying the foundations for a crisis: mapping the historico-geographical construction of residential mortgage backed securitization in the UK', *International Journal of Urban and Regional Research*, 33(2), 372–88.
Wallace, A., Ford, J. and Quilgars, D. (2013) *Build-it-Yourself? Understanding the changing landscape of the UK self-build market*. York: Centre for Housing Policy.
Wates, N. (1976) *The Battle for Tolmers Square*. London: Routledge and Kegan Paul.
Watt, P. (2021) *Estate Regeneration and its Discontents: Public housing, place and inequality in London*. Bristol: Policy Press.
Webb, B., Harris, N. and Smith, B. (2019) *Rural Housing Delivery in Wales: How effective is rural exception site policy?* Cardiff: RTPI Cymru.
Webber, R. and Burrows, R. (2017) *The Predictive Postcode: The geodemographic classification of British society*. London: Sage Publications.
Weber, B., Jensen, L., Miller, K., Mosley, J. and Fisher, M. (2005) 'A critical review of rural poverty literature: is there truly a rural effect?', *International Regional Science Review*, 28(4), 381–414.
Weber, M. (1978) *Wirtschaft und Gesellschaft: Grundriß der verstehenden Soziologie* [Economy and Society]. Berkeley: University of California Press (originally published 1921).

Weekley, I. (1988) 'Rural depopulation and counter-urbanisation: a paradox', *Area*, 20(2), 127–34.

Wei Yang and Partners and Freeman, P. (2014) *New Garden Cities: Visionary, economically viable and popular – entry for Wolfson Economics Prize*. London: Wei Yang and Partners.

Welsh Government (2012) *Practice Guidance: One planet development* (Technical Advice Note 6: Planning for Sustainable Rural Communities). Cardiff: Welsh Government.

Wetzstein, S. (2017) 'The global urban housing affordability crisis', *Urban Studies*, 54(14), 3159–77.

Williams, G., Bell, P. and Russell, L. (1991) *Evaluating the Low Cost Rural Housing Initiative*. London: HMSO.

Williams, N. J. and Twine, F. E. (1994) 'Locals, incomers and second homes: the role of resold public sector dwellings in rural Scotland', *Scandinavian Housing and Planning Research*, 11(4), 193–209.

Wilson, W. (2017) *Briefing Paper: A Short history of rent control*. London: House of Commons Library.

Woods, M. (2005) *Contesting Rurality: Politics in the British countryside*. Aldershot: Ashgate.

Woods, M. (2010) *Rural*. London: Routledge.

Woods, M. (2016) 'Reconfiguring places: wealth and the transformation of rural areas'. In *Handbook on Wealth and the Super-Rich*, edited by I. Hay and J. Beaverstock, 245–64. Cheltenham: Edward Elgar.

Wyatt, P. (2019) 'From a property tax to a land tax: who wins, who loses?'. *Land Use Policy*, 88, 104172, 1–10.

Yarwood, R. (2002) 'Parish councils, partnership and governance: the development of "exceptions" housing in the Malvern Hills district, England', *Journal of Rural Studies*, 18(3), 275–91.

Zayed, Y. and Loft, P. (2019) *Agriculture: Historical statistics*. London: House of Commons Library.

Index

Aalbers, M. B. 30, 32
ability-to-pay 89
'absorption rate' 171
access to housing x, 1–6, 13, 45, 146, 202
achievability 209
Action with Communities in Rural England (ACRE) 92
Addison Act (1919) 43, 56–7
adventitious buyers x, 52
AFA Planning Consultants 55
affluence 5, 91, 134–5
affordability x–xi, 4, 14–15, 19–22, 31, 53–6, 66, 73–6, 82, 85, 91–7, 100–3, 106–16, 129, 136, 144–7, 153–7, 161–2, 165–7, 170, 179–81, 193–5, 199–204, 207–12
Affordable Rural Housing Commission 20
Agricultural Dwellings Housing Advisory Committee 53
'agricultural ties' 79
Airbnb 28, 95–6, 211
allocation of housing 13, 15, 35, 51–2, 171–2
alms houses 74
amenity areas x–xi, 5–6. 17, 20, 36, 38, 44–5, 72, 82, 172, 195, 202–4, 209
anchoring (of people and communities) 6
Anglo-centric perspectives 3
applications for planning permission 141
Arch, Joseph 49
archaeological investigations 114–15
Article 4 directives 142
asset-backed securities 30
assetisation of housing 1, 15, 19–20, 25–32, 38–9, 46, 138, 211
assets of community value (ACVs) 123–4, 136
Attlee, Clement 50–1
Australia 103
authenticity 206
authoritarianism 138
'automatic consent' system 36
availability of land 165

Baker, K. 25, 27
balanced communities 37, 212
Bank of England 29
bank lending 23
banks 30
the Barbican 72
Barker, Kate 155

Barlow, J. 92
Baxter, D. 92
Beard, M. 43
beauty in development 142
Beer CLT (East Devon) 161–3
beneficiaries 104
Benenden Parish Council 162
Benson, M. 173
'best value' 16
Bevan, Aneurin 50, 68, 71
Borsodi, Ralph 104
Bourdieu, P. 134
Bradford and Melksham Rural District Council 68–70
Bradwell Springs 130–3
Brexit 35, 55, 156, 212
Bright, J. 194
Britain 5; *see also* England
Brown, T. 194
build costs 66–7, 179, 181
Building Beautiful, Building Better Commission (BBBBC) 142
building groups 180
building programmes 164
building societies 28–9
Burrows, R. 9
Buxton 57
'buy to rent' 21
buyout 136
by-right system 141

Cabinet Office 212
Cannonmede Cottages 95–6
capital gains 157
capital gains tax (CGT) 154–7, 199
capitalism 30
carbon 190, 200, 202–7
car-dependency 206
case-by-case permissioning 141
centrality of housing to national economy 155
Centre for Cities 141
challenges related to housing 3, 46, 209–10
Chamberlain Act (1923) 58
Chambers, D. 92
Chapel Stile 105–7
charitable incorporated organisations (CIOs) 75
Charities Aid Foundation (CAF) 160–2, 167
charities and charitable companies 72–5, 158–9, 200

223

Cherwell District Council 175, 193
Christophers, B. 32
Church Hall Cottage 105, 107
Churchill, W. 65, 145, 165
Circulars 22/60 and 24/73 54–5
city life 1, 7, 10, 20, 57
'clientelist countryside' 11
Clifford, B. 193–4
climate goals 207
Cloke, P. 9–10
Coalition Government (2010–15) 212
Coelho, M. 34
co-housing 179–82
collaborative ventures 179
collective approaches to housing provision 22
colonisation 10
Colonsay 149–52
commodification 5
common land 47
communitarianism 91, 102–3
communities 3
  need for 'tailoring' 143
  support for x, 103
community action and involvement 5, 102–13, 119, 134, 166, 208
community benefit societies 74
community build 179–80
community control 153, 166
Community Housing Fund 158–62, 208
community interest companies (CICs) 75, 90–1, 103, 106
community involvement in planning 141
community land ownership 108
community land trusts (CLTs) 22, 74, 89, 93, 102–12, 116, 120, 124, 137, 147, 153, 161–3, 174, 179–81, 208, 211
community-led housing projects x–xi, 115, 130, 144–5, 153, 158–73, 180, 199–202, 208–11
  finance for 135–7
  impediments to 133
community ownership 190
Community Ownership Fund 135, 158, 161
community right to bid 123–4
community right to build 120
community right to challenge 124
community self-help 91
community use 93, 147
companies engaged in housebuilding 164, 170–3, 194
  absence of 172
compensation payments 147, 153, 166, 208
competition for land 195
compulsory purchase orders (CPOs) 146–7, 166–7, 208, 211
conditional consent 91
constraints on provision of housing xi, 14, 39, 203
constructivism 11
consumption
  essential and *inessential* 210, 212
  housing production triggered by 14–15
'contested countryside' 11
converted property 45, 142
co-operatives 74–5

Cope, H. 75
Cornwall 83
council housing 14, 23, 28, 38–47, 51–3, 56–74, 92, 163–5, 169, 194, 202–3
  current decline in 138
  disposal of 89
  in the inter-war period 60–2
council tax 23, 155, 157, 167
counter-urbanisation 4–6, 10–12, 23, 34, 44–6, 54, 71
countryside 5–11
  ideas of 7
  nature of 9
  seen as a *productive space* or a *space of consumption* 5
  types of 11
county councils 59
county structure plans 12–13
county towns 12
COVID-19 pandemic 23, 156, 204–12
credit 13, 15, 22
crofting communities 148
crowdfunding 158–60
cultural capital 31, 93, 102–3
cultural identity 7
current use value 146–7, 163, 166
custom housebuilding 172, 174, 179

Dartmoor 95–6
de-assetisation 167
'deliberative' model of housebuilding 180
demand for and supply of housing 23, 209
democracy 206
dependence of villages 12
depleting areas 6–7, 170
depopulation 3
deregulation 142, 166, 171, 208
developable land 14, 90, 140, 145, 153, 171
  availability of 37
development, rejection of 36
development controls 5–6, 36–7, 142
development costs 39–40
development orders 119–20, 124
Dickie, J. 206
discontent with housing outcomes 202
discretionary decision-making 89, 141
displacement 6–7, 73
distributive justice 203–4, 207
downstream effects 89
drivers in the housing market x, 1, 7, 20–4, 31, 39, 202

economic policy 206
Edwards, Sir George 49
elderly residents 129
embedding 11
empowerment of communities 144, 166
enablers 92, 97, 134–5, 166, 194, 207–8
Enclosure Acts 47
endowments x
energy-saving 200
Engels, Friedrich 30
England 16, 26, 30, 36, 41–5, 52, 103, 116, 138–41, 153, 161–3, 173, 201, 203, 207, 212

English Rural Housing Association 162
entry-level exceptions 100–1, 165
environmental protection 44
estate duty 42
estates in the countryside 43, 56, 85
exceptional planning permissions 89–93, 100–2, 112, 165
exchanging areas 6–7, 13, 15, 35, 154, 172, 204
exclusion from markets 7
externalities 39
  negative 17

Fairlie, S. 185, 190
fairness x, 210
farming sector 3–4, 42, 49, 129
farmworkers, housing of 51–5
'Ferring' case 120–3
feudalism 47, 144
financialisation 19, 23, 26, 29–30
Field, M. 172
finance xi, 103, 133–7, 158–67, 167, 172
  barriers to 39–40
Fine, B. 134
Finland 103
'First Homes' framework 100, 102, 165–6
first-time buyers 101, 211
fiscal drag 157
'flight' 209
food security 3
'footprints' 190, 200
Forgebank 181–5
foundations *see* charities
framing 150
France 45
'free' houses 50, 52, 58
fund-raising 158–9
funding regimes 60, 76
future prospects 141, 143, 169–212

gain 89, 145
Gallent, Nick (co-author) xii, 17, 21–3, 92
garden cities 147
generational transfers 156
gentrification xi, 1–2, 23, 73, 140, 143, 166, 169, 204, 209
geography
  'cultural turn' in 9–10
  rural 9
George, Henry 105, 139
gifting 158, 162–3
global financial crisis (2008) 26
'golden shares' 112
government intervention in the housing market 16–18, 27–8, 46–50, 53, 56, 59, 66, 72–3, 76, 91, 163–4, 207, 212
Grand Designs (tv programme) 174
grant-aided houses 60
grants 40, 76, 200
Graven Hill 175–9, 193
Great Chart (Kent) 8
'greening' 206–7
Greenwood Act (1930) 58–9
growth, economic 210–11
growth areas 141
Guinness, Arthur 56, 74

Halfacree, K. 9
Halton (Lancashire) 181–5
Hamiduddin, Iqbal (co-author) 173
Hampstead Garden Suburb 108
Harris, N. 189
Harvey, D. 29–30
'high-end consumption' 17, 172, 174, 206–8
Hilber, C. A. 210
Hill, Octavia 56
Hilton Young Act (1935) 58–9
Hockerton Housing Project 190–3, 200
Hoggart, K. 9
holiday lets 23, 52, 54, 106, 167, 209, 212, 2
Home Builders Federation (HBF) 171
homeownership 3, 33, 46, 71, 154, 156
  benefits of 24–7, 31, 167, 211
  centrality of 155–7
  rates of 19, 22
house prices 4, 20–1, 24–6, 29–34, 66, 95, 145, 154–7, 171, 174, 207–11
housing associations 73–9, 85, 99–100
housing classes 34
Housing Corporation 76
housing estates 72
Howard, Ebenezer 147

Iden Green 162
imputed rent 25–8, 154, 166
incentives
  to buy a house 28
  for housing consumption 208
'inclusive' policies xi, 207, 212
income 6
  from farming 3
  lower bands of 16–17, 33, 169, 212
incomers 4–5
industrialisation 41
inequality linked to housing 3, 7, 19, 31, 202, 207–11
infill sites 147
inflation and inflationary pressure 29, 48–52, 155
infrastructure 4, 37, 90, 161
inheritance tax 157
'intentional community' concept 180
interest rates 155
intergenerational transfer 25–7, 32
investment in housing 6, 20, 24–8, 31, 52, 54, 71, 85, 156, 158, 209, 211
  in towns and cities 90–1
Ireland 6, 144

joint ventures 171

Kentish villages 17
key workers 210
King, Slater 104
Kingsley Wood Act (1938) 58–60
Kinlet (Shropshire) 98–100
know-how 170

Labour Party 147, 157
'ladder' of homeownership, getting on to 25–6, 32
Lafford Homes 194
Lake District 80–2, 105, 210

land
  concentrated ownership of 144
  as a critical ingredient in housing development 170
  as a financial commodity 37
  market in 138–40, 146–8, 153, 169, 171
  'natural' control of 144
  public- or community-owned 144
land acquisition 112
land availability 148, 165
land banks 171
Land Fund 136
land reform xi, 145, 148, 158, 166, 201, 208
land transfers 43, 46, 97
land trusts 91–2, 98, 130, 136, 166, 199; *see also* community land trusts
land use 140, 146, 166
  changes in 89
  planning of 6, 102, 118
land values 14, 21, 39, 71, 90, 96–7, 140, 144–8, 153, 158, 190, 199, 207
landlords 47, 56
landowners x, 11, 43, 47, 165–6, 171, 199, 202
  rights of 138
Lavenham (Suffolk) 125–9
Law, C. M. 42
'left-behind' communities 204
legislation 58–9
leisure pursuits 5, 12
Letchworth 108
levelling down 210
levelling up 142–3, 211
Liberal party 50
Lichfields (consultants) 125, 171
lifestyle 206
limited liability partnerships (LLPs) 75
Lincoln 194
Little Stocks Close 98–100
local authorities 53, 60, 73, 75, 82, 125, 148, 164, 170–1, 174–5, 178–9, 193–200, 204, 207
  leading on village housing 164–6, 193–9
  numbers of houses completed (1947–59) 67
  setting up trading companies 164
  strategic role of 76
local development orders (LDOs) 119
local need 44, 53, 80–3, 92–9, 107, 110, 114–15, 129–30, 139, 143, 208, 210
Localism Act (2011) 148, 164
Locality (organisation) 159
location of land and housing 24, 38
Locke, J. 139
London 212
'London prices' 145
low-cost building 174
low-impact development 170, 185–91, 199, 200, 203
lower-income households 169, 212
Loxley (Warwickshire) 136, 148, 159
Lyons Housing Review 147

Maclennan, D. 24
Madeddu, M. 23
market pressures xi, 143, 211
market towns 1, 12, 209

markets
  left to determine distribution of housing 203–4
  support for 210–11
Marlborough, Duke of 49–50
Marsden, T. 10
Martin, E. W. 43
Marxist analysis 30
Maxey, L. 185, 190
micro-management 70
middle-classes 4, 10–11, 91, 203–4
Ministry of Housing, Communities and Local Government (MHCLG) 141–2
Mirrlees Review 157
mismatches 4–7
'Mitchell' case 82
mix
  of age and social groups 16
  of localities 36
  of state, third sector and/or community action 39
'mixed economy' of housing solutions 74–85
mixed function of housing (for investment *and* utility) 20, 24–6
mobility 4
model housing 56
Monbiot, G. 145–6
monopoly in land 144
'monumental' countryside 204
Moore, T. 112–13
Morphet, J. 193–4
mortgage interest tax relief 154
  at source (MIRAS) 28
mortgages 27–30, 154–5
Murphy, L. 92

National Agricultural Centre Housing Association (NACHA) 77–9
National Community Land Trust Network 104
National Farmers' Union (NFU) 48–9
National Loans Board 164
National Lottery 159–61
National Model Design Code 142
national parks xi, 72, 80–1, 95–7, 102, 170
National Planning Policy Framework (NPPF) 100–1, 119, 142, 166
National Trust 43
National Union of Agricultural Workers (NUAW) 48–51
neighbourhood planning 89, 94, 116–37
neo-liberalism 16, 19, 143, 203
Netherlands, the 5
New Communities Inc. (NCI) 105, 108, 112
new towns 44, 147
Newby, H. 52, 203
niches 190
NIMBYs ('not in my back yard') 35
'no-go' areas 212
North Kesteven District Council 194
Northumberland 194–5
nostalgia 4–5, 206

occasional occupation 45
occupancy conditions, agricultural (AOCs) 41, 47–8, 51–6, 79–83
off-grid development 169–70

Office of Fair Trading 171
off-site manufacture (OSM) 100
'one planet' development 189–90, 201, 206
'one size fits all' approach 140
open housing markets 13, 15, 52, 72, 199
overcrowding 60
Owen, Robert 56
owner-occupiers 32, 34
ownership 200
   of land 145, 148, 190
ownership shares 180

Pahl, R. E. 9
parish plans 117–19
Parker, G. 116, 125, 134–5
'paternalistic countryside' 11
pay comparisons 3
Peabody, George 56, 74
Peek Close 125
Pendall, R. 35
permission for development 140–1, 145, 199
   for alternative use 146
   'in principle' 141
   not needed 142
permissioned sites 153
philanthropic gifting 39, 74
Phillips, M. 206
'placeless-ness' 171
place-making 180
planning committees 141–2
planning costs 37–8
planning system x–xi, 4–6, 12–17, 20–2, 34–9, 45–6, 54, 81–2, 85, 89–91, 102–3, 110, 116, 139–44, 171, 190, 207–8
   fixated with orthodoxy 143
   flexibility of 140
   future shape of 141
   key role of 13
   principle-based 90
   reform of 31
   what it can do 143
   see also reform programmes
planning–land–tax–finance nexus xi, 138
playground management 206
Pluckley (Kent) 10, 17
Plunkett Foundation 159
plurality in housing provision 171, 190
Policy Exchange 141
policy on housing 100–1, 119, 146, 207
population changes 3, 42, 45
post-carbon future xii, 202–7
'post-rurality' perspectives 8–9
poverty 6, 210, 212
'preserved countryside' 11
priority assigned to rural housing 3, 190
private consumption 38, 138, 144, 202, 210
private enterprise 39, 71, 85
private housing, tax treatment of 154
privatisation 144
   of planning 38
problem of rural housing 2, 8–7
property rights 15, 34, 138–9, 146
'protected' areas 3, 140–2, 207
providers of housing 13, 160–3
   registered (RPs) 74–7, 162–3, 200, 203

public good and public interest 35, 38, 138–9, 146, 199
public investment 90
public ownership of land 146, 200
public policy 14–16
Public Works Loan Board (PWLB) 164
pubs 133

quality of housing 3, 42–3, 171

rationing of land 146
reconfiguration, social 5, 209–10
recurrent taxes 153
redistributive justice 157
reform programmes 31, 141–6, 167, 203, 207
   advocacy of 144
   for land, planning, tax and finance 79
   in urban areas 141
remote areas 11, 172
renewable energy 206
'renewal' areas 141–2
Rent Acts 48–51
rentier class 211
rents and renting 20–1, 28–34, 41, 48–54, 95, 145; *see also* imputed rent
resale values 180
researchers, work of 4
residualisation 71–2
restrictive covenants 189
restructuring 3, 6
retired people, housing for 5, 7, 20, 45, 202
return on sale of land 165
'reward myth' 202
right to bid 148
right to build 174, 179
right to buy 23, 33, 71–5, 144, 148, 164
right to the city, and to the rural 199
right to housing 209–10
right to land 208
rights, allocation of 13
roads and road-building 71, 94
Robinson, S. 17
romantic views 203
'roots' in an area 210
Royal Town Planning Institute (RTPI) 171
running costs 200
'rural', use of the word 7
rural areas x–xi, 1–11, 20, 42, 49, 89–90, 101, 154, 157–8, 165–8, 174, 203–7
   advocacy for 143
   dynamics of 143–4
   extended definition of 73
   role of 143
rural districts and their councils 58, 60, 66
'rural idyll' notions 3
rural spaces, political 11
rural studies 9
rurality 2, 7–11, 207
   index of 9
   nature of 11
Ryan-Collins, J. 29–30, 34

'safety net' provision 76
St Ives (Cornwall) 82–5
Salter, K. 134–5
Satsangi, M. 45

Saunders, Pater 19, 32
Savage, W. G. 42
'save the village' interventions 38
scaffolding in housing markets 26, 51, 204, 207
scale, questions of 11–13
scarcity of housing xi, 13, 17, 20, 26
  generation and preservation of 90
'Schedule A' tax 28, 157, 167
Schöni, O. 210
Scotland 123, 135–6, 144, 148, 153, 163, 166, 203
seasonality 4
securitisation of debt 30
second homes 4–5, 20, 23, 28, 36, 38, 45, 54, 73, 95, 106, 109–10, 113, 155, 167, 208–12
Section 52 agreements 92
Section 106 agreements 91, 96–7, 101–2, 110
Section 157 (Housing Act 1985) 102
security of tenure 52
'seed-corn' 159
self-organised building (self-build) 5, 22, 148, 169–75, 180–1, 189, 199–200, 203
Semington (Wiltshire) 68
service sector 7, 211
settlement policy' 16–17, 140
settlor 103
shared ownership 211
sharing economy 28
Shaw, D. 129
Shelter 72
Sherrod, Charles 104
Sherston (Wiltshire) 62–6
shops 135–6
shortages 45
  of housing 3, 71
  of labour 70
  of land 144
Shucksmith, M. 33, 80–1, 210
Silverton (Wiltshire) 62–6
site exceptions 90–3, 96, 99–102, 145, 165
slums 57
small locations 2, 153, 165
small projects 40
sociability 180. 199–200
social capital 93, 102–3, 133–6
social change 204
social class divisions 1, 32, 43, 47
social diversity xi
social exclusion 6, 39, 143, 175
social goods 91
social housing 15, 20–1, 33, 47, 74–5, 102, 160
social representations 9
social structures 4
socialisation of rents 146, 199
societal goals 190
socio-economic factors 1, 7, 46
Sopworth (Wiltshire) 61, 64
South Shropshire 175, 180
South Tawton (Devon) 95–6
Spacehive 159–60

specialist providers of housing 76
speculation 14, 22, 79, 112, 138
'squirearchy' 43
stamp duty 22, 156–7
Stamp Duty Land Tax (SDLT) 34–5, 155, 157
'staycations' 45
stewardship xi, 167, 169, 190, 211
Stirling, Phoebe (co-author) xii
Stroud District Council 195
studies of housing 2
Sturzaker, J. 36, 129
subsidies 21, 27–8, 40, 44, 51, 57–60, 66–8, 71, 180, 200
suburbs 7, 206
Sullivan, Louis 10
supply
  of housing 26, 31
  of labour 41
surplus value 139
sustainability 106, 113–14, 130, 189, 194, 199–200, 209
'sustainability trap' (M. Taylor) 16–17
Swann, Robert 104
Swindon Borough Council 175

TAN6 development 189–90
taxation xi, 1, 22–3, 34–5, 139, 153–8, 165–9, 208
Teignmouth District Council 175
tenancies 47–53
'That Roundhouse' (Pembrokeshire) 185
Thatcher, Margaret 73, 76, 163–4
theorisation 19
think tanks 141
'third sector' of housing provision 39, 41, 73–7
three-party fiduciary arrangements 103–4
tied housing 38–9, 42–3, 46–57, 202
  decline and possible abolition of 52, 54
  need for 49–53, 56
Tir-y-Gafel (Pembrokeshire) 186–90
tourism 7, 45
Town and Country Planning Act (1947) 54
town dwellers 45
trade, global 42
trading up to bigger homes 156
transition in rural housing 85, 202
'trickle-down' effects 204
'trophy' property 5
trusted partners 171
trustees 104
Twine, F. E. 73

unfit dwellings 59–60
United States 3, 104–5, 112, 147, 206
  Office of Economic Opportunity (OEC) 105
Upper Eden 129–30
upstream effects 89
urban areas 2–4, 9, 210
urban–rural classification 76
urbanisation 42
use classes orders 142
user involvement in housebuilding 173
utility 154

vacant housing 6
value added tax (VAT)) 22, 153
value capture 146–700
value distribution 146
Village Housing
  as focus of the present book 2
  structure of the present book 18
  as title of the present book 11
village planning 107–8, 116–17, 124, 130, 137, 154, 158, 165
  impediments confronting projects 165
  led by local authorities 193–9
villages 102, 202–3
  characteristics of 22–3, 31
  life cycles of 16
  meaning of the word 2, 11–12
  problems of 143
  urban 12
voluntary sector 75
volunteers 115, 134
voting 5

wage levels x, 5, 15, 45–53
Wales 92, 200–3, 206
Walker-Smith, Derek 44
wealth 5–6
  distribution of xi
  in housing 138, 202, 210–11
  raising, accumulation and transfer of 25, 31–2, 145, 156
wealthy households 91
Webb, B. 92
Webber, R. 9
Weber, Max 19, 32
Welsh Government 189, 200
Welwyn 108
Wheatley Act (1924) 58–9
Williams, G. 92
Williams, N. J. 73
windfall gains 97, 145
Woods, M. 7, 42–3, 85
working classes and working population 5–6, 56, 208
Worth Matravers (Dorset) 113–15
Wroxton (Oxfordshire) 205
Wu, Meiling (co-author) xii

Youlgrave (Derbyshire) 109–12
young people 156

zoning 65, 89, 141–4, 165

Lightning Source UK Ltd.
Milton Keynes UK
UKHW021253211022
410866UK00009B/28